CW00763556

LONDON POLICE

THEIR STORIES

80 years at the sharp end

The Best of the *London Police Pensioner* magazine

Merlin Unwin Books

First published in Great Britain by Merlin Unwin Books, 1998

This edition and selection © London Police Pensioner Magazine 1998

Published by

Merlin Unwin Books
Palmers House
7 Corve Street
Ludlow
Shropshire SY8 1DB
U. K.

A CIP catalogue record for this book is available from the British Library

ISBN 1–873674–36-8

Designed and produced by Merlin Unwin Books, Ludlow
Typing: Tina Mulliner
Jacket design: Hamlyn Design, Ludlow
Printed in Great Britain by Redwood Books

Contents

page

1. A Whitehall Warrior. *Alan Jackson* — 1
2. Anywhere But Spain. *Dick Kirby* — 2
3. Croydon's Street Characters. *Harry Score* — 4
4. More About Gertie. *A. Bettis* — 6
5. Paper Jack. *Len Simms* — 7
6. Oliver Pudvine. *Ted Dilley* — 7
7. Doing Things the Pudvine Way. *Donald McLean* — 8
8. Man's Best Friend. *Alan Marshall* — 9
9. Old-time Policing. *Emrys Jones* — 11
10. The Stork Cometh. *Alan Jackson* — 12
11. A Winter's Tale. *Rick Harrington* — 13
12. Crepitus. *S. Cooper* — 15
13. The Raj Prince. *F. N. Cook* — 16
14. Alpha and Omega (almost). *G. M. Winterflood* — 17
15. Small Favour. *Alan Wheeler* — 21
16. The Old Rivals. *W. G. Tilbury* — 23
17. Thanks for the Memories. *Geoffrey Taylor* — 23
18. Riches from Beyond the Grave. *Frank Rawlings* — 24
19. It's a Bumpy Ride. *George Price* — 25
20. How Mulligan Found the Limehouse Orphans' Box. *S. Powers* — 27
21. Sent for a Purpose. *Paul Phillips* — 29
22. Tempus Fugit. *Derek Peckham* — 30
23. Fascists & Commies. *Dick Pamplin* — 30
24. In a London Pea-Souper. *Mrs E. Mitchell* — 32
25. Smoggy Days. *Douglas Lloyd* — 33
26. Peeping Toms and Wooten Lamps. *Denis McNamara* — 33
27. I was Press Ganged. *Frank Marley* — 39
28. Anyone Will Do. *Harry Joyce* — 40
29. The One That Got Away. *Dave King* — 41
30. A Helping Hand. *Peter Inman* — 44
31. Never a Dull Moment for Albert. *Albert Hunt* — 44
32. Look Before You Leap! *Alf Hogg* — 46
33. The Art of Dying Tidily. *Charles Hasler* — 50

34. Christmas Cheer in Acton. *Cyril Green*   55
35. At Your Service. *Arthur Gadd*   56
36. A Case of Appeal. *Arthur Fanning*   58
37. Over the Edge. *Ken Bell*   59
38. Crime Reporter of the Old School. *Norman Clark*   60
39. Children and the Police. *Mrs D. Barrett*   61
40. Jack Thyer's Royal Visitor. *John Thyer*   62
41. Coronation Day. *Dennis Picco*   63
42. Eve of Coronation Day. *Peter Gidley*   64
43. A Long Wet Wait. *Reg Clift*   65
44. King of Siam. *Philip Hoggard*   66
45. The Palace of Varieties. *Alan Jackson*   68
46. My First Day on Duty. *Ken Richmond*   70
47. Wellington Arch: Monument and Police Station. *Doug Lightwood*   71
48. Fanny of Wellington Arch. *Doug Lightwood*   74
49. Attempted Murder in High Places. *Geoffrey Taylor*   76
50. Another Attempted Murder of a Commissioner. *Geoffrey Taylor*   78
51. Bermondsey Ghost. *Geoffrey Taylor*   80
52. The Memoirs of Chief Inspector Monk. *Chief Inspector Monk*   81
53. A Child in the Arbour. *Mrs French*   83
54. The Real Inspector Bucket. *Arthur Fanning*   85
55. Redcaps on Madagascar. *Arthur Wood*   87
56. Proud Moments: the Met at War. *Geoffrey Taylor*   89
57. Bow Garage: Blitz-Style. *Geoffrey Taylor*   90
58. Evacuating the East End Youngsters. *Geoffrey Taylor*   92
59. Waiting for Hitler. *Arthur Scougall*   93
60. First Prisoners of War? *Frank Reynolds*   94
61. Fate Deals a Hand. *Don Milburn*   95
62. Bert Mead, Spycatcher. *Bert Mead*   99
63. Walter Haycock's Private War. *Bert Mead*   102
64. German Bomber in Difficulties. *Albert Kennard*   105
65. Feeding the War-Time Coppers. *Kate Fuller*   105
66. The Making of a WAPC. *Kathleen Farringdon*   106
67. Canadian Soldiers Murder Epsom Policeman. *Geoffrey Taylor*   110
68. The Hand Ambulance. *Eric Oddy*   113
69. Give Him a Hand. *Tom Land*   113
70. On Yer Bike. *Pat Moorhead*   115
71. Service in the Saddle. *Ron Marke*   116
72. Watch Out. *E.R. Boast*   117
73. The Accident That Never Was. *Ken (Dinger) Bell*   117
74. Macmillan was Right. *Geoffrey Taylor*   118
75. Retirement. *Lady Jennifer Hilton*   119

	page
76. After Sheehy. *Anon*	120
77. Mobile Column. *Adrian Collins*	120
78. Ever Onwards. *Fred (Chalky) White*	122
79. Always Remember Your Brake Test. *Terry Butcher*	125
80. Black Rats. *John Back*	126
81. Salute to Bow Street. *Alan Webster*	127
82. Learning the Ropes, Commercial Street Way. *Eddie Twitchings*	130
83. To Mother, with Love. *John Primeau*	131
84. Gray's Inn Road. *Cliff (Taffy) Sankey*	132
85. The Wapping Nightingale. *George Ludlow*	134
86. Sweet Memories of M. *John Livett*	137
87. Tottenham Court Road. *Percy Ledger*	139
88. Adventures at Norwood Green. *Percy Ledger*	140
89. Tottenham Court Road in the Thirties. *Percy Ledger*	144
90. Private Schwartz, H Division. *John (Jan) Fillery*	147
91. A Spot of Bother in the Rotherhithe Cells. *Bryan Billings*	148
92. On the Plank. *A Jackson*	150
93. Swifting them in. *Dick Brown*	152
94. The Hackney Elephant. *Fred White*	154
95. Pink Elephants. *Dennis Picco*	154
96. Life in the Saddle. *Geoffrey Taylor*	154
97. A Dignified Retreat. *Bill Knapp*	156
98. The Sport of Kings. *Jack Sadler*	158
99. Mad Dogs & Brockleymen. *Bert Kennard*	159
100. The Horse in the Fulham Charge Room. *Reg Humphries*	160
101. The Downfall of Flannel Foot. *Roland Swanborough*	161
102. Getting at the Creep. *Deryck Stanley*	163
103. Your Sins Will Find You Out. *Cyril Green*	165
104. The Incredible Adventure of Moby Dick. *Jack Sadler*	166
105. A Magnanimous Gesture. *Ben Hogg*	170
106. Police Discretion. *Bert Blake*	173
107. Gipsy Hill in the Twenties. *J. Coxhead*	176
108. Constables and Cubicles. *Alan Jackson*	177
109. In the Bleak Mid-winter. *Eddie Twitchings*	179
110. No Justice in This World. *Donald Bond*	181
111. A Dangerous Profession. *Geoffrey Taylor*	182
112 Jellied Eels by Scroby Sands. *Ted Aram*	185
113. Laughter in Court. *Bert Blake*	186
114. Nailed in Spain. *Bob Roach*	189
115. The Marquis of Granby Rules. *Alan Marshall*	190
Glossary of Police Terms & Abbreviations	194

Foreword

I have just seen the first draft of this book and although I have previously read most of the contents in our publication, *London Police Pensioner* magazine, they have once again provided me much pleasure in the reading. I am sure that *London Police: their stories* will be well received, for it records a real history of the police, much of which would otherwise be lost forever. I wish it and the charity it is supporting, the Police Pensioners' Housing Association, every success.

Ralph Dyson
Chairman, London Branch
National Association of Retired Police Officers

Introduction

The original idea for this book was not mine, but that of a non-police subscriber to *London Police Pensioner* magazine. The idea would not leave me, so I mentioned the proposal to Karen McCall, the Editor of the *LPP* and to Geoffrey Taylor, a prominent contributor to the publication. Both were thrilled with the idea. So my next step was to begin the selection of the best articles published in the *LPP* since its launch in 1972. That selection was my contribution. Geoff has provided all the 'venture capital' and Karen who has acted as the book's editor, has given her time free. All of us have a common aim: to raise funds for the Police Pensioners' Housing Association, a national charity which provides sheltered accommodation for retired policemen and women, their spouses and widows, from Forces across Britain.

We hope this project is a huge success: if so, we may consider a second publication. All retired and serving police officers have a certain story to tell, funny, sad or interesting, and this book and hopefully, any future editions, will save these accounts for future generations. Most importantly of all, *London Police: their stories* is helping to raise money for the PPHA. Hundreds of police pensioners are asking for help with sheltered accommodation. Please help by buying a book for yourself and your friends.

Norma Brown
Committee member
London Branch NARPO

Proceeds from this book

The Police Pensioners Housing Association are indebted to Norma Brown and others who have spent time researching through back-issues of *London Police Pensioner* magazine to produce a book to enlighten people about the way police officers have undertaken their duties in former years.

All donations and profits will go to our Association, and will help us to provide sheltered accommodation for retired police officers and their widows.

We have fourteen PPHA apartments in Yapton in Sussex; and for those who do not wish to move far from their present location or their friends and relatives, we also offer assistance by finding sheltered accommodation for retired police officers, their spouses, widows and widowers, that is both suitable and affordable.

Colin Burgess
Honorary Secretary/Treasurer,
Police Pensioners' Housing Association

Acknowlegements

The editor and publishers wish to thank all those who have so readily given permission for inclusion of the anecdotes which appear in this volume. The writers or their widows and widowers have co-operated with this venture, without a single exception. Every effort has been made to trace the writers of the letters. Inevitably, we have not always met with success in tracking down the writers of articles published many years ago. To those whom it has proved impossible to trace, we offer our apologies and hope that they will find pleasure in the reproduction the their articles in this book.

We would also like to thank all those whose photographs have appeared on the jacket, and whose names appear on the next page. Thanks also to those who have given their time free on this publication: Merlin Unwin who has acted as consultant on all print and publishing matters, Geoffrey Taylor for providing the advance financing of the project and for dealing with permissions, Ralph Dyson for his advice, Rayner Unwin for proof-reading, Norma Brown for masterminding the whole project and to all the organisations, magazines and publications who have helped us to promote this book.

Cover Illustrations

Front cover (clockwise from top left)

1. Sent in by ex PC John Hopkins, who spent several years on duty in Downing Street when Harold Wilson was Prime Minister. 2. Sent in by Jim Beard. Photo of Tariq Ali who lead the anti-Vietnam war demonstration when 110,000 marched on Downing Street, October 1968. 3. Photo submitted to LPP by Jack Bunker, Warrant Number 144887, archive photograph. 4. Ron Spendloff, ex PC 285F, Coronation Day, Queen Elizabeth II. 5. S. Powers, who writes of the photo, 'Despite what many may think, I stopped the gentleman by hooking his legs from under him with my right arm as he ducked past me. I know this regrettable action was frowned upon by authority at the time, but I'm sure it was the last time he tried to breach a police cordon.' 6. Submitted by T. Shaw of Lady Hicks and Sir Seymour leaving All Souls Church, Spanish Place, Marylebone, after the wedding of their daughter.

Back cover (clockwise from top left)

1. Ron Spendloff, ex PC 285F, police vehicles of the 1960s. 2. Photograph submitted by Susan Kellerman, whose mother WPC Ella Moody took part in this training exercise in the late 1930s. 3. Phil Williams, GM, ex DT6. The Traffic Patrol Unit of the Anguilla Police Unit, manned by the Metropolitan Police on secondment during the Emergency, September 1970. 4. William (Bill) Barrand, 127636S, ex PS 38H, sent in this photograph of Sergeant Bissell, self-defence instructor, showing how to arrest Chummy.

A Whitehall Warrior

Odd and eccentric characters from these shores could always be found at any time of day or night at AD (Cannon Row's) ground. The proximity of Parliament and the Royal Palaces may have been an added spur to their pilgrimages. Some of them could be awkward when they wished to be, though the majority were docile.

However there was the odd exception! Shortly after leaving Peel House. I was sauntering up Whitehall towards Trafalgar Square near the Whitehall Theatre, where a man was shouting, waving his arms about, and in somewhat of a frenzy. He was big - very big; complete with a huge bushy beard. He looked as though he had just stepped ashore from a Viking long boat.

He was about to meet a Saxon. I touched his arm in a perfect Peel House manner, said 'What seems to be..', when I was seized by my tunic lapels, and lifted bodily against the wall, the toes of my shiny 'Royal Stags' just touching the pavement.

He stared at me from a foot or so away, and started to deliver a very long tirade. I heard Convoys, MPs, Pension Rights, War Office, their Lordships at the Admiralty and I think even the Balkans were mentioned. I was aware of my tunic buttons pinging off at short intervals, and my freshly starched blue shirt collar pressing deeper into my jaw.

Events then took a Whitehall Farce turn. A man and woman approached the pair of us. Could this be the public-spirited citizen we had been told would come forward in our moment of need? In a lull when the Viking drew breath, the man said 'Where is the nearest petrol station?' Peel House had done a good job on me. 'Under Hungerford Bridge,' I gurgled, 'Get me some assistance'! 'No we don't require assistance, just petrol.' Off they went.

A Q car drew up, Echo 11, a Wolsey 6/80 I recall. Their contribution was the advice that I should not get beaten but should hold on to him - a TA car was on the way. A TA car drew up, a 6/90, complete with a cadet on the rear seat.

Do you recall in the Fifties and Sixties, following any incident or commotion, when reporters arrived, every bus queue had a Kathleen Harrison character. Their comment was usually along the lines 'I thought it was students larking about.' I imagined one over at the bus stop saying 'Students larking about again I suppose.'

Back to the story. After a struggle three of us managed to feed the Viking into the rear of the TA car. 'Hang on to him, cadet,' we shouted. Pushing the cadet aside, Thor grabbed the steering wheel, and with what seemed an effortless action, twisted the wheel into a positive non-steering shape. The driver, envisaging a crash, cried, 'Out with him!' So we had the job of untangling him out of the car.

I heard AD's van bell sounding, tearing up Whitehall, flat out at 28mph. Could it be Dusty Miller at the wheel, nose up to the screen? I began to see this being a long tour of duty. He appeared with the cadet's cap clamped between his teeth, the cadet's face displaying a look of: perhaps I should have been a plumber.

After a rocky ride to AD he was eventually lodged in the Charge Room. 'What have we here?' enquired the station officer, as we did a Military-Two-Step around the charge room.

The necessary forms completed, we headed for St Francis Mental Hospital at Tooting. What a journey! A male nurse met us, and gave the Viking an injection of paraldehyde, and then peace.

No pint of course. I wound down by stitching buttons back on my tunic.

I often reflected later, on what terrible wartime experiences that man and others I encountered had probably endured to leave them in that state.

Alan Jackson AD, AH, CTS, LK, TDM, TDP, TDR, B10

Anywhere But Spain

I was a junior DC on a murder squad in the early 1970s. The murder had occurred in London's tough and colourful East End but in stark contrast to the same area today, in those days if police said that they wanted assistance from the general public, they got it.

I was deputed to interview a young man, who in response to the police request, had walked into the police station to tell me that although he had been in the general vicinity at the time of the murder, he had neither heard nor seen anything suspicious. I therefore took a negative witness statement from him, thanked him for his time and he left the police station. It was then that the result of the routine search that I had requested at Criminal Records Office came through; it transpired that he was circulated as being wanted by Interpol. I swiftly despatched a brace of Aids to intercept him twixt police station and home and scrag him back in.

Having accomplished their mission, the suspect was casually deposited into the cells (as suspects were, in those halcyon days) and the Aids wandered off, quarrelling amongst themselves as to whose diary he should appear in.

I went down to the cells, where I confronted a very angry young man. 'This is a nice thing!' he cried. 'I come in here to help you out and I get chucked in the cells like a common criminal!' 'You're here, because you're circulated as being wanted for failing to appear,' I replied. Genuine bewilderment flooded over his face. 'Failing to appear?' he echoed. 'That's rubbish! I've never been in trouble with you lot in my life! Where am I supposed to have failed to appear?'

'Spain,' I replied, and the perplexity was swept from his face, as though it had been wiped with a cloth, to be replaced with a look of absolute terror. 'Spain!' he screamed. 'Don't send me back there! Oh Christ, you can't ! I've got to get out of here!' And with that, since I was the only barrier in the cell doorway standing between him and freedom, he launched himself at me. I had to severely rebuke him for his outburst and eventually, he sat trembling on the edge of his cot. 'Just take it easy,' I said. 'I'll see if I can find out a bit more about this.' He nodded dumbly, looking at me with blank, unseeing eyes.

'Yeah, I've got it here,' said the laconic Detective Sergeant, telephoning me from the Interpol office at the Yard, having checked the reference number I had given him from CRO. 'It's a warrant from Torremolinos for theft of a purse.' 'So when do I get to take him over there Sarge?' I said excitedly. My naive remarks enriched the DS's otherwise boring existence at the Yard, because for nearly a full minute, he was convulsed with laughter. 'You don't, you chump,' he laughed. 'It's just a local warrant. What it means is, if he ever goes back over there, he can be lifted, but not otherwise. You won't get a trip out of this one!' 'But,' I said stupidly, my dreams of far off sunny beaches suddenly dashed, 'but I've got him in the cells.' 'Take my advice, tell him to f** off and not to do it again!' He was still laughing when he put down the telephone.

I was smarting from being jeered at as I returned to the cells, but when

I saw the pitiable look on the face of the Spanish suspect, looking at me in much the same way as a condemned man might regard the prison Governor, in the forlorn hope that he might be carrying a stay of execution, I felt so sorry for him that I promptly repeated the news that I'd received from Interpol. The poor chap all but kissed my hands as he snuffled out his thanks. I said, 'Of course you're free to leave any time you like, but if it's not too much trouble, why were you in such a state?'

The young man wiped his eyes. 'I went to Spain with some mates in June about five years ago,' he replied. 'One night we all went out to a nightclub. We all had a few drinks and then, all of a sudden, this girl who was sitting near me reckoned that she'd had her purse nicked. The next thing I knew, the local coppers came and dragged me outside.'

I nodded. The local coppers he was referring to would, in those days, have received their pay cheques from General Franco. 'It doesn't make any difference now,' he continued, 'but it's God's truth, I didn't nick that girls purse and I don't know who did. But those coppers dragged me down the nick and gave me the full treatment. Christ, was it rough! Boots, fists, rifle butts, the lot! After a couple of minutes of this, I'd have stuck my hands up to nicking the Crown jewels! I said, when they ran out of breath, 'You want a confession? I'll give you one!' One of them, a horrible-looking bloke, with a tooth missing, grinned at me. 'A confession, Senor?' he said, 'We don't want no steenkin confession. We doin this, because we like eet!'

I shook hands with the young man at the door of the Police Station and I saw him no more.

Dick Kirby ex DS, Wt no 157728, J, K, N, COC1, C8, NCIS

Croydon's street characters

In the 1930's there were some unforgettable eccentrics living in Croydon. Those I came across in the course of my duty were: 'Gertie' or 'Duppas Hill Kate' and 'Paper Jack'.

Gertie was buxom and always wore a large flowered (Ascot type) hat and in her drunken state would almost every Saturday give the local youths their weekly thrill by stripping off right down to her birthday suit - except she never removed her large straw hat.

On at least three occasions, to my own embarrassment, I had to place my cape round her shoulders and large front and walk her along the few hundred yards to Fell Road nick, always accompanied by a crowd.

Once inside she would be placed in a cell and for at least a couple of hours the staff would be entertained by a recital of almost everything that Shakespeare ever wrote. She was very good, but after a while everyone got fed up with the dramatic or moving words and at the first opportunity the Station officer would declare her sober and get rid of her. The funny thing is that I never can remember her being charged. She must have been but I certainly never went to Court as the arresting officer.

Now we come to Duppas Hill Kate. She was another buxom lady in her 40s who lived and slept 'rough' in the Duppas Hill area. She was spotlessly clean and if you were on night duty during the summer months you could expect to see Kate having a dawn bath in one of the building workers' water tanks or having a shower under the hose pipe on one of the numerous building sites in the area. If she saw you she would deliberately turn towards you and try to have a conversation.

She also used the toilets on the Hill as a laundry by plugging the bowl tightly with paper and then continually pulling the chain. I never did find out how she dried her washing. As far as I know she was never arrested for any offence although it was rumoured that she would provide 'certain services' for four pence (old money). On a weekly wage of 55 shillings I don't think that many young coppers availed themselves of this doubtful pleasure.

Finally we come to 'Paper Jack', a gentlemen whom I looked on as a friend. He was dressed from head to foot in brown paper, held together with string and rubber bands but his feet were always clad in pieces of lino. He was highly intelligent and was usually surrounded by school children, helping them with their home work.

The people in the Waddon and Purley Way areas would allow him to sleep in their garden sheds and some would even leave a blanket for him to use. Many a driver would pull up for a chat and offer him money but his answer was always the same: 'Sir, I am far richer than you can ever hope to be'.

One day some youngsters threw what were then known as 'coloured matches' at him and on a warm summer afternoon one of the matches fell between the folds of his brown paper suit. Fortunately I was nearby, seeing the kids out of school, and I ran over and by rolling him on the road managed to put the flames out. He was scorched but not badly burnt. I remember a story and photograph appearing in the local newspaper all about Paper Jack and this young copper.

I was only at Croydon for two years. I think the Superintendent felt that with naked ladies who seemed to strip off when I was about and an eccentric friend that I used to roll on the roadway, I was far too young and innocent to keep such company (or was he jealous?)

I did hear several years later that 'Paper Jack' had been knocked down and killed on the Purley Way. If it was so then he died without leaving an enemy in the world except for some small boys with coloured matches.

Harry Score 122688

More about Gertie

I was patrolling the area of Croydon during the last war in the black-out and as I approached a disused public house, formerly known as The Crown but then being partly used as an air-raid shelter, I heard a muffled scream. On entering a door leading down to a cellar, I saw a bundled-up woman entangled with a perambulator on the foot of the stairs. On closer inspection she appeared to be unhurt, but very drunk. After ensuring that she was safe to be moved, I arranged to take her into custody for her own safety, complete with the old pram.

On arrival at the station some PCs present immediately recognised here as 'Gertie', a regular customer who made a living as a flower-seller in Croydon. She was subsequently charged for being drunk and incapable and in addition for not possessing an identity card.

The following morning she appeared before Croydon Magistrates with whom she had an ongoing camaraderie, pleading guilty to both charges. The Chairman of the Bench asked why she carried a bottle of methylated spirits with her, to which she replied, 'I have it to oil me pram'. He also asked why she didn't have an identity card, to which she answered, 'Why should I? Everybody knows me'. Her replies caused much laughter in the Courtroom. With 97 previous convictions behind her for the drunk and incapable charges she was once again convicted, sentenced to one day's imprisonment, and immediately released when the court completed the hearings.

With regard to the identity card, I was lumbered with her once again, and had to escort her to the registration office and also pay for it.

PC A Bettis ZD 129313

Paper Jack

I well recall two of the characters who roamed London pre-war. First of all Duppas Hill Kate - as she was known to us - her real name was Gertrude Hedson. She had many convictions for drunkenness in her time. I clearly recall her was one Sunday morning. My mother and father called me into their bedroom, and in the field opposite our house, we watched Gertrude washing her underwear in the cattle trough. I never knew if the cattle drank from it again.

Paper Jack, as he was called, was a very well-educated person and I knew him well. His real name was Priceby. A neighbour of ours used to let him sleep in her coal shed and I've had many a conversation over the fence. He was a harmless old man and for some unknown reason, had cut himself off from his family. He was dressed in paper winter and summer.

Unfortunately his death was a tragic one. He was knocked down in Waddon Park Avenue, Croydon and killed by a car one winter's evening. This would be about 1936.

Len Simms Ex Z

Oliver Pudvine

Those whose service stretches back to the Fifties and before will well remember an officer whose name itself was worthy of Dickens - Oliver Pudvine.

Tales about him are legion - many no doubt apocryphal - but I have a store of reminiscences, having served on the same relief as him during the twilight of his long career.

I remember the surprise I felt when I first transferred to King's Cross Road, then known as EK, to find in the parade room line-up an elderly gent with a big pink face, incongruously dressed in the uniform of a PC.

I soon got to know him better, although I never found out whether he had ever had a wife; he seemed the perfect bachelor. His extensive vocabulary was delivered in a manner suggesting the strictest confidence, his hand often covering his capacious mouth; the delivery was slow, deep and rumbling - the ideal voice-over for dog food advertisements.

Indeed, he was deeply devoted to his food which required, at grub time, an entire table whereon to lay out a wondrous selection: cheese, meat, pies, salad, vegetables, bread and butter, all carefully parcelled in individual paper bags, together with two mugs, one containing tea and the other hot water.

To these, between making pronouncements on the terrible state of the country (which was all the fault of the Yanks), he would devote loving attention. No 45 minutes was so well spent. While the rest of us wasted our time playing darts, cards or table-tennis, Ollie was servicing his formidable appetite.

On the street he favoured the cape, and he became the terror of the parking motorist in the Clerkenwell area, descending upon a line of cars like a rotund Batman, at times lying prone on the pavement to check exhaust systems. The result of his labours was a stack of process books, mostly for unnecessary obstruction. These books were masterpieces of calligraphy, erudition and legal argument: a barrister would have been hard-pressed to find a loophole in Ollie's cogent pleadings. That the evidence section of the book was three times as long as most of our thin and miserable contributions goes without saying.

Ollie had a distinct rolling gait, and it was as well to leave a couple of feet of clearance when walking with him. One priceless sight was of him and another large constable with a similar nautical roll returning to the nick from night duty crashing together at regular intervals like cymbals.

He was a pastmaster of the delicate art of mumping (scrounging) and, such was his knowledge of human frailty and such his outrageous nerve, that he had transformed it into an exact science.

In the Italian Quarter of Clerkenwell Ollie was a well-known and much-admired figure - a sort of latter-day medieval squire moving among his subjugated tenants.

By and large Ollie was a great man. He certainly brought some colour into the drab existence of us poor creatures struggling to get through the last two long hours of night duty, or the even longer first two of early turn. He was an original and a constant surprise.

Ted Dilley, ex M, J, N, G, Y, S, D8.

Doing Things the Pudvine Way

After being posted to Kings Cross Road, old EK, at the start of the 1960s, I was summonsed before Superintendent. Wharton, the Officer in Charge. I was told that my process figures were not up to standard, so I would be posted to process patrol with an experienced officer.

Next day I was accosted by a portly figure, round faced, helmet on the back of his head, wearing a flapping cape. Ollie Pudvine in the flesh.

Within a short time, like Batman and Robin, we had descended on the unsuspecting motorists of Farringdon Road. Ollie, with some relish and a little help from me, started to report every motorist in sight for obstruction, no road fund licence and many other offences.

After a short time I had to retreat into a doorway to avoid the irate motoring public, only to hear Ollie being told by one such person, to 'do something useful, you old F...'. This was met with a blank stare and another name in the book.

After a wet afternoon of trouble and strife, a young and chastened probationer followed his mentor back to the station to laboriously write out a pile of process books, which were then handed to an irate station officer (who before the advent of admin. units, typed all process charges with his own fair hand).

I would mention, that our return journey to the station was made by Ollie walking into the middle of the road and hailing a bus. Needless to say, we did not pay for the journey!

I slunk off to the Section House utterly exhausted, and in the evening had a well deserved pint to steady my shattered nerves.

Ollie was a character. Once worked with, never forgotten.

Donald McLean PC 237E, 237N, 148611

Man's Best Friend

PC Dave Latcham, alias The Chinese Hooligan or Late Turn Latch, was a slim consumptive-looking officer with drawn Mongolian cheek bones, and a slightly longer than regulation hair cut. His oil-stained uniform was usually embellished with a sprinkle of dandruff and just a touch of cigarette ash.

Dave had an insatiable appetite and could clear the canteen tables of left-overs quicker than a gannet. He derived his nickname from the fact that he looked like an untidy chinese 'lay-about'. He relished working late shifts, as he found early rising far too uncivilized and unflattering for his chalk-like complexion and Dracula-type life style!

Dave found no trouble swopping his early turn shifts with many willing officers, for this ensured a few extra hours in bed daily. One afternoon our hero was sitting in the police canteen devouring a third portion of somebody's leftover bread pudding, when the duty sergeant asked him if he would kindly attend the scene of a housebreaking, (a) as he was the only officer available and (b) because he was well over the time of his official refreshment break.

If ever there was a willing officer, it was Dave. He walked the short distance to the alleged scene of the break-in, a typical council house with its privet hedge, concrete path and Crittal windows which of course displayed the compulsory chipped alabaster alsatian dogs facing each other on the front windowsill like some prized antiques.

Dave was not unduly alarmed or surprised to be joined at the front gate by a huge mud-splattered german shepherd dog. Man and dog were ushered into the hall by the informant, a one-eyed shifty looking gentleman, who probably just had the edge over Dave for oil stains and unkempt appearance.

The great dog slipped knowingly into the rear kitchen, where it commenced devouring a bowl of cat food, whilst the cat appeared to be standing on stilts on top of the gas stove. Dave removed his helmet as he entered the inner sanctum and dusted down the ash-covered chair that he was offered.

Reclining on a couch opposite was 'One-eye's' spouse, a corpulent dyed blonde with dark roots highlights. She was wearing a tight fitting egg-tarnished blouse and a mini-skirt that displayed much, if not all of 'One-eye's' supper! This smoking vision of loveliness was set against the obligatory Gaugin print of the green-faced lady dominating the wall and a large television turned down slightly in order for Dave to be heard.

He had just completed recording the relevant details in his pocket book, when the great dog wandered into the room - sat down by the fire, and commenced to divest itself of fleas. The creature then belched loudly - walked over to the television and cocked its leg up against the screen. Five eyes looked searchingly at each other but not a word was spoken!

Dave declined the kind offer of a cup of tea from his host who stood by picking his ear with the handle of a table fork. As Dave was making his way to the front door, 'One-eye' shouted after him, 'Hey don't forget your dog mate!' 'Dog?' queried Dave, 'I haven't got a dog.' 'Well he ain't my bloody dog,' retorted One-Eye. 'I thought that he was a flipping police dog!'

Alan Marshall ex PC560P

Old-time Policing

Two incidents in the mid Thirties which caused considerable mirth amongst the troops at Lewisham, concerned one PC 'Lofty' Platt, an old timer, nearing the end of his service. He was reluctant to commit himself to writing reports and much preferred direct policing.

One wet morning Lofty was patrolling in Rushey Green, Catford, on a fairly busy main road, heading towards the station and a well-deserved breakfast, when he heard the squeal of brakes and turned to see a large open-top lorry had stopped at the kerb. A small mongrel dog was lying to one side of the front wheels.

The lorry driver alighted from his cab, looked at the dog, and pronounced to Lofty that it was dead. This was agreed. The dog had no collar and it was obvious that it was a stray. It was agreed that the driver could proceed on his way to Coventry and although it was a serious incident, Lofty would not take further action in the matter.

The driver got into his lorry and prepared to move off. Lofty picked up the dead dog and placed it in the rear of the lorry! Imagine the driver's reaction when he arrived at his destination!

The same PC was on night duty in Crofton Park, Brockley, and it was his usual practice to call at a certain bake house there, presumably for a 'mike' and a smoke. The Section Sergeant on this particular night was Tom Elliot, better known to the boys as 'Got a fag boy'. He and Lofty were not best friends.

Lofty called at the bakery as usual in the early hours of the morning, took off his helmet, and settled down on a chair for a few minutes.

Meanwhile one of the bakers popped outside for a bit of fresh air, but he quickly returned and tipped off Lofty that the Sergeant was approaching rapidly. Lofty immediately took off his tunic, stuffed it under the table together with his helmet, donned a white baker's apron and proceeded to the end of the bakehouse where, with his head bent, he appeared to be kneading some dough. The sergeant briefly glanced in at the door, exchanged a word with a baker and after satisfying himself that all was well, departed.

Lofty who did not wish to lose his pensionable increment, lived to plod another day.

Emrys Jones ex SPS M 125916

The Stork Cometh

Gracing our ranks during the late Fifties at Cannon Row was a certain PC 678 Charles Burgess.

I still smile when I see a shot of No 10 Downing Street on TV, with a grim-faced Diplomatic Protection Group PC outside, complete with bullet-proof vest necessary in the time we live - and I think of yesteryear when the only threat would be a milk bottle or half a brick thrown through the window by a disturbed man or women as a protest against a pigeon cull at Victoria Station!

Charlie had the bearing of an 'old time copper' and the size to match. However, he was softly spoken, and had a rather posh accent (or so I thought, being a northerner). He had been an MP (Redcap variety) at the Shape HQ near Paris, a lovely posting I always felt.

Like the rest of us at that time at AD, we did not relish the month's tour at and around the door of No 10. Two PCs were posted there, on Two and Three protection posts. Post two was the armed post.

One day around lunch time, the then Deputy Commissioner, Sir A Robertson, was enroute to his Club in St James on foot. He came up Downing Street, intending to walk through Treasury Passage onto Horse Guards Parade.

Outside No 10 stood Charlie, gazing across at the usual group of tourists. Now Charlie displayed a propensity to wearing a cape. Not a common sight then on A Division. The Dep. Comm. stopped in his tracks, when he realised the PC on the door appeared to have only one leg. Charlie was indeed balanced on one leg, the other being bent back at the knee, and held there with both hands.

Those who recall Deputy Commissioner Robertson will be aware that this phenomenon would not be ignored by him. He went hot foot up to Charlie, announcing himself. History does not record if Charlie asked for his silver token. Robertson demanded to know if he possessed two legs. Still on one leg, Charlie explained he had been studying the stork, and how it managed to remain in one position, on one leg, for long periods. Before this could be explained in detail, it became obvious that Mr Robertson was not in the least interested in the mechanics of stork's legs. Charlie was ordered on two legs.

Red faced and no doubt even more hungry, Sir Andrew continued on his way. He must have had a good lunch, or saw the funny side (the former, one thinks) for nothing more was heard of the incident.

Tourists, especially Americans, did photograph the one legged PC, and no doubt Charlie still adorns photograph albums all over America. When the question was posed 'What happened to the guy's other leg?' the answer would depend on who was the PC opposite. If it was PC 398A Harry Bacon, the loss would be explained as either that Charlie was knocked over by the Commissioner's horse, or that, when in pursuit of a would-be assassin, his leg had been trapped in the cogs of Big Ben's clock. 'Not to worry, Sir, he has a spare leg in number 10.'

A PC fresh from the Training School had been put on Number Three protection post, and was giving Charlie a hard time, grumbling that he had joined the police to make London's streets safe, not simply to adorn Downing Street. Also, he was keen to get in the Traffic Branch, and how could he do Process charges outside number 10? During this time a coal lorry had stopped opposite and the driver and his mate started to unload bags of coal. Without a word, Charlie had pencil and Process book out and reported the driver for several offences. He walked back to the PC, replacing pencil and book. 'You were saying..?

Working traffic point in the Mall (another delightful posting) Charlie espied the officer from the Household Cavalry trotting down the Mall to dismount the guard at Whitehall Palace at 4pm. In the prescribed manner Charlie gave The Lord Lieutenant a signal to stop. It seems the brakes on the horse did not work, and Charlie was pushed aside by his Lordship's nag. Charles was not amused. The upshot was that Charlie was posted to FH Notting Hill, much to his delight.

Was that the last we would hear of him? Of course not! I saw the headlines of the Evening News sometime afterwards. 'Glubb Pasha's son arrested'. I read on... 'PC Burgess told the court...'

We had plenty of characters at AD with a sense of humour and you needed one - a month's posting on night duty outside No 10 would be enough to tax anyone's spirits.

Alan Jackson, 148490 PS ex AD, AH,CTS,L,TDP, TDR,B10

A Winter's Tale

As a young man in the Fifties, I was based at Kensington FK. One night duty I was on 9 beat and wandered off it across the Cromwell Road into Stanhope Gardens. It was about 3.30am and I was walking past a row of derelict houses when I heard a piercing whistle.

I went to the house concerned and gingerly made my way down the broken stone steps leading to the basement, then through the downstairs door flapping on its broken hinges in the cold November wind.

It was pitch dark inside and I noticed a dark shape against the banisters. Hurriedly I switched on my torch, but as usual, it took about three tries before it worked.

Imagine the sight that greeted me. Chained to the banisters was a good-looking young man in his twenties; dressed on that cold winter's morning in a thin open windcheater with an exposed bare chest. He wore a pair of khaki shorts and a pair of wellington boots.

It took me a couple of seconds to take in this apparition and then I blurted out something like 'What are you doing here?'

The man told me that he had been in a pub and some men had done this to him. My first thought was that he was a queer and had propositioned the wrong man, but on reflection didn't really believe it.

Going up the road I found my mate John Watts religiously checking the parked car registrations on his 'stolen' list. I shouted to him.

'Hey John, come and see this body chained up down here,' and he replied with his inimitable charm, 'Sod off! What are you doing off your beat?'

I persuaded him to come down, and a look of concern spread over his face. One of us stayed at the scene and the other went to Fourteen post, on the Cromwell Road and phoned the nick.

A DC nicknamed Whiskers, because of his RAF handlebar moustache, attended the scene with the duty officer, Inspector Sims. The Fire Brigade arrived and cut the chains and the man was taken back to Kensington Station.

It later transpired that he had buried his clothes under some rubble and chained himself up with a couple of snap locks. He, in fact, was a masochist and was duly released.

The tragic sequel to this was that three years later the same man was found dead under a manhole in a disused naval camp in Devon. Only an ID gave his particulars as the same man from Stanhope Gardens. I learned that he had been a university student and the son of a naval sea-captain.

Rick Harrington ex PC 349F

Crepitus

Our First Aid sergeant instructor when I joined Peel House in the winter of 1935 was a gruff but not unkindly man and he was always on about Crepitus. For those who may have forgotten, it is the scraping sound from fracture bones.

Crepitus became his name. Everyone called him that. He used to fix us with a glittering eye and say: 'if the infirm is conscious give him 'ot tea, 'ot coffee, 'ot cocoa, 'ot as can be drunk!' It became a catch phrase. Meeting in the corridors of that gloomiest of buildings we used to shout, 'As 'ot as can be drunk' and laugh.

Then the war came. I and 1,695 others were released from the Metropolitan Police to become Aircrew. In April 1945 I was a flight engineer on a flying boat operating from the Bay of Bengal. At that time our business was long range air-sea rescue. First Aid boxes were used. I asked who was going to deal with those. My gallant Captain said 'You are, because you are qualified.' My certificate was years out of date. Well, that's war for you.

We had a call. An American B29 bomber had come down near the Burara Coast. There was a reliable fix and we were off. We found five airmen in the sea, none too soon, for one in particular was in a poor way being badly burnt.

I had to hurry off to play my part in getting the flying-boat air borne, so I said 'Put that burn cream on them and give them all the hot sweet tea they can drink.' I don't remember saying 'as 'ot as can be drunk' but I might have.

When I returned, the rescued were an extraordinary sight. The burn cream was bright purple and had been liberally applied. They looked like ancient Britons. The copious tea produced a need and we only had ration tins, emptied through the rear hatch on the long grind back to India.

Medical opinion as I remember was divided as to the efficacy of the treatment, but they all lived. The crew went to see them in hospital. One of my lads said they ought to thank Crepitus. They didn't understand. Well they wouldn't, being Americans.

Sometimes, thinking about all this, I hear a chuckle from the place where all good First Aid instructors go for their just reward and I always know it's old Crepitus.

S Cooper

The Raj Prince

Any Sunday morning visit to the street market in Petticoat Lane during the Thirties and Forties would inevitably afford a sight of that well-known purveyor of racing tips at 6d a time, the one and only Raj Prince Monolulu. His tall figure, well over six feet, and his flamboyant and many-coloured costume, topped with three coloured ostrich feathers in the band around his forehead identified him from afar and if you were still in any doubt his raucous call of 'I gotta horse, I gotta horse' confirmed his identity without question.

He was undoubtedly one of the best crowd-pullers I have ever known and such was his fame, he could bring Petticoat Lane to a complete standstill without really trying. Yet on the many times I had to move him on, he was always cheerful and courteous and complied with directions, only taking time to apologise to his audience for ceasing business.

It was at an Epsom spring race meeting that the Raj Prince came into this story. After a winter spent on Commercial Street manor, a day on the Downs was a great pleasure. We had arrived on the Downs long before the general public and had paraded on the course in front of the Grandstand to be posted to our respective duty posts.

I had been posted on one of the race starts and Jack Milsom had been posted on the Downs which was on my way, so together we made our stroll to duty. Crossing a car park we met the Raj Prince Monolulu who greeted us warmly and after a few words of banter, he tipped three horses: Cider-apple, Sandal Wood and Julian. Personally, I wasn't interested but Jack expressed his intention of backing them if he could get someone to put the money on for him. To cut a long story short, Jack managed to back all three and all three went down the pan.

When racing was over I met Jack on the way to book off and again we ran across the Raj Prince. Jack went over to him and, with a broad grin on his face, said to the Prince 'Show your face down the Lane on Sunday morning and your feet won't touch.' The Prince returned the grin and produced a handful of sixpenny pieces saying, 'You can't win 'em all but this should cover the stakes.'

The sequel to all this occurred some six weeks later, again at a racecourse, as I had been posted with others to an evening meeting at Alexandra Palace. Several of us PCs were walking through the park to the course when who do we see sitting on his shooting stick but the Raj

Prince who, as we passed him, was murmuring 'a little cider for the Policeman' which he repeated several times. My immediate companion was PC Jack Grace, an inveterate gambler. He opened up his copy of the Evening News which he had bought solely for the racing details, and discovered that Cider Apple was indeed a runner. 'I'll have a bet on that,' said Jack. Unfortunately I had to put my oar in with a statement, 'I wouldn't, Jack. That was one of three he tipped Jack Milsom at Epsom six weeks ago and they all lost.'

As you have probably guessed, Jack didn't back it and, surprise surprise, it won at 8-1. When I met Jack later that night he told me things about my ancestry I couldn't possibly believe.

F.N. Cook Ex PC 488G/125309

Alpha and Omega (almost)

Whatever merit is lacking in this, my first attempt at literary composition, at least my story is true, and it also supports the contention that truth is stranger than fiction.

In 1932 I joined the Met. I was sent with 20 or so other young applicants, to the training school at Peel House in Victoria, London, for a ten-week course on How to Become An Efficient Police Constable. It was the toughest ten weeks of my life.

Daily, except Sundays, we were awakened at 6am and at 6.30 the whole school (nine other classes) were running around the Tate Gallery and its environs until 7.30. Breakfast at 8; and at 9 o'clock the day's work started. There were lectures on law, police procedure and self defence till 5pm with a break for dinner from 1-2pm.

Officially that ended the day, but we soon learned it was imperative to devote every spare minute, including Sundays, to the private study of our bible, the Instruction Book, if success in the final examination was to be hoped for. It was necessary to learn by heart whole chapters of the accursed tome and the task was colossal. It proved too much for some and weekly resignations were not uncommon.

Another aspect of the course which some found difficult to take was character training, not a specific subject but a policy permeating every part of the syllabus, designed with one intent and adhered to relentlessly by each of the many instructors.

The object: simply to toughen the individual mentally, and to instill and develop self discipline without which a man cannot control others and command respect. The means: a constant barrage of sarcasm, facetiousness, ridicule and something at times near to downright bullying. All very juvenile but in the main effective, and it worked. Some took it hard; others, like me, learned how to cope and benefit.

There were among us a number of ex-service men, men already inured to parade-ground pressures, and from them I learned quickly how to deal with the fearsome assault of our persecutors. A sense of humour helps: it can dull the edge of sarcasm and castigation if one can see the funny side and laugh (secretly of course) at one's tormentor; but the great thing is - not to resist. When the adversary is too strong for you, you fall in with him, in the same way as a wise man never fights nature; he gets along with it and uses it.

I found that by going along with the instructors and really trying to comply with demands, stupid as they were at times, the risk of abuse was reduced and it became a matter of pride to execute commands to the best of one's ability.

We learned to control ourselves so that later we could control others. We also learned how to control traffic, crowds and arterial bleeding, how to collect evidence, give evidence in court, take statements and write reports. Above all, we learned how to complete reports. So much was made of this that I began to suspect that what happened was never so important as the way it was reported. 'Date, time, place: every detail to be recorded accurately, omitting nothing, adding nothing, remembering that a policeman's report might easily hang a man.' We had capital punishment in those days.

I became a good recorder of events; at least I think I did. Nobody ever told me so, but a report accepted without comment had to be a good one and in later years few of mine were questioned.

Well I got through the ten weeks all right and gained sufficient marks in the final examination to win an 'Honours' tie. I still have it.

Finished with Peel House, I was posted to one of the big outer divisions in North London and found myself stationed at Hampstead, a lovely spot in those days but a poor training ground for probationary constables. Largely heathland, the rest of the manor was a high-class residential district, quiet, pleasant, but dreadfully boring for a young policeman eager to make a name for himself.

When eventually allowed out on my own I prowled those quiet, select byways diligently searching for some opportunity to put my vast, acquired knowledge to use. But nothing happened and there was nothing to report, at least for a long time. My big chance came late in November.

Leaves from the Heath trees were falling faster than the roadmen could sweep them up and the weather was seasonally wet and miserable. One night it rained heavily for ten hours.

Next morning, on duty in a road bordering the Heath, I turned a corner and nearly got my feet wet: the road was flooded. I knew exactly what to do: inform the Borough Council and stand by to divert traffic and assist pedestrians as necessary. I did the former by phone then stood by importantly to assist traffic and pedestrians in distress.

Neither appeared, but in due course a council lorry drew up and three men with brooms and shovels made short work of the leaves blocking the drains. In a few minutes the road was unflooded and I hadn't raised a finger to divert traffic or carry a little old lady to safety. Oh well! not quite what I had hoped for to christen my virgin pocket book, but something anyhow. I retired to a convenient spot and wrote a report worthy of another tie.

Later I met my sergeant. 'All right, boy?' he inquired gruffly. 'All correct, sergeant,' I replied smartly, 'but I have a report.' I handed him my pocket book. He read the report and turned slowly on me with a look of utter disbelief. 'What a load of bloody rubbish,' he snapped.

Surprised, not to say hurt, I asked 'What do you mean, sergeant?' 'Mean?' he retorted, 'I mean this is a load of bloody tripe! Getting the council out to clear a few leaves from a drain!' 'What else could I do, Sarge?' I wailed. 'Do?' he snarled, 'you could have got your stick out and cleared the bloody leaves yourself.' Humiliated, I apologised. 'Sorry, sergeant; but that's what we were told to do at Peel House.' He relented a bit. 'Well you're not in Peel House now, boy. You've got to forget what they taught you there and learn to use your common sense.'

So that was my first lesson in how things should not be done. Of course the sergeant was quite wrong in saying I must forget all I had learned. Without that knowledge, I would have been up the creek many times during the next 26 years. What he really meant was that I must learn how to use it, tempering book learning with common sense. This takes quite a time, but when achieved one is said to be experienced.

Some 25 years later, I was still in the same division but at a different station. I had survived a war, married and raised a family and was on the verge of retirement.

It was November again and I was on night duty. It had been raining heavily all day and when I paraded for duty at 9.45pm I was given the temporary rank of Acting Sergeant and sent straight out to report to an Inspector at the junction of two main arterial roads which ran through our area.

I found the place flooded. The junction lies in a hollow and the River Brent which flows parallel to one of the roads had burst its banks in places and turned the area into a sizeable lake. The roads were invisible but here and there an abandoned lorry, up to the top of the wheels in water, bore witness to abortive attempts to beat the flood.

I found my Inspector who said it had been like this since early afternoon. Council road engineers had been down but could do nothing until the water had subsided a bit. It seemed the trouble was in the main culvert which they could not get to. These two roads carried a vast amount of traffic and a serious problem had built up rapidly.

Every policeman in the surrounding districts had been mobilised to implement a vast diversion exercise devised at short notice and commendable speed.

The situation had been under control for some hours and the day duty men were being relieved piecemeal as the night relief came on. Nothing more could be done other than maintain a watching brief and pray that the rain, which had eased off about the time I arrived, would not start again.

The Inspector said: 'I shall have to leave now but will be back about midnight. If anything happens, get hold of me through the station.'

He left and I visited as many of my men as possible to relay orders. Then I viewed the scene and pondered. My mind drifted back 25 years and I heard the Sergeant's voice: 'You could have got your stick out and cleared the bloody leaves yourself!'

Walking along the raised river bank at the north of one of the roads I reached the western limit of the flood area then continued along the pavement in the same direction until I came to an iron grating of a road drain in the gutter. Continuing west, I paced the distance between this drain and the next, then on again to the next. The distance between drains was about 30 paces so there was a fair chance that the first drain under water to the east of the one I had started from would also be 30 paces away.

I cut myself a branch from a willow tree growing on the river bank and from the first exposed drain walked east into the flood water for 30 paces.

I prodded with my pole and stirred up a mass of sodden leaves.

Almost immediately there was a 'glup-glupping' sound and a small whirlpool appeared, to be stifled as soon as the stirring ceased.

Satisfied my hunch was correct, I stuck the pole upright into the drain as a marker and gathered together three of my men to cut themselves similar tools. We found three more drains (obligingly they all adhered to the same 30 paces rule) and we all stirred merrily until every drop of water in the immediate vicinity drained away.

Then further into the flood we went for similar assault on the next four drains, and so on until the lake had completely disappeared. The whole operation took less than half an hour. It would be good in terms of dramatic effect to end my tale thus: 'And so my first and last cases were in essence the same and the success of the last resulted directly from the lesson of the first, after 25 years'.

I am tempted to do so, but it would not be true. Being, thanks to my Peel House training, a man of some considerable self-discipline and therefore captain of my own soul, I can resist the temptation and shall confine myself to plain, unadorned fact: and that, I feel, would give my Peel House instructors exceeding joy.

No, it was not the last report of my career: I did not in fact retire until several months later, during which time I compiled many more; for the life of me I cannot remember the last.

In fact I never reported the above incident at all. That duty fell to the Inspector and I did not even see it, but I am willing to wager it contained no mention either of me, my zeal and perspicacity, nor my devotion to duty.

G. M. Winterflood PC558S/122392 SH & SY (Known as Stormy Weather).

Small Favour

On the manor, we had a butcher who was kindly disposed towards the CID. Every Wednesday evening he would leave his motor by the back gate of the nick with the ignition key under the driver's mat. If we weren't too busy, the car was ours for the evening and we would leave it in the same place at closing time, after visiting a few hostelries on the manor and investing our half-a-crown out-of-pocket expenses on purchasing refreshments for informants while seeking information.

In those days aids on F District were only allowed this half-crown for incidentals a week unless you had an arrest, in which case the Detective Inspector let you charge 5/-.

On one particular Wednesday I was duty driver and away we went. The car was a wooden-bodied Ford Pilot Estate with plenty of poke. After about our third pub the lads piled aboard but the car wouldn't start and soon the battery was dead. While we were trying to push-start it, along came the area car, driven by a marvellous character who will remain anonymous, as I wouldn't wish to embarrass him.

Seeing our predicament he immediately had the solution. He would use the area car to push the Ford - bumper to bumper - and when he hooted I would declutch from second gear and we would be away. However the Ford had a rather high compression ratio and we came to a halt with my engine running but the back bumpers of the Ford had over-ridden the front bumpers of the area car, with not inconsiderable damage to the radiator of the police car.

After much huffing and puffing (and comments about throwing a bucket of water over them) we got the two vehicles apart. We asked what we could do - like knocking up a panel beater - but the driver said 'Not to worry, you haven't seen me,' and away he drove. We got back to the nick about 10pm and booked off.

I started to walk back to Paddenswick Section House and down a side road, in the shadows. I saw the area car, which in those days went off duty at 11pm. I went over and asked if they'd managed to fix the radiator. The driver was looking somewhat apprehensive as he still had a large dent in the front end. He said what he needed was a 'shout' which necessitated the entire crew leaving the car, so the damage could have been caused by some careless, or drunken driver.

Unfortunately, that evening things were quiet and they hadn't had a call. Nearby were a couple of phone boxes. I dialled 999 and putting on my best Oxford accent told IR 'I have just seen two men climb over the fence into Ravenscourt Park and they were carrying a heavy suitcase'. The reply: 'thank you sir, may I have your name and address?' (you must be joking). As I left the phone box the area car drove past me and the driver bid me 'Goodnight, and thanks mate'. After all, one good turn deserves another.

Alan Wheeler ex F, B, V, Heathrow, COC13.

The Old Rivals

There has always been tension between uniform officers and those in plain clothes. We uniform officers must have been a healthy lot. Of course, the CID were never exposed to the elements, most of their duty was spent in a warm office or the local pub. Any job in bad weather got the response: 'Sent the Aids out to keep 'obo' on it.'

I always remember an old SPS at East Dulwich giving a lecture to me and another 'rookie'. He said, 'If you ever get a good 'knock off', stay in the charge room until you have signed the Charge Sheet, otherwise the CID gits will creep out of their office, tell you to get back on your beat, then they would sign the Charge Sheet and get their DI to get them in for a commendation.'

The SPS in question was an extremely smart man, uniform always immaculate with numerous World War 1 medal and campaign ribbons. He really disliked the CID and would refer to them as men unfit to be seen in uniform.

W. G. Tilbury, ex PC 301P/126303, PW, PR, DT8.

Thanks for the memories...

• Milk sold from a shining 20 gallon can on a two-wheeled hand cart hinged in the middle, with a pint measuring can.
• Empire Day, 1 May, with Union Jacks everywhere.
• November 11, when all traffic stopped, and everyone stood still for two minutes.
• Sugar scooped from a sack and wrapped in thick blue paper rolled into a cone with the sharp end pushed in.
• Winter butter tasting strongly of mangel wurzels.
• In sweet shops, tiger nuts, locust beans, gob-stoppers and Woodbines (five for 2d) in open-ended envelopes.
• Bowling hoops, whipping tops, home-made sledges, gas mantles, and rag rugs with a sacking base.
• Gypsies by the roadside making clothes pegs from willow branches.
• Winkles on a cart on Sunday afternoons, and the cat's meat man.
• Sunday School trips to the seaside with our eyes full of soot from the steam engine.

• The lamp-lighters and the barrel organ man with his pet monkey.
• The annual horse show with magnificent heavy horses bedecked in shining harness, brasses and rosettes.
• The ploughman at work in the rain with a folded sack over his shoulders and a bottle of cold tea in the hedgerow.
• The fishmonger delivering herrings to the door for 14 a shilling.
• Drinking-water collected from a communal pump with a shoulder yoke to carry two pails.
• Nine gallons of cider delivered free up to 100 miles for £1 (1931).
• A suit of Plus Fours made to measure for £1.50.
• The village baker baking the Christmas cake for one penny.
• Carbide bicycle lamps and the carbide also used for home-made fireworks.
• Out with the village poacher to pick up snared rabbits only to find the gamekeeper had taken the snares, together with the rabbits.
• The hand-operated fire-tender drawn by four horses at full gallop, and the crews called out by the Church bells all rung at once.

Those were the days!

Geoffrey Taylor, 124133 H, DT7

Riches from Beyond the Grave

While I was paying a night visit to Richmond Station, a lad was brought in who had escaped from a Borstal institution and was found to be in possession of a number of £5 notes. His story was that on his first night of freedom, he had found suitable accommodation in an old air-raid shelter at the rear of an empty house, where he came upon an old tin box full of fivers.

As he found it well nigh impossible to carry all the notes, he had buried most of them under a grave adjoining a church. He knew neither the name of the church nor where it was situated.

Deciding to take the boy by car to the numerous graveyards on the Sub-Division, we first drove to Richmond church, then to Petersham, where Captain George Vancouver, the discoverer of British Columbia, is buried, but to no avail. Finally we came to Old Mortlake Church which, according to the boy, seemed similar to the place he had concealed the notes. Scaling the iron railings, a search began among the graves.

It was an unusually dark and blustery night making it more difficult.

At last we came to a grave consisting of a large stone slab and headstone, under which he thought they were hidden. It took two of us to raise the heavy stone, but before we had time to focus our torches on it, a sudden gust of wind blew fivers in all directions.

Needless to say, there was a rush to recover the notes, some having blown well away from the gravestones.

Whether all were accounted for is doubtful in the circumstances; and anyone visiting the old Mortlake church might still be lucky enough to find a weather-beaten fiver caught in a crack of some ancient tomb. Subsequent enquiries were made on T Division to find the rightful owner.

Frank Rawlings

It's a Bumpy Ride

The Hand Ambulance, popularly known as 'the barrow' was a contraption with two large wheels at the front and a prop-stand and smaller wheel at the back. It had a perambulator-like hood at the top, a wooden body platform and two great thick leather straps to fasten down recalcitrant or insensible bodies. I was at Marlborough Street with Tommy Land and can testify that the barrow was in constant use, particularly on Friday and Saturday nights, when, owing to the vagaries of the licensing hours, we at Marlborough Street could look forward to minor (not always so minor!) riots. The pubs in Marylebone - the Selfridges side of Oxford Street closed at 10.30pm but those in Westminster (the opposite side of Oxford Street) closed at 11pm.

The favourite drinking spot for the Irish labourers was the Marble Arch end of Oxford Street. As soon as time was called there was a concerted rush for the *Gloucester* pub on the corner of Park Street and Oxford Street. Unfortunately for us it was on Marlborough Street ground. There they were, pushing and shoving to get as many in as possible before 11pm which without exception led to a challenge to fisticuffs and there was no shortage of takers. Police with the utility van and the barrow were soon in attendance, making, or trying to make, arrests.

When sufficient reinforcements arrived, arrests were made and peace restored to the *Gloucester.*

The recalcitrants who couldn't be taken in the van were strapped to the barrow and taken on what we used to call the long ride home. This was via Upper Brook Street and South Molton Street to the *Haunch of*

Venison Yard which was the object of the exercise. For this particular Mews thoroughfare was cobble-stoned and was traversed at as great a speed as the pusher was able to muster. This caused the miscreant's head to beat a rapid tattoo on the wooden body of his conveyance which resulted in one of two responses. Either he increased his vituperation in obscenity and volume or he became absolutely silent. In either case you had made your point!

When quite a young recruit, I was called to the *Coach and Horses* pub by the licensee who requested that I eject an abusive drunk who wouldn't leave. As we were hurrying to the pub I was going through the procedure in my mind which we had been taught at Peel House - drunken men: method to be used for the ejection from public house. I went over it silently. If he refuses to leave peacefully push his left shoulder at the same time pushing his right shoulder towards you - this will have the effect of swinging him around with his back to yours, then put your arm around his neck and drag him from the premises.

On entering the bar, I was confronted by a huge man. This is him, says the licensee, hastily retiring behind the bar to a position of comparative safety. I asked the drunk to leave and he told me in concise if not too coherent words that he had no intention of doing so. Right, I thought, you asked for it, and with that started to put into action the ejection procedure.

Unfortunately, neither my pushing nor pulling managed to budge him. Ah, I thought, tact and conciliatory methods called for here. Eventually on promising to get him a cab, he came outside with me.

Two cab-drivers refused to take him and I was beginning to realise this was not my day. I then noticed that he was standing with his heels against the kerb. I curled myself up and took a running leap into his chest, over he went on his back and I sat on his chest.

Right, I thought, what now? By the grace of God, around the corner came Inspector Pitt. He was a short, very rotund man and greeted me with the usual, 'What's up lad?' I told him I had arrested the man for being drunk & disorderly. With that we each took an arm and marched him to the nick. I am not sure who took whom to the station but it must have been an unusual sight to see Inspector Pitt and myself being given a ride by swinging on the prisoner's arms. We got him inside and charged him. The following morning he was most contrite and apologetic.

George Price 121685 C,K,V,T.

How Mulligan Found the Limehouse Orphans' box

My tale begins in the days before the spread of Chinese restaurants all over our green and pleasant land but we had many Chinese hostelries on our ground for all the varied licensees and media workers who gravitated to Limehouse after their evening's toil was done.

The general effect of this was that 'coppering' at HH was at its busiest between midnight and 4am. But when some special attraction elsewhere kept the nocturnal wanderers away, HH relaxed and became a more normal type of police station, where some small transgressions passed unnoticed.

One of these small transgressions was a quick game of pinky. Now pinky is a dreadful corruption of the game of snooker, sometimes called scrub which is played with only one red and all the coloured balls with the pink ball being a sort of 'no mans land', any movement of which by any means cost the person in play his complete score. The object of the game is to score 31 with only two odd numbers, the black and green, which could only be potted in the two bottom pockets in the case of the black, and the top right hand pocket in the case of the green. A game which gives rise to much hatred and the use of strange words which could not be used even in canteen company.

Serving at Limehouse at the time were a young active sergeant and an older wiser Station Sergeant, both refugees from A division where they were only missed by the divisional rugby team.

The SPS had pondered for some time over his young colleague's obsession with this diabolical game when he would have been safer in the front office, and probably richer. He decided that sheer terror was the cure. Coming into the front office for a visit on one of the quiet nights, he found it as thickly populated as the Marie Celeste. Reconnaissance soon disclosed that the attention was on the snooker table from whence came muttered 'You've still got to get the black' and the click of the devilish spheres interspersed with expletives.

With his duty driver he decided to introduce the spice of danger for his sergeant to bring him back to reality.

The driver, as always, had his screwdriver handy and within a matter of moments, the Orphans Box left its safe home on the counter and nestled in the bottom of the young sergeant's clothing locker, in the Sergeant's room.

Having struck his blow for 'good order' the SPS continued his arduous pilgrimage up Burdett Road, Bow Common Lane and various other East End beauty spots to Poplar, and finally around to the Isle of Dogs where the swing bridge outside 12 gate of West India Dock had its own Police Box.

At this point Mr Mulligan enters the story. The SPS, having 'the gift of tongues' introduced himself to the Communications officer with the news 'My name's Mulligan, I work for Wimpey, I was on my way to one of our jobs and I see that your little police station here has been robbed, a little tin box with Orphans on the front of it but there's no money in it.' A deadly silence from the other end followed by a strangled gasping voice: 'Stay where you are mate', to which Mr Mulligan said 'I've got to get on now but I'll take the little box with me and if I come this way I'll drop it in at the big police station up the road, but if I don't come back, I'll drop it in at Scotland Yard on my way back to Hammersmith'.

Putting his handkerchief back in his pocket, the SPS carried on to HI, where the lights were flashing furiously and he was informed by his errant sergeant, in a broken voice, of the loss of the orphans box.. 'and I've only been out of the office for a few minutes at the toilet and what's more I don't think it was there when I took over at ten.' I should mention that he had been warned the previous week of the date of his 'oral' promotion board for SPS, having succeeded in the 'written'. In due course the SPS returned to HH having sadistically allowed time for terror to have its full effect.

The matter was considered whilst all eyes watched the door for Mulligan's arrival. A suggestion by the driver illustrated the dire straits which had been reached, 'Sarge, if I run you down to Arbour Square and you take the station officer into the reserve room, I'll pinch their box off the counter'. The sergeant was outraged, 'Don't be daft, then we'd both be in trouble if you got caught.' 'Well I wouldn't do it if there was any chance of being caught, but you're the one who's going on a promotion board.' The desperate young sergeant said 'Have you got a screwdriver then?'

The duty officer, conscious of the fact that Jack held the key of the safe in which there was a revolver and ammunition, reminded them that the box always had the Superintendent's signature across the bottom so it couldn't be interchanged. After a short pause, Johnny the driver produced the second of the solutions which had been prepared enroute between Isle of Dogs nick and HH. 'Tell you what, Sarge, when this geezer comes in, I'll go out and come in behind him to the counter and we'll nick him for stealing the Orphans Box.'

Protests from Jack about the grave injustice of such an action were met with the 'It's up to you Sarge, you're the one going on the board'. Jack put on another couple of years whilst he pondered and then demanded an assurance that Mr Mulligan must not be ill treated in any way, no thumps, no stick out. The duty officer who only seemed to be able to raise objections said 'but didn't he say it was empty? This time of the month its half full of half crowns and even notes, why would he bring an empty box back and there's no way you can get that amount of money to put in it.'

With that unhelpful contribution he announced that he was 'going to get round the ground' and left Jack in his own individual cloud of gloom and despair, whilst desperately trying to estimate how much change there might be in the canteen till.

As the duty officer was driving out of the station yard, the side door of the station opened and loud and clear across the Limehouse skies rang out 'You bloody Irish B....d!' I don't know what took him to his locker just then.

S Powers BEM.

Sent for a Purpose

I was on duty in the Archway Road one morning, doing a school crossing. The road at this point was very steep and busy and was deemed too dangerous for a school crossing patrol. It was sheeting down with rain. Archway Road was awash from kerb to kerb.

A young cyclist drew up beside me. He had a drop handled racing machine, cape and sou'wester. 'Can you tell me the way to Camberwell please officer?' Well you can imagine my response, I dared not take my trusty A-Z out and try to explain the way from Highgate to Camberwell in that weather, so I quickly said 'Follow the signs to Central London, cross any of the bridges over the Thames and you'll pick up a sign to Camberwell.' 'How far is it?' he asked. 'Oh it must be all of nine miles, ' I said as I looked at this drowned rat. 'Is that all?' he said as he replaced his foot in the pedal straps and sprinted off. 'I've just come from Birmingham.' I felt as flat as a pancake and I'm equally sure he felt nine feet tall.

On another occasion I was standing outside the Police Box at the Nags Head , on the Holloway Road/Seven Sisters junction when a giant of a man came up to me. He was obviously a navvy by profession and his hair hadn't been washed for a few months. He was clutching the scruffiest bit of paper and envelope. In an almost incomprehensible Scottish accent he bashfully asked: 'Officer will you kindly write a letter for me to my wife up in Scotland? You see, I can't read or write.'

Then he explained how he had come down to London six months previously to look for work and somewhere for him and his wife to live. He had just succeeded on both counts and I had the privilege of drafting the good news as if I was writing to my own wife. So I took him into the Police Box and did just that. He did manage to write his name at the end.

We shook hands and he was on his way. I often think of him, and feel sure I was placed outside that Police Box on that day for that purpose.

Paul Phillips ex PC 178N

Tempus Fugit

Here are some of my own observations on the subject of growing old.

Shop assistants call you 'Dear'
You pay someone to do your DIY
You eventually realise that this is it.
Its years since you bought a new suit.
Market researchers in shopping precincts ignore you.
You can remember A.R.Ds and Form 29.
(Men only) A woman offers you her seat on a bus.
You look in the mirror and your father/mother looks back at you.
You discover Saga, paracetamol and your prostate.
When someone mentions 'The War' you ask 'Which One?'

Derek Peckham

Fascists & Commies

In the last few months of 1946, our easy life was disturbed on a weekly basis by having to go as Aid to G Division every Sunday to help police fascists' and communists' meetings at Ridley Road, Dalston. Fortunately, the area was quite familiar to me, I was a frequent visitor to Ridley Road Market. Street markets always held a special fascination for me.

There was really only one recognised pitch for a meeting at Ridley Road on a Sunday afternoon, and the two opposing parties would try to arrive early in order to book the site before each other. As soon as the market closed on Saturday night they put down a box and claimed the ground for Sunday afternoon. The losers in this weekly competition tried to start up a meeting on the opposite side of the road, so they finished up just yards apart with a certain guarantee that verbal exchanges would soon develop into physical violence. The numbers actually attending to listen to the speakers were never more than two or three hundred, but thousands of other people turned up just to see the fun when the police closed the meetings down.

We used to have to form a double line, back to back, between the two opposing factions, and attempt to keep order so that the meetings could be conducted peacefully. Needless to say it was a forlorn hope and we found ourselves the meat in the sandwich as the two diametrically opposed groups tried to get at each other and the meetings had to be, almost invariably, closed down early.

Chief Superintendent Charles Satterthwaite of G Division was usually the officer in charge and he always made his presence felt. I remember on one occasion seeing him struggling to arrest a soldier in uniform who was shouting rather unpleasant things about the fascists. As Mr Satterthwaite pulled him by one arm, the soldier's wife or girl friend was pulling on the other. With all the crowds I did not see the outcome nor was able to assist in any way.

Very late the same night, while we were parading at Dalston Police Station prior to our dismissal, I saw a uniformed soldier sitting in the Charge room and heard the Station Officer making an appeal for his arresting officer to make himself known. I gather no one came forward because shortly afterwards he was released without charge but warned to keep away from the area on Sunday afternoons. I never did know whether he was same soldier that I had seen with Mr Satterthwaite earlier, but I like to think that he was.

On a subsequent Sunday I was moving slowly down one side of Kingsland Road, trying to disperse the crowds, when I saw a milk bottle thrown from my side of the road to the other. There was no way that I could see who had thrown the bottle but I did see it land on the helmet of a colleague on the opposite side of the road. When I arrived he was helmet-less, struggling with a man he was trying to arrest. It appeared that the moment the bottle struck his helmet he turned and grabbed the nearest person to him and was determined to make an arrest for assault on police. I had to spend several minutes trying to calm both of them down, and then convincing my colleague that he had to let his suspect go. I escorted the 'injured party' back to the Police Station, but as far as I know he did not suffer any real hurt except damaged pride.

I hope that these reminiscences will remind others of those Post War days when we were constantly reminded that the signature on our Warrant Card was not yet dry and how easy the 'Job' was compared to the Pre-War days.

Dick Pamplin Wt No 128917 ex PC 192J and PS 16H

In a London Pea-Souper

I found a newspaper cutting in Australia this year whilst we were visiting my sister. There is a photo of a fog-shrouded PC in the cutting, which refers to the four day 'pea-souper' London smog of 5 December 1952.

My husband at the time of the smog was a PC on A Division. I remember the smog well. I had a young baby then and couldn't go out. My husband was on duty at Hyde Park Corner 8-4pm or 4-12 midnight, all traffic duty and responsible for opening the Wellington Arch gates for the Royal family.

I know that like a lot of other men he was there for King George VI's funeral and of course later for the Queen's Coronation, but coming across a newspaper picture of a smog-obscured London Bobby on point duty surprised me.

I was wondering if anyone knows who was photographed at Hyde Park that day because there were six others there, all much the same build and height and he could be any one of them.

My husband tells me he nearly ended up in the Serpentine coming home on his bike. He knew the gravel path very well, having travelled it for a few years, but suddenly he ran out of path and was on grass and could see water nearby.

It was a PC from Hyde Park nick who helped him on the right path home. I thought it might interest other men who were on duty during that smog time when day never came and up to 4,000 Londoners died of bronchial problems. What a horror it was. I don't remember anything like it since.

Mrs E Mitchell

Smoggy days

I was reminded of an incident during the smog of 1952 by Mrs Mitchell's letter. I was then a PC at West End Central and was called by a bus driver who couldn't find his way out of Hyde Park Corner and asked me to help. This I tried to do, but once I left the kerb, I too got lost. He might still be going around Hyde Park Corner!

On another foggy tour of duty I was finished at midnight. Earlier in the evening I had seen the late Bernard Raby who was going to wait for me as we lived two roads apart on the north side of Clapham Common.

From West End Central we got to the Mall without any trouble, then thinking we had got to the Victoria Memorial, we turned left to head for Buckingham Palace Road, but we had turned much too soon and found ourselves by the lake in St James's Park. Later, on the journey home on Chelsea Bridge Road as we approached the bridge we were on the wrong side of the road and in front of a car which fortunately for us was going very slowly!

Douglas Lloyd

Peeping Toms and Wooten Lamps

I was demobilized from the RAF in January 1948, having been called up in 1945. The war ended three days after I joined. In the light of that, if I'd joined in 1940, I could have saved the world a lot of aggro.

I went to Kirkham to pick up a demob suit. That was like winning a prize of 'One minute in a supermarket - as many items as you can carry out, keeping your hands in your pockets'. This was different in that the only train leaving Kirkham was going in 20 minutes and the boxes containing suits, by 1948, were empty.

I came out in a greenish jacket that wouldn't do up at the chest and sleeves three inches above my wrists. The trousers were chalky grey - that is, they were grey with chalk marks all over. I wasn't sure whether they were long shorts or short longs. No turn-ups.

The hat was a pork pie type which probably started as a bowler in 1945, but by 1948, pork pie was a better description. You had to wear a hat so you could salute. Can you imagine that? No hat, no salute - hat, salute! I bet the guy who dreamed that up is Sir Something or other.

Not to be diddled, I walked up to the complaints department. A thumb just jerked towards the exit door. After two years in the services you learn 'never ignore a jerked thumb'. I went past numerous windows which opened, thrusting wads of papers in my hand. The last two doors had indiscreet signs on them. One said 'Big something or other...' I was being hurried along at a fair lick. I thought 'Go for it!' The door slammed shut as I went through and I found myself out in the street. I thought 'Is that it?' Two years in the Airforce and out on my ear ten minutes after going through the demob gate.

I found my way to the station, bought a newspaper and sat down in a carriage to look at some of the junk I'd been given. Ticket to London. Note saying to sign on for a further three years' service, you can keep your old rank. So that's why they made me a Corporal two days ago.

The only gun I'd fired in two years of service was a sten gun, in training, that was like a bit of gas pipe with a slot in the barrel half way up into which you slotted a clip with about twelve bullets. The only safe place was directly in front of the barrel, anyone behind you stood a good chance of being hit. I think the Airforce bought a job lot off Hitler.

Two years in the Airforce and never been in an aeroplane. In fact I hadn't even seen an aeroplane. How can you explain that to your kids when you get home. 'What did you do during the war Dad?' 'Oh, I was in the Airforce.' 'Did you fly fighters or bombers Dad?' 'No, I shot the guy behind me with a ...' 'What did you do that for, Dad?'

Leave pass. Three months leave. Can't be bad. Pity the money they gave you would only last about a week. The train started to move off and I had a quick look at the newspaper. Wanted, experienced mechanics for Police vehicles. That's not a bad idea! What do I know about cars? Four wheels, except trucks, tyres, engine, windscreen, various bits and pieces in between. Can't be that difficult. Write for interview.

Letter about a week later. Call at S. London address re. your application. Not like the Airforce, shy with their aeroplanes, the Old Bill had cars from ground to roof, you could touch them and look at them. Something to tell the kids: 'Did you fly an aeroplane Dad?' 'No but I touched a Police car'.

Very pleasant Superintendent. I knew he was a Superintendent, it was written on his door. He had a uniform with buttons and things on his shoulder. Indeterminate age because when you're 22, anyone 23 or above is old.

He quizzed me on my knowledge of the internal combustion engine which lasted about three seconds. 'By the time I've taught you what you've got to know, we'll both be old men. We could do with big young lads like you in the Police. Come and join.'

It's never ceased to amaze me, the variety of ways people in authority have to dismiss you, from a look, a nod, a smile, a frown, to a 'get out!' But finding myself on the street, I assumed I'd failed the interview.

How about the Police? Not really me. Still, I suppose it's better than walking the streets (joke there somewhere!). As most Policemen nowadays don't walk but ride, they wouldn't get the point.

The idea kept growing in my head and after speaking to a City of London Policeman, (in those days I think their minimum height was six feet, add to that a foot of helmet and an inch or so of boot leather, and you had an impressive lawman). I asked him where the nearest Police Station was, he smiled, nice white teeth, nice complexion and a deep voice, directed me to a nick.

He was the first person in authority I had ever spoken to who was pleasant and helpful. Most would say, 'What are you looking at? Stand to attention! Get your hair cut!' And they were the ladies. I daren't tell you what the blokes said.

In fact that guy was the first Policeman I'd ever spoken to. Where I came from, the sight of a bobby's helmet and we were off.

I found the Police Station and timidly walked in. 'What can I do for you son?' An elderly Police Sergeant, again nice complexion. In fact all the Old Bill in those days had good complexions; must have been the wind and rain. 'Can I see the Manager, Sir?' I asked. He grinned. 'I'm the Manager here, what do you want?' 'I thought I'd like to join the Police, Sir,' I said. 'Sarge, not Sir. Fill these in and good luck'. He gave me a few forms to fill in and again I found I'd been expertly dismissed. Is it some sort of course these people go on, to learn this art of dismissing? They never say 'You're dismissed'. Just a - a what? It just happens, one minute you're talking merrily away, next thing you're out, but cleverly out, not halfway through a sentence.

I filled in the form, not easy. They wanted to know everything about everything. What you had for dinner fifteen years previously. What school did your Great Granny go to, and they wanted referees. Not being a footballer, I though I'd be struggling a bit with that one. Finally I sent it off.

Weeks went by and I began thinking of going back into what I did before the call-up. Toolmaster's apprentice, nah Carpenter's improver, nope, don't fancy that. Letter. See you at Beak Street, 10am for physical and mental test. Physical, no problem, mental, yes, I am a bit mental, still, give it a run.

I turned into Beak Street, it looked like the Army, Navy and Airforce were playing there. There were hundreds, a few in posh civvies, most in various officer ranks. Was I glad I didn't have my old Corporal's lot on. We'd had to hand our uniforms back in, officers owned their own uniforms, probably all they had, poor sods. 'Can you hear what I'm saying?' Right ear, left ear, same message, 'Hurry up plonker' or something like that. The hundreds reduced to dozens, I couldn't believe it.

Before a Board of five Policemen, senior rank officers, asking various questions. I must have done OK in front of them because I was invited back with about twelve or so for educational tests. I got through although I don't think I passed. I think they were one short to make a bus load and they let me go.

I don't know if many of you have ever felt the pain of having various parts of the body punched, bored or countersunk, but over the next thirteen weeks or so my brain ached with pain. One of the nastiest forms of mental torture was a black book, twelve inches by nine inches by two and half inches approx. One paragraph of about six or so lines had to be learned word perfect by the next day. That was given to us in the morning; by late afternoon we had several pages of complete twaddle, no rhyme, music or meaning, which had to be learned word perfect by the next morning.

Suffice to say I spent the first week crying on my bed, when I wasn't being bullied into learning. It took me nearly two months to learn the small paragraph, in fact never being questioned on it, I don't think I ever did learn it.

I passed, just, and was sent to the East End of London. I was the first post-war recruit on our relief, where I walked the various beats with one of the experienced guys. None of them wanted to talk to me. I began to wonder whether I smelt or something. It's hard to walk with someone for eight hours and they don't want to talk.

I was amazed at the amount of local knowledge these guys had, obscure roads and alleys, names of all the local trouble-makers, doctors, nurses, vets. They were walking encyclopaedias.

Thankfully after the first month we changed to night duty - 10pm to 6am, with half an hour break which came so that someone was out when you were in. When I say 10pm to 6am, that's not strictly true. You came on at 9.45 and you were booked off at 6.15. Most times we were away shortly after 6am.

The first thing to grab when you came on at night was a Wooten lamp. That was the name of this huge torch which had an accumulator battery charged up during the day. If you were first in you could get a bright one which, at its best was like a dying fag-end and at worst no light at all. Sometimes there would be an actual beam if the night was black enough but the beam would disappear before your eyes if you had it on for more than a second or so.

This wasn't the only drawback. Being an accumulator it weighed about 4lb, would spill acid if you weren't careful and the spring return handles were so strong it took a good grip to hold them together for long.

I was posted to a cycle beat and pushed my bike up the road, making myself as inconspicuous as possible, hoping no one would ask me anything. I'd just stopped at a corner for a few minutes as I'd seen the older chaps do, when this big car screeched to a halt. The driver yelled 'Where's Katherine Road guv?' I frowned as if searching my brain for Katherine Road amongst the mass of knowledge I'd got stored away. I sensed his impatience as he revved the engine. 'I'm sorry, I'm new here, but the Police..' I didn't get any further, rear wheels spinning, he shot off like a scalded cat in the direction of the nick.

I hardly had time to yawn when he came screeching back, did a right turn and roared off into the night. I thought Katherine Road must be up there somewhere and as I turned to go in the same direction I saw a large fluorescent sign saying 'Katherine Road Tyres'. I thought 'What a plonker, what a start!' I got on my bike, it was about 10.30pm, and I started to cycle up Katherine Road.

It was cold and dark and I'd just left the last of the shops behind. 'Bloody hell, what's that?' I nearly fell off my bike. Corner house, light in ground floor back window, from my bike I could see a head, yes, a head definitely a head, moved. I could see over the wall and, cycling onto the pavement, standing on the pedals, a head moved silhouetted against the light.

My heart was racing. Call the Police! No, silly bastard, you are the Police. Get Help. No, he might be gone by the time we get back.' 'What would these old guys do?' 'Suppose it's not a he, but a they, could get your head kicked in'. 'What were we taught?' 'Allo, allo, allo, what 'ave we 'ere then?' 'Put bike in safe place in case it gets nicked. That's the last thing you want.' I took the bike across the road and hid it in a front garden. Thinks; 'Creep up, grab him, Got you, you bastard. No can't do that.' I crept across the road, climbed the low front garden wall, up on my toes, crash, kicked a couple of milk bottles. I froze, edged forward. He's still there, must be crazy or bloody deaf. Opened gate, crept up behind him. I touched him on the shoulder. 'Uh! Uh!' he squealed, turned round, spotting me he said, 'Crikey guv, you frightened the hell out of me.'

I grabbed his sleeve, my confidence coming back, I was a lot bigger than him. All cocky-like I said, 'So what are we up to then?' I looked towards the lighted window, I couldn't believe it. I looked at the chap, he was now looking at the same as me. Naked lady, completely starkers. I tell you, in 1948 you never ever got to see a naked woman. I mean, I'm 22 years old, I've honestly never seen a naked woman. Neither had he by the way he was ogling her. At that time even my wife undressed in the dark. I said 'You're looking at her.' He said 'So are you.' We were both looking at her.

First she put her hair up, then she put it down. All in front of a big mirror. I thought, 'Say something you twit' 'What are you doing here?' 'I, er, I live here.' 'Well, we'll find out.' I shifted my hand up to his collar, although at this stage I wasn't sure whether or not he had committed any offence. Mind you the bint must have been deaf as a post. She hadn't heard us and we were making a terrific racket, so it seemed at the time.

I tapped on the front door, nothing. Louder, still nothing. I was trying to keep it as inconspicuous as possible. Bang, Bang, Bang, I crashed out on the knocker. The guy cringed and said, 'Blimey mate, you'll wake the street.' The door flew open, Miss Starkers (still starkers) glared at us: first me then him, back to me. Her breasts stuck up. 'What the hell do you want at this time of the night?' I was still looking at her breasts. I was thinking of saying 'More front than Selfridges'. 'Well?' She was certainly in a bad temper. 'This man said he lived here.' 'No 'e doesn't'. 'I caught him looking at you in the back garden'. Straightaway she said, 'Well he can watch me if he wants can't he?' I definitely felt the guy smile. 'Well,' she yelled again, 'Don't just stand there.' I remember looking at the ground, my foot, I looked up in the air. I let the guy go. 'Am I staying here all night? Say something!' I said 'Do you mind if I stay and look as well?' I don't really know what happened after that. I seem to remember her grabbing a stick of sorts, the guy ran and I followed. I was handicapped by this bloody Wooten lamp hanging from my belt. As I turned the corner my buckle gave way bringing my belt and lamp down round my knees. I heard the guy yell out, 'See you tomorrow night guv.'

I recovered myself, got my bike, cycled towards the nick. Sergeant came up 'Everything Ok?' 'Yes Sarge, nothing happened, these Wooten lamps are useless.' 'For a light they are but they're better than a truncheon in a punch up.' Sadly I never had the opportunity to go back up to that house.

Denis McNamara ex PC344 KF, KW, PS 23G, PS 135 Wt. No 133406

I was Press Ganged

A pal and I cycled from East Ham to Wembley on Saturday 28 April 1923, to see the first FA Cup Final to be played at the new Wembley Stadium. It had been built on the site of the British Empire Exhibition which was due to be opened in the Spring of 1924. We both paid 2/- entry and three old pence for a programme (eighty souvenir programmes for a pound!)

This was the last year of an apprenticeship served by me after leaving school during the Great War, for which I was paid 8/- a week, rising by 2/- a year to 18/- for my last year. My pal was the son of an SPS at East Ham Police Station and a short time after the Cup Final we were both told by his father to be at the Police Station at 6pm one evening. We both pondered on what our movements had been during the last few days and what skirmishes we had been involved in, if any.

Upon arrival at the appointed time, I was taken into the Charge Room, put against a brass 'stick of inches' fixed to the wall, then a tape measure place around my chest. Then SPS Hiles asked me the names of two neighbours which he wrote down - these were the first words spoken and he then told me to sign my name on a folded form.

I asked him what it was all about and he replied, 'You have just made an application to join the Metropolitan Police.'

Protests were in vain as he explained all the advantages - wages increased from 18/- to £3 10s, promotion, pension of around £150 per year, free medical service, one day off a week and 12 days annual leave a year, taken when I chose!

Upon reflection, I felt a great deal better - following demobilisation after the war the Government of the day had asked industry and all employers including the police to take on as many ex-servicemen returning from the war as possible. Munition production had eased and the fairer sex who had tasted the advantage of being employed were loath to give up that source of income.

Consequently, employment was getting harder to find. I subsequently received my 'calling up' papers from Westminster to attend Scotland Yard for medical and educational tests.

Service did not start until you were posted to a division and shortly after that I found myself on duty from 6am to midnight at the opening of the Exhibition at Wembley.

Two years later came the General Strike, another two weeks of extended duty (12 hours a day) and all leave stopped. No overtime was paid in those days but the extra time incurred could be taken off in the 'exigences of the service'. Overtime was first paid about the time of the formation of the 'Courtesy Cops'.

I dare say the press gangs of years ago have gone but I was certainly shanghaied into the Police. Still, there were very few jobs that carried a pension, so in the end, I certainly don't regret it.

Frank Marley Wt no 112675

Anyone will do

Whilst still at school, I had a job delivering milk to residents of Huntingdon and in that capacity called daily at the homes of serving officers. It was then known as the Huntingdonshire Constabulary. Thus it was that I became well known to many local police officers who watched me grow up.

After leaving school, a clerical job at a depot of Shell Petroleum Co. became available but I opted for a police career. With that in mind, I called at Huntingdon Police station and was received by a sergeant who knew me well. He greeted me by saying 'Are you in trouble boy?' 'No sergeant,' I said. 'I want to join the Police Force.' I too, was then placed against a large wall stick of inches struggling to gain every possible fraction of an inch in height, whereupon the sergeant said, 'Go home boy, and eat some more pudding.' I was about to leave, thoroughly dejected, when he called me back saying, 'You could try the Metropolitan. They take any bugger.'

Thus you hear another true story and that season I joined the world's premier Police force to complete and enjoy 30 years absorbing service.

Harry Joyce, No 123518 ex Det Supt

The One That Got Away

I am relatively young, 53 years old, fit and well with no medical problems, stress or history of medical problems.

On the evening of the 30 September while at home on my computer, my left arm literally slid off the keyboard and fell to the left side without any prior indication or warning. Despite efforts, it failed to respond to any action to move. It was completely limp as was the hand.

Having seen a few of these while in the Job I realised that it could be a stroke. I stood up and my head started to spin. Fortunately I was at home, and adjacent to the bedroom. I cleared what I was doing and went and laid on the bed to await developments.

I digress here a little. Many years ago, the late Pathologist Professor Keith Simpson, who was most informative in his advice whilst performing post-mortems to any bystanders, ventured one of his theories on such attacks.

A stroke is the common name for a coronary haemorrhage, which is, roughly, the exploding of a blood vessel in the brain. It may be an artery of which there are three in the brain. This explosion causes permanent damage to the brain cells and dependent upon the severity of the attack, which is always sudden and unexpected, is the degree of damage. The affected side of the body is always opposite to the side of the brain that sustains the damage.

Strokes are the third largest killer in the UK after cancer and heart attacks. In about 55% of the cases the attack is fatal. Of the remainder about 35% will have some permanent disability and those that are left should have no permanent disability.

Dr Simpson had a theory that if the original attack was not fatal, then there was no reason why, if the circumstances were available, the damage could not be limited quickly enough for the damaged brain cells to be substituted by other undamaged cells in the brain, which could take over the duties of the damaged cells. His theory was that the brain could be stimulated into this 'replacement therapy' by a sudden shock to the heart that would stimulate the undamaged brain into action.

His suggestion was that this stimulation could be induced by the subject at a given time standing beneath a running shower of cold water for about 20 minutes. This, he argued, would stimulate the brain enough for the 're-education' of the damaged parts of the brain to take over the actions of the damaged cells. At the time of this advice I had listened attentively.

I now return to lying on the bed with no power at all in the left arm and hand. Then the left side of the face started to drop and tingling started in the left leg and foot. I now recalled Dr Simpson's theory. I undressed and walked unsteadily to the adjacent bathroom, where with much effort I managed to lift the by-now partially powerless left leg into the bath and turn on the cold shower.

I stood under the shower for some 20 minutes, during which time the tingling sensation in the leg and foot ceased and the body became numb from the cold. I did not lose control of any of the body systems or functions. After this immersing I managed with some difficulty to get out of the bath and return to the bed.

Now most medical manuals will indicate immediate medical aid for a stroke or such an event. Alas I have a dear wife with multiple sclerosis who is dependent upon me. To call the doctor would entail a stay in hospital, maybe for a couple of weeks. It would also give my wife stress, a major cause of MS tension and to be avoided at all cost. Immediate medical aid therefore was out of the question.

My wife saw me lying on the bed and sensed I had problems. However also knowing my warped sense of humour, she laughed when I told her I had had a stroke; 'You'll be alright in the morning dear.'

About two hours later I decided I was strong enough to take a hot shower and did so. The left side of the body was now very weak and with little or no speech too. Problems were obvious. However, the hot shower did wonders and I found that, with determination, the leg was quite capable of movement and the arm would move if pushed.

I decided to sleep on these problems and returned to bed. Sleep - you must be joking. I laid there working out the possibilities and decided to walk the very thin line between determination, prudence and stupidity.

The following day I got up, certainly a bit unsteadily, the left side a bit weak, (understatement of the year!). I had something to eat and went for a slow walk around the block. The left-hand judgement was none too good and the walking was a little unsteady, but everything worked roughly.

I took it easy for a couple of days and with exercises to the limbs managed to get the leg working quite well and then movement into the arm. The harder the exercises the better the results.

After five days I went to see my doctor expecting an almighty rebuke for not contacting him earlier. I was able with some difficulty due to speech problems to give him an exact story and also explain why I had not been earlier.

He set in train immediately a sequence of actions that by the end of the week had had me X-rayed, scanned, tested, medicated and apart from some speech problems, nearly back to normal. His care, understanding and assistance were superb.

It is now 10 weeks since my stroke. I have had every test there is, been examined by a neurologist and, with care, rest and slight but reducing medication, all will be well, including the speech by Christmas. By Easter all will be repaired by nature.

I have gone into this in some detail for there is not too much documentation on what happens to you when you have a stroke. I can tell you, it puts the fear of everything you ever dreaded into you, and then VAT too. But afterwards, you appreciate life much more.

However, the specialists to whom I have had the honour of being examined have now declared that I am once again fit well and healthy. Apart from the slowly recovering speech, I am felt to be 'as fit as a fiddle.'

To anyone who suffers a stroke, though I appreciate it is a generality, maybe you can profit from the advice that the very learned, wise and friendly Dr Simpson gave me many years ago. If you are still alive after the initial attack, get under the cold water, you've nothing to lose and everything to gain.

Thank you Dr Simpson. For once, one stayed off your slab and it was all thanks to your advice.

It would of course be very remiss of me to berate immediate medical aid, for it is only in hospital that you can receive all the superb care and attention that the NHS can lavish upon you in these events.

However, for those on holiday or in difficult situations where such normal remedies cannot be available, I have hopefully given you all some hope. If you're determined to get better then you will. It's all in the head.

Dave King 147096 PC ex L, Z & W

A Helping Hand

A PC whose name I have forgotten had been called to an old lady, who had locked herself out. He suggested gaining entry by breaking a pane of glass in the door, to release the catch.

She declined this offer, saying that she could not afford to have the glass replaced. He decided to attack the door with his shoulder. This was successful, except that he tore the door from its hinges. As it fell, it connected with the hall light, smashing the bulb.

Undeterred, the officer said. 'Leave it to me madam.' He helped himself to a chair and stood on it, to remove the broken bulb. The chair collapsed, leaving the officer hanging by the flex, which pulled the rose and a lump of plaster from the ceiling. The officer, trying to make amends, volunteered to make the lady a cup of tea. She declined the offer but he insisted. He then made the tea with coffee bags.

It would appear that she was a very understanding person, because she later invited him back for tea. I was serving at Esher VH during the Sixties when I heard this true story.

Peter Inman, 135413 ex DC,Y,L

Never a Dull Moment for Albert

Soon after starting early turn one summer's morning in 1924, I was patrolling the Thames Embankment at Chelsea when a passer-by called my attention to a man lying at the bottom of a flight of steps leading to the shingle of the river. The tide was rising and my informant thought he might be is some danger. I went to the spot indicated, looked over the parapet and there, indeed, was a young man. He was lying full length on the bottom of a flight of steps leading down to the beach and he seemed to be fast asleep.

I called down to him, 'You'll get wet if you don't get up.' No reply. I repeated my remark but got no response. I thereupon climbed over the parapet and went down the steps to shake the young fellow. He murmured, 'Leave me alone.' I told him he couldn't stay there and that he had better get up. No reply. I spoke to him again, but still there was no movement or reply. By this time the rising tide was almost touching him so I literally dragged him to his feet and half carried him up the steps and got him over the parapet onto the pavement where he remained quite inert.

I got help from the PC on the adjoining beat who fetched a nearby police hand-ambulance (this was in the days when police hand-ambulances were still scattered about the Metropolis). Together we pushed him to the local hospital. The sister in charge examined him and then said to a nurse, 'the usual treatment in this case.'

The latter took the young man away and very soon I heard screams coming from a nearby room. I looked in. It was my 'customer' lying fully clothed in a bath full of hot water and he was shouting and struggling to get out. I said to the nurse, 'that seems to be drastic treatment,' to which she replied, 'It is, but it's the only way. He is absolutely riddled with maggots through self-neglect and his flesh is being eaten away. The water is hot but not too hot to burn him and it is the only way to get him clean and free from vermin. Just watch.'

Sure enough, after a short time, dead maggots began to come to the top of the water and soon the surface was literally covered with them. After a while, when the patient had recovered a little, I managed to get his personal particulars from him and left him for further treatment.

A few weeks later I took a casualty to the hospital and saw the same sister. I asked her how the 'maggoty' young man had got on and she told me he was all right. He had, she said, been out of work a long time, was half starved, emaciated and neglected, but they had found him a job in the hospital and he was now doing well.

One night in 1925 while on night duty in Chelsea, I had just finished my refreshment break and had resumed patrolling my beat when, at about 3am, a nearby street door opened and an elderly woman wearing a dressing gown hastily thrown over her night attire, came out. She saw me, ran up to me, and in a most agitated voice implored me to 'get the doctor quick, please, my daughter is going to have a baby.' Telephones were not so plentiful in those days.

I got the Doctor's address which was nearby and told her to go back and look after her daughter and I would fetch him. I quickly reached the

Doctor's house and rang the bell. After a while an upper floor window opened, a head popped out and a sleepy voice demanded, 'What do you want at this time of night?' I told him that a woman was about to have a baby and her mother had asked me to fetch the Doctor. 'All right,' he said, 'I know the case, I'll be down in a minute, wait for me.'

Wondering what he wanted me for, I stayed until he came out and said, 'I'll want you to help. The mother is useless and helpless. Her daughter's husband is away and there's no one else in the house.'

What a position to be in! Here was I, a young bachelor who knew nothing about what to do in this field (we had never been taught anything at Peel House about what to do in a case of this kind) and I never felt more embarrassed or uneasy in my life. I demurred, telling the Doctor I knew absolutely nothing about these matters, but he was adamant. 'Isn't it your duty,' he said, 'to help a member of the public who needs urgent assistance? This is one of those cases.'

I had no answer to that so we quickly went to the mother's house where her daughter was, indeed, in a very advanced stage of pregnancy. The Doctor told the young woman's mother, who was in a state of nervous collapse, to bring hot water and towels, and to me he said, 'Get your helmet and jacket off, find an apron and I'll tell you what to do.' During the following half hour I learned more about child birth than I had ever known either before or since. The young mother had a baby daughter and afterwards I sometimes saw her pushing her out in a perambulator.

Reflecting on this episode of some 65 years ago, that baby, if still alive, could be a grandmother!

Albert Hunt, ex Supt CO SB, Wt no 112271

Look Before You Leap!

At long last, after all the training and learning, he was finally on his own. He had completed over three months in Training School, during which he had seen other lesser mortals fall by the wayside. He had been on the street for a period of at least two weeks under the watchful eye of a man experienced in the art, but now at last, he was alone.

Casting an approving eye over himself in a shop window, he had to admit he looked an imposing sight. His was now the power that could decide any argument, in fact he was 'the law', and even he had to admit that in his new uniform he was as much a sight to strike terror into the heart of any potential lawbreaker as he was also a most welcome presence to all elderly women in fear of being mugged. Yes, at long last he was the copper on the beat.

'Please God now let something happen so that I can prove my worth to the community,' he prayed.

For over an hour now he had been walking the streets, but to his amazement and mortification nobody had so much as glanced in his direction, let alone shown some appreciation of his presence. Then, having decided nothing untoward was going to happen to brighten his first tour of duty, he decided to do something about it.

Coming towards him he espied a scruffy individual carrying over his shoulder a sack which appeared to be full and heavy. Bearing in mind the statement from his instructor in Training School that a great percentage of all stolen property was being carried through the streets at any one time, he decided to stop this individual and find out just what the sack contained. Placing himself squarely in front of the pedestrian concerned he announced in as commanding a voice as he could muster: 'And may I ask what you have in the bag, Sir?'

Our hero had been instructed at Training School that on being asked such a question, the suspect would do one of three things: (a) he would offer a polite and perfectly reasonable explanation; (b) he would run away taking the sack with him; or (c) he would try to bluff it out by offering a false explanation and giving a false name and address.

Being well prepared for the suspect to do any of these three things, our hero was nonplussed at the reaction: 'Oh no! Not now, you idiot,' replied the suspect, dropping the sack and disappearing into the nearby doorway of a large well-known multiple store. 'Oh dear!' thought our hero, 'they didn't tell us how to cope with this one.'

Quickly making up his mind however, he at once brought into action his personal radio, and explained to the voice at the other end what had happened. 'Not to worry mate,' was the reply to his call for help, 'We'll get a car to you as soon as possible.'

It was then that he realised that he could follow two courses of action: (a) he could follow the suspect into the shop and try to find him (he had already realised that there were a number of floors and exits in the store), and leave the sack and its contents on the footway, or (b), stay where he was to direct the other officers and cars when they arrived, in the meantime finding out just what the sack did contain.

Deciding to adopt course (b) our hero firstly had to tell the crowd, which to his consternation was growing larger by the minute, to stand back whilst he examined the contents. Having finally cleared a space he up-ended the sack to find himself staring at a large heap of steaming horse manure. His discomfiture was not aided by the merriment of the crowd, the majority of whom were laughing their heads off.

Whilst he was wondering how on earth he was going to get it all back into the sack without a shovel, and already beginning to worry about the Sergeant's reactions to his story when he arrived back at the station, he was aware of the sound of police sirens and the eventual arrival of a Panda. His dilemma was not helped by the fact that his comrades at once joined in the general laughter and the loud comment by one of them that 'my roses could do with a bit of that'. He then had to give both men the description of the suspect and they at once went into the shop to commence a search, leaving him to clear up the mess made by the manure.

Meanwhile more Police cars arrived and each officer was given a description of the suspect and the net spread ever wider. A nearby shop-keeper helped out by providing our hero with a hand shovel and he also consented to hold the sack whilst the 'law' shovelled it all back in.

Eventually, and with every PC throughout the district looking for a person fitting the description of the suspect, our hero was obliged to use his personal radio yet again to get the van out to take him and the sack back to the station, both of which were by this time smelling a bit high. The manure, having been disturbed by its upheaval on to the footway and subsequent return to the sack, was by this time steaming and smelling strongly, and our hero was not at all pleased with the comments of the van driver who was complaining about having to fumigate the van before he could take it out again. When, eventually, the Sergeant found time to attend to our hero his first comment was that he would soon be known throughout the force as the PC who had lost a prisoner during his first tour of duty.

It soon became evident that although the Sergeant was familiar with most aspects of the case, nobody yet had had the temerity to inform him of the contents of the sack. So, after upbraiding the PC on committing this unforgivable sin, he said: 'Well let us see what we have in the sack, my lad.' In some trepidation the PC then told the Sergeant that he had already discovered the contents and eventually mentioned the dreaded words: 'Horse Manure'. 'It contains WHAT?!!,' shouted the Sergeant.

'Horse shit,' replied the PC who had formed the opinion that the Sergeant did not know what 'manure' was. After a thorough roasting, the poor PC was told to go to the canteen to have a cup of tea whilst the Sergeant calmed down and decided whether to class the horse manure as Prisoners Property (escaped), or Property found in the street.

So the PC, having been told that he should always obey the Sergeant, was very dejectedly sitting in the canteen drinking a much-needed cup of tea and wondering why, as each person entered the canteen, he sniffed the air and carefully avoided the table occupied by our young friend.

He had almost finished the cuppa and was preparing to return to the Sergeant to find out whether a decision had been reached about the horse manure, when the door to the canteen was pushed open by a scruffy individual in civilian clothing, who carefully looked round and then made his way over to the table occupied by our hero.

As he walked across the canteen towards him, the PC recognised him as the suspect who was at that moment being sought by every PC at the Station. At the same time our hero realised that he had made a terrible mistake and one that in future was going to be difficult to live down. He was therefore not in the least surprised when the individual concerned introduced himself as a Detective Sergeant attached to the station, who after congratulating the PC on his initiative, then took up the roasting he had already received from the uniform Sergeant and said: 'Thanks to you I have lost the trail of a man we have wanted for some time. By the time that I had entered the store and come out through a back door the crook had long since disappeared.'

Apologising profusely the PC asked: 'I can understand the scruffy appearance and also the sack over the shoulder, but why on earth did it have to be manure?' To which he was informed that the Detective Sergeant was off duty and had collected the manure from a local stables. He was on his way with some to his allotment when he saw a man whom he had been seeking for some weeks. Suspecting that the crook was engaged on yet another nefarious operation he had decided to follow him and catch him red handed.

So, having apologised still further to the Detective Sergeant, and having assured himself that the uniformed Sergeant had not yet entered the manure into any book and that it was about to be collected by its rightful owner, the PC changed into a uniform that did not smell quite so high, and prepared to leave the station for the few minutes left in this, his memorable first tour of duty.

But, as he was about to leave the station there was a sudden commotion and two PCs struggled into the Charge room with a suspect dressed very similarly to the description given by the PC and who was quite naturally vainly protesting his innocence.

'Now see what you've done,' said the uniformed Sergeant who had spotted our friend leaving the station, 'You've not only lost a prisoner on your very first tour of duty, but you have also deprived a CID Sergeant of clearing up some back crimes and to cap it all it looks very much as if I will have to deal with a complaint against the police.'

At this stage the PC decided that he should make himself scarce, and resumed his presence on the street, a much wiser and more mature officer who decided that in future he would proceed with caution until he had got to know every CID officer at this and the surrounding stations.

I am now coming up for 83 years of age: I retired in 1958 as a Sergeant at Enfield Highway - in other words, long before the advent of personal radios and Panda cars.

Alf (Ben) Hogg ex PS 26N 122814

The Art of Dying Tidily

I am told that the first thing most readers do when they receive their copy of *London Police Pensioner* magazine is to turn to the back page to check the obituary columns. No doubt most are relieved to see their name has not yet been recorded, but although the longevity of some old police officers is legendary, even the most optimistic of our members will accept that it is only a matter of time before they make the back page.

When that day arrives many will leave behind a widow who, while still suffering from the stress of bereavement, will be expected to cope with all the problems that arise, some of which can cause real distress and hardship unless speedily resolved.

While aware that I run the risk of being told that Grandma has already learned to suck eggs, I have compiled this article in the hope that the information it contains will, in some small way, be of assistance to our members and their dependents. I have tried to present the facts accurately as they are today, but future Government legislation may materially alter them.

A Will

The one most tangible benefit any of us can give to our surviving spouse and other relatives is to make a Will. So often this is something which is put off to another day until it is too late and one dies intestate. This can cause considerable problems since there are strict rules under the Administration of Estates Act which govern the disposal of the estate, and may result in financial hardship for the widow.

Another serious problem is that upon death all bank accounts etc. are frozen until Probate is granted. This can also lead to financial problems for a widow because it can take several months to settle the estate and in the meantime she will not be able to draw on funds from the estate to settle outstanding accounts, except for funeral expenses. One solution to this is a joint bank account. Joint ownership of building society deposits or other savings accounts can also be useful in these circumstances.

Essential requirements

One of the first requirements after a person dies is to register the death with the local Registrar of Births & Deaths, whose address is usually in the local telephone directory, or can be obtained from your local Post Office. The Registrar will require to see the Death Certificate issued by the doctor and the deceased's Medical Card before making an entry in his register and providing a certified copy. Since a number of interested parties are likely to request a copy of the Death Certificate, it is advisable to ask the Registrar for some extra certified copies at the time.

Pensions

The next important step is to notify all the sources from which the husband was receiving a pension. Naturally, in the case of a police officer, the first of these will be Pensions Branch, whose address is shown on all pension advice slips. When writing to notify the death of a pensioner, the pension number as shown on the advice slip should always be quoted and a certified copy of the Death Certificate enclosed.

Immediately upon receipt of this notification, Pensions Branch will commence the necessary action to replace the deceased's pension with the relevant widow's pension. Naturally Pensions Branch will require proof that the person claiming a pension is legally entitled to it, so in the first instance an explanatory letter and claim form will be sent to the widow with directions for its completion and return to Pensions Branch, together with a certified copy of the death certificate. If there are any problems about completing the form, ring the number quoted on the letter head or contact the London Branch Secretary (whose address is published in *London Police Pensioner* magazine) for further advice. In exceptional circumstances, a local Welfare Officer will be asked to visit you.

Generally speaking, to qualify for a widow's pension, the claimant must have been married to her husband whilst he was a serving police officer, and still married to him at the time of his death.

However, since 6 April 1978, provision has been made for payment of a widow's pension in cases of post retirement marriages, but only in respect of the husband's police service after that date.

While every effort is made by Pensions Branch to effect the transition as quickly as possible, inevitably there will be an interval of four or five weeks before the first widow's pension is paid and this can often cause money-flow problems. Where the husband retired after 1972, the widow will receive for the first 13 weeks after his death a 'temporary' pension equivalent to the pension he was receiving at the time of this death, but this does not apply to widows whose husbands retired before that date.

From September 1998 the responsibility for paying all Metropolitan Police pensions has been transferred to a service company. Full details of the company address have been given on your Pensions Advice slip.

If the husband was in receipt of a National Insurance Retirement Pension being paid direct into a bank account, the Central Pensions Branch DSS, Newcastle-upon-Tyne NE98 1YX must be informed, quoting the Pension reference number and enclosing a copy of the Death Certificate. Where payment was being made locally on a weekly basis through a Pension Book, this should be taken to the nearest DSS Office together with a copy of the Death Certificate.

In the event of a widow continuing to have her widow's pension paid into a bank account, she can obtain a special card from the Central Pensions Branch to produce as evidence that she is entitled to concessions as a pensioner. When applying for such a card remember to quote the correct pension number.

A number of ex police officers take up further employment within the Civil Service and eventually qualify for a short service pension. If this applies, the Paymaster General, Sutherland House, Russell Way, Crawley, West Sussex RH10 1UH must also be informed, quoting the Pension Reference number and enclosing a copy of the Death Certificate. Others may be receiving a pension from a private employer, and in such cases they will also need to be informed enclosing a copy of the Death Certificate.

Taxation

HM Inspector of Taxes, Public Dept 7, Government Buildings, Ty Glas, Llanishen, Cardiff CF4 5YF should be informed as soon as possible, quoting the Income Tax reference number, which will be found on the Annual Notice of PAYE coding or any other correspondence from the Tax Office, and enclosing a copy of the Death Certificate.

If a widow is over 65 years of age, she is entitled to Age Allowance and should claim immediately since the allowance is not automatically awarded. The Inland Revenue will of course want to know details of all sources of income including any investment earnings.

Separate taxation for husband and wife simplifies this particular problem because the wife will already have a tax record of her own to refer to when corresponding with the Tax Office.

Other interested parties

There are a number of other organisations who will need to be informed of the death by letter and in those cases where they are holding monies or assets due to the estate of the deceased they will require a certified copy of the Death Certificate before releasing those assets.

The length of the list will depend upon the personal circumstances of each individual but could include any or all of the undermentioned. Their addresses will normally be found on the relevant correspondence but in cases of doubt the telephone directory or local Post Office will be of assistance:

1. Bank Manager(s) of all branches where the deceased had an account.

2. Manager of any Building Society holding investments in the deceased's name or where a mortgage has been taken out. In both cases the roll or account number should be quoted.

3. Managers of Investment Trusts and other shares.

4. All Insurance Companies, giving number and details of any Policy(ies) held. This includes House, Furniture, Personal Accident and Car Insurance policies.

5. National Savings Bank.

6. National Savings Organisation.

7. Premium Bonds, Lytham St Annes.

8. Motor Vehicle Licensing Authority, giving details of vehicle tax disc and driving licence.

9. Hire Purchase Companies where there are agreements in the deceased's name.

10. Local Water Authority if account is in deceased's name.

11. Local Authority to whom Community Charge is being paid. 12. Private Landlord or Local Authority if living in rented accommodation.

13. TV Licensing Authority if agreement is in deceased's name.

14. TV Rental Company if agreement is in deceased's name.

15. Electricity Board, Gas Board and British Telecom where accounts are in deceased's name.

Helping Agencies

As already stated, if serious problems arise, arrangements can be made for a local Welfare Officer to visit, but there are a number of other agencies which are available in certain circumstances.

To begin with, in cases of financial hardship, help can be sought from the Metropolitan Police Widow's Relief Fund. If the husband's death was the result of injury or illness received in the execution of duty, the Police Dependents' Trust will also help.

If there are dependent children, help will be given from the Metropolitan and City of London Police Orphans Fund.

Non-Police agencies and facilities include:

1. Meals on wheels - a WRVS service.

2. Home Help Service from the Local Council.

3. Red Cross - Nursing and Surgical Aids.

4. Home Library Service for the housebound. Details from any local library.

5. Citizens' Advice Bureau will give help on a wide range of subjects including free legal advice in many instances.

6. Most local Councils have concessionary bus travel schemes.

7. Rail companies will supply details of concessionary rail travel schemes.

8. Your doctor can supply details of any local Chiropody services, etc, for elderly persons.

9. Age Concern, Astral House, 1268 London Road, SW16 4ER, Tel: 0181 679 8000, publish a number of useful pamphlets including *Instructions for my Next of Kin and Executors upon my Death*, price 25p,

which is a very useful document to obtain and leave behind you! If there is a local Age Concern office near you, they will be happy to help you with your problems.

10. Finally, the DSS publish a number of useful booklets free of charge which can be obtained from any DSS office. They include:

FB29 *Help when someone dies*
D49 *What to do after a death*
NP49 *A guide to Widows Benefit*
RR *A guide to housing benefit*

I hope that this information is of assistance to some of you.

Charles Hasler, 128763

Christmas Cheer in Acton

It happened many years ago when I was serving as a young Detective Constable at Acton Police Station, which at that time was on X division.

It was about 1pm on Christmas Eve when a poorly-dressed elderly man was shown into the CID office. He informed me that he was employed at a local bakery and that he had been paying into a Christmas Loan Club at the factory throughout the year, so that he could provide Christmas fare for himself, his wife and sick children. I knew of this man and his family as they lived in a cottage quite close to the Police Station, and I knew they had a struggle to make ends meet. He told me that the Loan Club money should have been paid out at noon that day when the factory closed, but when it came to his turn the treasurer had told him he had no more money. This meant he had very little money with which to buy food and presents for his wife and family. He gave me the treasurer's name, but unfortunately did not know his address.

I told the man I would see what I could do and asked him to call back at 6 o'clock that evening. My first call was on a friend of mine who carried on business in Crown Street, Acton, and whom I thought might know the treasurer's address. I explained the position to him and mentioned the old man's plight. He could not help me, but referred me to an acquaintance who lived at Shepherds Bush.

I had still not been successful in tracing the treasurer when I returned to the station at 4pm and was greeted by the Station Officer with, 'What's all this about an old man being robbed of his money? I've been swamped with Crown Street tradesmen bringing in parcels for him. I've got one of the cells half full of them.' I was flabbergasted when I saw what was in the cell - joints of meat, bags of fruit and vegetables, sweet, chocolates, flowers, decorations, etc. Having been told the story the Station Officer said, 'I'll give you a hand to get it down to the CID officer,' which he did.

When the old man called at 6 o'clock that evening I asked him if he had a truck or wheelbarrow. He said he had and I asked him to get it. He returned a few minutes later with a wheelbarrow and I piled all the parcels, etc, into it. The old man said, 'What's this?' I said, 'It's yours with Christmas Good Wishes from the tradesmen of Crown Street'. The old man was speechless and tears ran down his face as he pushed his wheelbarrow out of the Police Station Yard.

I called at the bakery on the morning it reopened and this resulted in my complainant being paid his money in full by lunchtime. The old man came and thanked me and told me it was the best Christmas he and his family had ever had.

I later saw my business friend in Crown Street and asked him to inform all the tradesmen there of how much their generosity had been appreciated. I take my hat off to them, they were a good lot.

Cyril Green

At Your Service

During the early 1930s, a well-to-do professional man and his young bride lived in a large detached house near the centre of Epsom. Sadly, the man died prematurely, and from that moment on, time stood still for his widow. Her late husband's American car was put on blocks in the garage and the door locked. Thereafter, the widow rarely ventured outside the limits of her garden.

Apart from the occasional tradesman, the only visitors to the house were her doctor, and the local bobby enquiring about the lady's welfare. I am told that it was custom for the bobby to be given a glass of sherry and half-a-crown! Gradually the house fell into a state of decay and the sole occupant became a recluse, similar to Miss Haversham, in Charles Dicken's *Great Expectations*.

After some 40 years, frequent calls to Epsom nick (usually originated by the milkman) resulted in officers attending to ascertain that the elderly lady was still in the land of the living. Having become senile, she often did not bother, to collect the milk or groceries from the doorstep.

I happened to be late turn van driver at Epsom when one such call was received. With my colleague Geoff Moore (the station comedian), we went to investigate. After wending our way through the overgrown garden, we hammered on the front door and called through the letter box, with no response. Our efforts were repeated at the side and rear of the house, to no avail.

It was now dusk, and after considering our options, we decided to effect an entry. Selecting a small kitchen window, so rotten it almost fell apart, we entered. The light of our torches revealed an incredible sight. There were mounds of mouldy food everywhere, candle stubs, dead matches, and numerous mouse traps (some with grisly remains), and a general air of decay. Moving cautiously over the rotting floor-boards, we kept calling the lady's name, by now convinced we would be writing a 'sudden death' report. All the doors of the entrance hall were locked, (and probably had been for some years), dust and neglect was all around.

Suddenly, a small figure clad in white appeared on the upstairs landing, holding a flickering candle! I think the hairs on both our necks stood on end.

'What's all that noise?' the apparition asked. Realising that this was our missing occupier, we reassured her that we were police officers. Apparently the lady had not felt well for a couple of days, and had retired to her bed as her doctor was on holiday. We went upstairs and helped her back to bed and asked if there was anything she wanted. 'I would like my hot water bottle filled, and a cup of tea.' she replied. Keeping our gloves on - for hygiene purposes - we complied with her request.

Whilst speaking to the old lady, we noticed that although she was in bed, she was also wearing gloves! Subsequently, colleagues back at the nick, told us that she wore gloves all the time, rather like that other famous eccentric, the late Howard Hughes. We told her that we would arrange for the damaged window to be repaired, and noticing a phone by the bed, impressed upon her that if she had any problems, she had only to phone.

The next day I was on leave, but Geoff happened to be in the communications room when a 999 call was routed to Epsom from IR requesting urgent assistance to an elderly female in distress at the house of our old lady. Naturally Geoff said he would deal with it. This time on his arrival, the front door was opened. 'What's the matter love?' said Geoff. 'I'd like another cup of tea,' came the reply! After doing the honours, he informed the old lady that as it wasn't really what the police called an emergency, perhaps she could make the next cup of tea herself.

A couple of years later, the inevitable happened, and the old lady died. The house was sold, and a large tree growing in front of the garage doors was cut down, releasing the rare American convertible car from within. Thus the car came into the hands of a local garage proprietor, who lovingly restored it, and has it still. Several 'executive' type houses now occupy the site of the earlier house. I wonder if at odd times a small figure roams abroad in search of a cup of tea in the twilight hours?

Arthur Gadd 138401

A Case of Appeal

In August 1830, the Home Secretary Sir Robert Peel received a letter from an ex Police Constable 4576 Michael Riley, who had joined the Met Police Force on 2 July 1830 but was dismissed 28 days later by Mr (later Sir) Richard Mayne, one of the two Commissioners.

The letter constituted in effect one of the first cases of an appeal to the Home Secretary by an officer subjected to disciplinary proceedings, and is preserved in the Public Record Office. Here is Riley's sad saga:

I beg leave to lay the following statement of my case before you in order that you may judge of the Rigid Manner in which I have been treated.

I have to state that on Wednesday evening last at half past six, being employed on the New Police, I apprehended a man coming out of an unfurnished house in the Five Fields with carpenters tools and took him to the Watch House, from whence he was brought before a magistrate and committed for the Westminster Sessions.

I beg to observe that I was to search his lodgings at nine o'clock on Thursday morning from whence I was directed to proceed to Queen Square where I was in attendance until a quarter before four, and was again on duty at nine o'clock the same evening.

Being consequently greatly fatigued and my feet being extremely tired from the length of time I was on foot, about half past two the following morning I pulled off one of my boots which had become troublesome just for a moment to ease the foot.

At this particular juncture the sergeant happened to come up. He

observed it was not correct and that he would report me, on which I told
him that I had only that moment pulled it off for the purpose above stated
and for the condition my feet was in from the hours I was employed.

On Friday morning, I was accordingly called before Mr Mayne, and
without a hearing was told I should forfeit a day's pay.

Now Sir, having faithfully performed my duty and being such a length
of time on foot I did not think that I deserved to be fined for such a trivial
matter, therefore, I made an objection to pay it when my services were no
longer required in consequence of my refusal.

Now, Honoured Sir, I request from your well known Goodness that you
will cause justice to be administered to me, as I do not conceive that I
have committed any fault to deserve my dismissal.

I have further to state that my father lived as book keeper for a
number of years with Colonel Silvester at Manchester and that I served
my time to Mr Marsden Cabinet Manufacturer, St Ann's Square,
Manchester.

I shall take the liberty to await the honour of an answer, or if your
Honour should please to favour me with such a written answer, I beg
leave to subjoin my address,

I am Sir, with due respect,
Your Very Hum. Servant
Michale Riley
42 Hart Street, Covent Garden

One cannot but feel sympathy for poor Riley and I am sorry to have to
tell you that his heart-rendering tale had no effect - his appeal failed.

Arthur Fanning

Over the Edge

Harry Gladish and Bernard Hales were both Traffic Police at DT7 with
me. Both good lads. One Monday morning, Harry came on early turn a
little quieter than usual and slightly pale, and later over a cup of tea I got
him talking. 'Well Dinger,' he said 'My roof started to leak so when it
stopped raining I borrowed an extending ladder and a roof crawling board
that fits over the ridge and went up to see where the trouble was.'

Now Harry was living at the time in East Ham in a two storey slate-
roofed Victorian house, a tall thin structure with a cast iron gutter.

Having climbed the ladder he then transferred to the crawler board and started up it, when to his horror, the board which had not properly secured itself over the ridge started to slide back down the slippery slate tiles! Eventually Harry ended up flat on his face on the slates, the board having pushed the ladder away and fallen into the back garden. He slid back slowly at first, he gradually gathered speed thinking 'If I can grab the gutter I'll be alright.' As he came over the roof, he grabbed the gutter, which promptly snapped and he fell, landing flat on his back on the coal bunker, which had a felt and lathe lid.

'I had to call an ambulance,' he said. 'My next-door neighbour heard the crash as the crawler board hit the floor, rushed our to see what was happening, saw me fall off the roof and collapsed.' Harry, I am glad to say, was quite alright, just a few bruises and scratches from his adventure and slightly paler and quieter than Monday morning.

Ken 'Dinger' Bell H, DT7, DT8, PB, TDR

Crime Reporter of the Old School

I was a crime reporter on the old News Chronicle in the late twenties and early thirties and struck up acquaintanceship with Crime Squad officers sent from the Yard whenever Chief Constables of the County Police Forces required their expertise.

We used to rub shoulders with them in the bar whenever the day's work was over, and I recall Chief Inspectors Hambrook and Percy Worth among others.

Big murder cases I covered in those days were the Brighton Trunk murders, the Cheltenham Torso mystery, the Rouse Burning Car case, Gracie Golledge and Norah Upchurch murders, as well as the Dartmore Prison Mutiny. All that's going back a bit, but I wonder if mention of them strikes a chord in any of your pensioner readers?

In those days it was almost a crime in itself to approach the police for information but by dint of carrying out parallel investigations ourselves we often came up with material matters that assisted the inquiry. It was foolish to deny us access to police information, despite the issue of a Press Card explicitly giving us the right to such data at source.

The 'Green Door' room on the Embankment, with its row of telephone boxes based on the American plan, served no other purpose than to gag us by providing only odd paragraphs of street accidents and minor crime. This had the effect of sending us to second-hand sources - with consequent distortion of an investigation - and the buying of Christmas turkeys and other emoluments for our contacts.

How different from today when enlightened policy has the scene of crime officer giving Press conferences and fully up-dated situation reports. Such Press old hands as Stanley Bishop of the Herald and later News Chronicle, Perry Hoskins of the Express, and Hugh Brady of the Mail would turn in their graves at the easy time today's crime reporters have when they themselves had their own ways of getting exclusives.

Brady, for instance, once carried the name of Boy Jacoby, the Savoy Hotel page-boy who was murdered, in his waistpocket for three days - and still gave the Mail a scoop! - while he recovered from an excess of alcoholic intake he had indulged in to get it.

Norman Clark, Surrey

Children and the Police

How many children ever speak to a policeman? Unless their fathers are policemen, small children never, or very rarely, have the opportunity to speak to one.

The only time they see them is on TV during scenes of violence at football matches, or on picket lines or at demos. Sometimes they see a white car with a flashing blue light as it passes on the way to an incident.

At home they hear derogatory remarks about the 'copper' who charged father with speeding or other crimes, but never a word of praise.

None of these things gives children a fair opinion of the police or creates a bond between them. When a policeman stood outside the school gate to see them safely across the road, the little ones trusted him and confided in him. The sweets and pictures which they gave to my husband each day were a sign of respect.

You only have to see the friendship which develops between small pupils and the school crossing lady, to realise that this is a lost opportunity to make children aware of the friendly policeman from an early age.

If a policeman could man a crossing even one day a week, I am sure it would bridge the gap between the police and the public. I know it isn't easy today, but if only we could start with the children.

Mrs D Barrett

Jack Thyer's Royal Visitor

The recent death of a much loved uncle recalls to my mind a funny incident which occurred in the early 1960s, at a time when I was residing in Police married quarters at Harriot House in Stepney.

At that time people had joined the Met from all far-flung corners of the British Isles, and the married quarters were something of a melting pot of accents.

There was nevertheless a good camaraderie and it was common for us to enquire of our neighbours how the family was and whether they'd heard from 'back home' lately.

One morning I was tending my little bit of garden, when the usual conversation took place with a passing neighbour, in which I was told they had had visitors but that they had now gone back. I replied that we ourselves were 'expecting a load at the weekend', meaning that my mother, father, brother and the aforementioned uncle were due to visit us from Scotland.

That to me represented a 'load' in our small quarters, with the consequence that some of us would be sleeping with a blanket on the floor.

However, unbeknown to me, the news apparently got around that Jack and Janice Thyer were expecting, not a 'load', but a 'lord', to visit them. Apparently the result of this was that the gardens were all put ship-shape for the weekend and the children put out to play dressed in their Sunday best.

It appears that when my visitors arrived they were rubber-necking around the precincts of Harriot House when a neighbour sidled up to my wife and indicating the aforementioned uncle, enquired (in all seriousness) 'Is that the one who's the lord?' Following on from this, the uncle, a noted thespian - no he wasn't bent, just a member of an amateur dramatic club - apparently did a tour of inspection of the gardens with an immaculate impersonation of a 'Lord Charles' type character, commenting on a bloom here, a leaf there, a blade of grass there.

This took place while I was late turn shift at West End Central, and I returned home that night much puzzled by the hilarity among my visitors.

A family inquest then took place as to what I'd actually said to the neighbour and it was concluded that when I said 'load' it did sound as if I was saying 'Lord'. All these years later my wife still complains that I sound my R's in the wrong places where I ought not to. Oops!

John Thyer ex PC C, G, S Divisions

Coronation Day

Shortly before Coronation Day, part of the Traffic Police DT4 motor cycle fleet was replaced. The older machines, stripped of leg-shields and other equipment prior to disposal, were retained as extra vehicles.

The big day arrived - together with pouring rain - and before day-light, a group of us arrived at CO on the old machines, feeling like drowned rats. We were 'reserves' and were allocated a small basement room in CO, insufficient in size, and in seats, for the number of motor cyclists who eventually arrived; and the smell of wet clothing and tobacco smoke left much to be desired. Small groups kept leaving for fresh air, and mid-morning found several of us on the steps of the main entrance of CO, where we could watch the carriages going along the Embankment, on their way to the Abbey.

The most memorable was the open coach containing the large Queen of Tonga and a small male companion (Noel Coward was later to suggest that he might have been her lunch).

A little later two PC's arrived with a well-turned-out Police horse, but why two grooms? I was soon to find out! From CO there emerged a small figure of a very senior Police Officer, wearing an 'admiral's hat' and a huge riding cloak which swept the floor. One of the grooms assisted the would-be rider to mount, whilst the second groom (the catcher) caught him as he slid down the opposite side. We left hurriedly, so that our mirth was not too evident.

At about 1pm the reserve motor cyclists were ordered to the Abbey, where we huddled out of the rain, against the glass wall of the temporary annexe which had been built. The glass had been etched with heraldic designs - which left much of it clear, and we found that we could look into the waiting room. Now the guests had spent long hours in their seats, and the well-corsetted ladies in their gowns and robes were very glad of a good scratch - under the watchful eyes of the peeping Traf. Pols. The Lords, meanwhile, were removing their coronets and producing fag ends and snacks from within.

The guests who were not in the Royal procession were to be escorted, via Victoria Street, to the rear entrances of the Palace. A rota had been made out and the cars were drawn up in the correct order. Unfortunately, the guests did not keep to the rota, and when a car pulled up to the door, and the wrong passengers appeared, the car was waved away. The Police motor cyclist allotted to the car, unaware of what was happening, tore off up Victoria Street with an empty car behind him, and was forced to do a U-turn and rejoin the queue.

Eventually, we got all the guests to the Palace (whether or not in the correct cars I know not). We were dismissed and returned to our garages. Another 12 hour duty was over. At least, I'd seen the Queen (of Tonga).

Dennis Picco 131210 W, DT4, CTS, TD8, CO

Eve of Coronation Day

On the eve of Coronation Day 1953, my relief paraded at 3pm for a Late Turn tour until 11pm. We went off duty for two hours and paraded again at 1am on Coronation Day.

The weather was grotty - rain and plenty of it. We donned leggings, macs, motor cycle helmets and gloves and rode the 10 miles from Thornton Heath to Cannon Row.

To ride with goggles on in driving rain and in the dark was an invitation to crash, so goggles were draped round the neck. That meant eyes were filled with rain and vision was impaired but it was the better alternative. It wasn't long before boots and gloves, were water-logged, the rain pouring down the inside of the 'waterproof' mac.

At Cannon Row we joined a mass of motorcyclists from other District Garages, all soaking wet and looking like a colony of penguins. The smell in the canteen was appalling, the air filled with the odour of soaking clothes and water-filled boots and gloves mixed with tea, coffee, food and tobacco.

At 3am it was time to move. I went to Hyde Park, Storeys Gate. The rain still hurtled down as we all left Cannon Row. It was a nightmare journey - just hanging on the motorcycle and praying that I didn't skid and crash on the wooden block surface in Whitehall as it was then.

We were in position at 3.30am, pitch dark, still raining, everybody 'full of the joys of spring'. My heart went out to all those poor devils who had stood all night waiting to see a spectacle that many would never see again. Gradually, the weather improved.

Then came the Coronation procession. Magically, the rain cleared. Near to me stood an elderly lady no more than 5ft tall. No hope of seeing over the top of the crowds, she cried.

I don't remember who it was who helped me but we grabbed hold of the little lady, lifted her up and sat her on top of a Traffic Patrol TAG car. She pulled up her skirt, put her legs round the roof-mounted speakers and enjoyed a perfect view of the Royals, Queen Salote of Tonga et al. She sat there for two hours. When she came down she gave us both a big hug! We forgot our wet clothes, life wasn't so bad after all.

Such a long spell left us a bit tired and I found it difficult not to fall asleep riding back to Thornton Heath. The long hours meant overtime. I remember the grudging way that our claims were dealt with. If it had not been for the magnificent efforts of our Constables' Rep Tommy Green, we would not have received our rightful dues. Tom used General Orders to insist that we were properly treated.

There are two sides to every story. Life in the Force was not a complete bundle of merry laughs and it does no harm to talk of these matters as well as those that were amusing.

Peter Gidley PC 747Z 131142

A Long Wet Wait

On Coronation Day, I was a PC at the old Rotherhithe nick, a Sectional Station of Deptford Sub-Division.

We paraded at 1.30am at Deptford nick and then were taken by chartered LT buses to our ground at Hyde Park Corner. There we spent a longer day than most in the pouring rain as all the military were camped in Hyde Park so we had them all passing us on the way to the parade, then the parade itself, and then we were still engaged whilst all the troops marched back to Hyde Park.

When they had all passed we were allowed to fall out to the side of the road where the fags came out. Then came the highlight of our day: the roads were opened to traffic which was chaotic. But as in those days most of us were ex-servicemen, no one volunteered to sort it out, and we stayed where we were quietly puffing.

Suddenly, out of the blue appeared the resplendent figure of a senior officer, Bertie Hefford, Chief Superintendent of M Division, who took up his position in the middle of this busy junction and spent the next half hour waving his arms about trying to sort out the traffic whilst we all gave advice - under our breath.

Bertie then came over and thanked us all for a good day's work and said we could all go home. Although in those days transport was provided to take you to your ground on ceremonials, nobody thought of providing transport to take you home.

A Deptford Sergeant and I then made our way on foot to Victoria Station hoping to get a bus but with the crowds this was impossible so we then retraced our steps to Charing Cross Station where we were lucky to get a train to New Cross. There I intended to get a local bus home but the Sergeant said we had earned a pint so we adjourned to his local pub, which had been open all day.

There we stayed until 10.30pm having a 'knees up' in full No 1s with medals jingling and the locals insisting on buying our drinks.

A memorable day, the only time in my service that I saw a Chief Superintendent directing traffic. I wonder if any of the lads who were with me that day are still about.

Reg Clift Ex Insp 135558 MR, LP, HH, ED, CB, COB8.

King of Siam

One Friday I was late turn driver. On arrival I was met by Superintendent Starkey. He said, 'At 7 o'clock I want you to be on Tower Bridge with the GP car, put your civvy jacket on so as not to cause interest. Three people will arrive by car and you are to bring them here to HL.' 'Who are they?' I asked. 'Never you mind who they are. Just be there at 7pm and bring them here - and don't forget!' Then he went off duty.

At about 6pm I was about to take my refreshment break when a call came to pick up a drunk-and-disorderly from Gardiners Corner. It turned out to be a huge Irish building worker about 7 feet tall with size 14 boots coated with concrete. We had great trouble persuading him to get in the van and even more at HL. We got him into the charge room kicking and struggling. PS (Dobbie) Dobinson was busy with some other charge so we dumped him in the detention room. He immediately began kicking the door and shouting, 'Let me out of here you so and so's'.

I returned to the canteen for my break and got into a card school with Les LeFevre, Alan Best and George Wheatcroft. Later George Wheatcroft said, 'Haven't you got to pick up someone for Superintendent Starkey?' It was a few minutes to 7 o'clock. I shot out of the canteen, grabbed my civvy jacket and by 7pm, I was parked on Tower Bridge. Seconds later a car drew up behind me and who should get out but Prince

Philip, the Commissioner and another civvy who turned out to be the PR officer. I'm sure the look of amazement that I registered was seen by the Commissioner. No one had any idea that such visitors were expected.

I took the long road back and drew up in front of the station. The Commissioner obviously sensed something was amiss and drew Prince Philip's attention to the building next to HL. 'This used to be the Garrick Theatre and there is a bust of him,' he said pointing to the building. I took this opportunity to dash through the station.

Our unwilling guest was still shouting and kicking the door. I said to Dobbie, 'Quick, Prince Philip's outside with the Commissioner,' unaware that the Prince was close behind me, 'I don't care if its the bloody King of Siam, take this man's bloody boots off!' He turned round and saw the Prince, his jaw dropped as he spluttered, 'I beg your pardon your worship, I mean your majesty.' Prince Philip grinned and said, 'You've got a rowdy customer there Sergeant, I suggest you have his boots removed.'

Our three visitors went off with the Duty Inspector, Mr Forest, to the Superintendent's office. Dobbie turned to me and said, with great feeling 'You and your bloody practical jokes.'

Later I drove the visitors around the various clubs and places of interest. On our return the ND Relief were parading. Prince Philip spoke to each member and saw them out. The LT Relief that usually booked off to the Station Sergeant paraded for dismissal.

The Prince spoke to each officer in turn. I had, by now, put on my uniform. As he reached me he started to ask what I had been doing when he corrected himself and said, 'Don't tell me, you introduced the King of Siam.'

Years later, Dobbie, then retired, was working as a clerk at the Limehouse Labour Exchange. One day, while in uniform, I called in to renew my passport. The counter clerk mentioned he didn't recognise me and I told him I was based at Leman Street. He said, 'We've got one of your ex-sergeants here, Mr Dobinson, do you know him?' 'Just tell him the King of Siam wants to see him,' I replied.

Dobbie entered with a huge smile and grabbed my hand. 'This so-and-so caused me loads of agro, but we sure had some laughs as Leman Street was a happy-go-lucky station.'

Philip Hoggard 127135H

The Palace of Varieties

AD, Cannon Row, was well known throughout the Met for the number of protection posts - 18 when I was there, plus five traffic points, and six beats. Even at Peel House, I remember men hoping they would not be posted to be 'Statue Minders'. What did add to the misery there was the thought of having to perform duty at Buckingham Palace, or 'BP' in the vernacular of the day.

It was usually night duty or late turn when you found yourself parading in the police room there. One place you were unlikely to be posted was on the front gates. They were for regular staff. We were deployed at the rustic rear of the Palace.

The permanent staff were mostly at the end of their service, and we had just started ours. They also roamed around the grounds, from dusk to dawn, with dogs. Labradors were used, and kept in kennels in Hyde Park. They were ferried to the Palace for late turn and night duty. If I'm correct the handlers did a few days' course at Hyde Park. It was not the same dog with the same handler, but all the time changing.

There was a small Police Lodge we used for breaks: the bare essentials, table and chairs, a few lockers, and the ubiquitous kettle steaming away. Unless you took sandwiches, it was a long walk to Cannon Row for refreshments.

We patrolled small areas, usually a section of terrace. From time to time, handlers and dogs would appear throughout the night, to allow you time off for refreshments, and a break. Being posted to the Palace for years spawned a few characters, and I met one or two.

One night I heard the opening lines of the Gettysburgh address, and out of the darkness appeared a PC with dog. As he approached me, he was getting in full flow. I was just about to say 'Good evening Mr President,' but he got in first with 'Go and get a cup of tea mate.' I was off, leaving the thespian to his speech.

Another PC there seemed to be the Palace Astronomer, and on clear nights, he was likely to open the conversation by looking skyward saying 'Jupiter is bright tonight.' He was soon pointing out other heavenly bodies. He still persisted, even when I casually mentioned, that there was a wonderful display of heavenly bodies at the Hammersmith Palace on Thursday nights. 'Crabbed age and youth, dear boy - go and have your tea.'

Most had an altruistic nature, and provided us with a cup of tea. There were no provisions for visitors. It usually worked out that on arrival at the Lodge, a regular was about to make a brew. Tea was the chief beverage drunk, and its preparation was worthy of an Oriental tea ceremony. They all possessed small tea pots, mostly brown, then a collection of small jars, and milk in a long-discarded medicine bottle. A spare cup would be produced from the locker, and tea and conversation would begin. Very nice!

Sharing our lonely vigils at the rear, we had a couple of sentries, from one of the Foot Guards Regiments. I knew from my Army days that young officers posted some outlandish questions to sentries so I tried to be in earshot, when he arrived with the Guard Sergeant.

One night I heard the following. At the approach of the Officer of the Guard, accompanied by the Guard Sergeant, the sentry sprang to attention and gave a rifle (303 Lee Enfield) salute. The officer saluted saying, 'You are ...?' The sentry replied in a broad Yorkshire accent 'Garthwaite Sir.' After a pause the Officer said 'I want you to imagine that after we have left, you hear a loud noise, and see a Russian T34 tank approaching the Palace with hostile intent. What are you going to do?'

It was a clear frosty night, and you could almost hear poor Garthwaite's brain untangling. 'I'd call out the Guard Sir,' said Garthwaite, rather pleased with himself. 'No one hears you Garthwaite, positive action, quick,' said the officer. 'Positive action Sir?' was all Garthwaite could say. 'The tank is still approaching. What are you going to do in this situation?' As a last attempt, Garthwaite played his trump card 'I'd put one up the spout, Sir.'

I should add, the Guard Sergeant was looking heavenwards, perhaps hoping for some divine intervention. The exercise ended there. We enjoyed a spot of schadenfreude as the officer tripped on his sword.

I sidled up to Garthwaite, to render my sympathy but alas, dear reader, I cannot commit to paper his comments. Before I leave the Palace, I must mention a piece of 'high tech' plus belt-and-braces action of the time. One duty we performed was to patrol in a small area of a courtyard. This was outside the police office. A window was waist-high, and you could see into the office. Likewise they could see you, unless you moved into an area of darkness.

At an appointed time, a curious ceremony took place. This was heralded by a 'rat-tat' on the window. The Sergeant then threaded black cotton through a small hole in the wooden window frame. The cotton was retrieved, and taken across the yard, and secured to a hook that was fastened in the wall. A signal was then given to the Sergeant 'Cotton secure!' or words to that effect The cotton was then attached to a switch in the police office, this in turn activated a loud alarm if thrown.

Imagine now, this black cotton, taut, waist high, unseen across the yard. The night wore on, one's thoughts drifted. Yes, you've guessed it, I along with many others walked onto the cotton, the switch was thrown, and off went the alarm. All hell broke loose! You could see the PS, PC, and perhaps an Inspector leaping to their feet. It just needed Corporal Jones to call out 'Don't panic Captain Mainwaring'. Outside would be a PC sheepishly holding the cotton, thinking up a suitable story.

At last dawn broke, the Monarch was safe, and it was over. Hot-foot down Buckingham Gate, over Victoria Street, to the top floor of the Section House, where bed awaited.

Alan Jackson AD, AH, CTS, LK, TDM, TDP, TDR, B10

My First Day on Duty

In the mid-Fifties, having somehow passed out from Peel House, I was posted to Sydenham, then part of the East Dulwich Sub-division. After a few days of 'learning beats', at six o'clock one morning I was released upon the unsuspecting public who had the misfortune to reside or pass through the area known as Sydenham Hill. this was an area where very little occurred at any time of day, let alone early turn. I can remember feeling very grateful for this fact.

Precisely on time (as per schedule in my little brown beat book) I made my first ring and later presented myself at the nick for my refreshments. I was invited into a 'chip school', a game in which I soon became quite proficient. PS Norman (Lofty) Lay and PS Fred Boyd were already at the table and initiated me into the hidden mysteries of dominoes - Sydenham style.

As I was putting my tunic back on in preparation for resuming my role as the protector of the inhabitants of Sydenham Hill, one of these worthy gentleman said to the other, 'Oh I see he has *****'s old number'. 'No he hasn't said, the other, 'He has ****'s number'.

Quite a heated discussion ensued as to whose number I had inherited. I left them to it as I had by then come to the end of my 45 minutes refreshment period, besides which I had just discovered that I had a rather urgent job to do. I went outside the canteen and could still hear their raised voices whilst I hurriedly changed my numerals over so that they read the same on both shoulders.

During my earlier life, I had worked as a draughtsman for the Vacuum Brake Co. Designing brake arrangements for steam locos - a job with a real future! This company had very strict Victorian standards particularly with respect to time-keeping. One was expected to be in the office and working well before 9am, and if anyone left before 5.15pm, they were looked upon as clock watchers. This training, coupled with three years in the RAF had a certain conditioning effect upon me. So having resumed my beat on Sydenham Hill and not wishing to be labelled a clock watcher, I remained there until 2pm before slowly ambling down Kirkdale and Dartmouth Road towards the nick, which I was approaching at about 2.10pm when I became aware of PS Lay who seemed quite agitated leaping up down on the front steps of the police station bellowing, 'Where have you been?' or words to that effect. I reported, 'All correct Sergeant', whereupon Norman Lay explained to me in no uncertain terms that all was far from correct, that the whole Early Turn relief had been kept waiting, that the Late had been held back from their beats, and most importantly, his wife had cooked him his dinner and it was getting cold.

I apologised, promised to do better and slunk away home.

Ken Richmond ex PC 143903/573P

Wellington Arch: Monument and Police Station

Wellington Arch, which dominates Hyde Park Corner, must be the only public memorial in the world to also have served as a police station.

In gratitude for the Duke of Wellington's great victory over the French at Waterloo in Belgium in 1815, a public subscription raised enough money to provide a fitting tribute to the Iron Duke in the form of a Triumphal Arch to be built facing Apsley House, the Duke's London home. Later an equestrian statue showing the Duke mounted on his favourite charger, Copenhagen, was placed on top of the arch.

Built in 1828 to a design by Decimus Burton the arch remained on its original site until 1880 when it was deemed to be in the way of increasing traffic and was moved some forty yards south to the top of Constitution Hill where it formed an impressive gate to the Royal parks. In 1912 a bronze sculpture by Adrian Jones was mounted on the roof.

The Metropolitan Police began to use the arch as a police station in 1831, and apart from three years between 1881 and 1884, when the arch was re-sited, there has been a police presence there for almost 150 years.

When A Division re-opened the police station in 1884, the west pier and the upper part of the arch was converted to become a section house and the home of the sergeant and the dozen or so constables stationed there. This use continued for 59 more years until it was closed in 1943, four years into WW2. The office on the ground floor dealt with all kinds of public service but lacked cells and a CID office, so all prisoners had to be transferred to Cannon Row to be dealt with there.

From its exterior appearance the arch is obviously a big building but there are few clues as to its interior size and functions. Architectually it has three main features: the east and west piers across the top of which is a great span. Each pier has four floors including a basement. The span which formed the third floor is built on top of the two piers and inside it is like a large oblong box; this served as a dormitory with ten beds. Above the dormitory is a rectangular area surrounded by high walls and in the centre of this is the plinth supporting the Quadriga. The east pier was the home of the royal gatekeeper and his family.

The basement beneath the station office was fitted up as a kitchen and messroom with two toilets and a pantry adjoining. The residents appointed a caterer from among their number who collected a few shillings a week from each of us and this paid for the ingredients of a good mid-day meal and enough to employ a cook on a part-time basis to prepare these meals for us. The office on the ground floor had a small annexe in which was the small PBX telephone switchboard and the air raid siren switch.

In 1962 an RT link with Cannon Row and Commissioner's Office was installed. On the floor above the office there was a library-cum-rest room, and on the second floor were two small PBX telephone switchboard and the air raid siren switch.

Ten constables slept in the dormitory which had a bathroom, shower and toilets attached. On the landing outside the dormitory was an iron stairway which led to a hatch, then to an iron ladder fixed to the wall of the plinth which led up to the flat base of the Quadriga itself, and from here a magnificent 360 degree panorama of London could be enjoyed.

Conditions inside the Arch were spartan for there was no central heating and the only warmth came from a small gas fire in each room. There was practically no natural light and in winter the three feet thick stone walls ran with condensation. Worse still, every time there was a storm the sewers beneath Hyde Park Corner could not cope with the sudden rush of surface water, and consequently the sewage flooded back into the basement and was forced up through the two toilets, filling the kitchen and mess-room with raw sewage a foot deep. We were helpless until the rain stopped and it then took two hours to bail out and mop up the mess.

Vacancies at the Arch were always filled by volunteers and despite the unhygienic living conditions there was never a shortage of these. I suspect that apart from the excellent camaraderie which existed there, AW was the only section in the while of the MPD with two authorised refreshment periods, and generally we were little bothered by supervising officers from Cannon Row.

For over 150 years the personnel of the Arch had a close affinity with the monument and their presence breathed life into what could otherwise be a cold and cheerless stone pile. Those who worked there over the years could tell countless stories of famous and infamous events which took place beneath its shadow. In 1850 Sir Robert Peel was thrown from his horse near the arch and died of his injuries a week later. On 16 July 1936, I was on duty on Constitution Hill when I witnessed what was at first thought to be an assassination attempt on King Edward VIII as he rode mounted at the head of a column of troops he had just reviewed in Hyde Park.

A disgruntled journalist named Andrew George McMahon, who was standing on the horse ride of Green Park, suddenly whipped out a revolver from his jacket and aimed at the King. In a flash a Special Constable named Dick from Hackney and three PCs from H division, threw themselves on the gunman and a struggle ensued in which the revolver was sent slithering across the carriageway to land at the hind legs of His Majesty's horse, causing it to rear up and almost throw him.

At his trial at the Old Bailey, McMahon pleaded that he meant no harm to the King but was making a public protest about the Home Secretary's refusal to grant him a licence to publish a newspaper called The Human Gazette. The court found him guilty of possessing a loaded firearm with intent to endanger life and sent him to prison for a year.

With the outbreak of war in 1939 the roles of the Arch and its police underwent dramatic changes, for the building became a Group Reserve Centre with massive increases in strength, covering the whole 24 hours, with squads ready to deal with any major bomb incident or other war-time contingency.

But in fact over the ensuing six months of the Phoney War, nothing very war-like happened; the overcrowded situation inside the Arch got on people's nerves and squabbles between regulars and auxiliaries were common. All this was forgotten when the bombs began to fall and all concerned realised high explosive bombs were incapable of distinguishing between the pros and the amateurs.

Throughout the Blitz and the V1 and V2 attacks, the only damage sustained to the building was caused by bomb splinters and it seemed to bear a charmed life as it was ringed by bomb incidents which caused much damage and some loss of life. Houses all around received direct hits and the squads from Wellington Arch were often on the scene first to be joined by colleagues from surrounding stations and the rescue squads. King George VI's former home at 145 Piccadilly was demolished by a direct hit and we helped to dig out the caretaker and his wife from the ruins.

But by far the most serious incident affecting us occurred on the night of May 10 1941, when two big bombs destroyed the Alexandra Hotel just down Knightsbridge from Hyde Park Corner killing over 40 guests and seriously injuring about 50 others, nearly all the victims being in the basement air raid shelter. Wellington Arch personnel were nearest and first on the scene to be joined shortly afterwards by officers from Gerald Road and the rescue squads; they all tore into the rubble in their efforts to bring out the injured and the dead.

Approaching the hotel from the rear PC Reg Oakes and two colleagues from Gerald Road heard the cries for help from a family of four who were trapped on a narrow ledge, which was once the floor of their suite on the fifth floor, and risked their lives in rescuing the entire family. PC Reg Oakes was awarded the George Medal for his bravery and his colleagues received commendations.

Doug Lightwood ex PC546A

Fanny of Wellington Arch

My tale of Wellington Arch police station and some of its occupants would not be complete without a mention of our cook. Fanny was an absolute darling and although she was nearer to 90 then she was to 80 she lived alone in Pimlico and braved the Blitz to come and do for us. Apart from cooking satisfying lunches for us she offered to darn our socks, launder our shirts, sew buttons on uniforms, and generally mothered us.

Emulating her late lamented husband, who had served in the East Surreys in the Boer War, she swore like a trooper and smoked like a chimney, getting through 30 Woodbines a day.

Fanny loved us all with one exception, and this was someone we called Joe who we had found almost frozen to death in the basement light-well of the Arch one morning in January 1940, in one of the bitterest winters of the decade. We brought him in, gave him a tot of whisky in some hot milk and put him by the oven door to thaw out. As police regulations did not permit strangers to stay overnight unless charged with some offence, we had to put him out when he was sufficiently recovered. But the next morning we heard a tapping sound on the pantry window. It was Joe who had spent another freezing night outside.

We took pity on him and allowed him back into the warm kitchen and decided to let him stay until the weather improved. It wasn't difficult to feed him despite our short rations, for if you have not already guessed, Joe wasn't human but was a starling named after Joseph Stalin, and our guest used to help himself to tit-bits from the edge of our plates as we were eating and pecked at Fanny's pies she left uncovered to cool on the stone floor. This enraged Fanny to the extent that she would flick him off with her oven-cloth and yell, 'I'll wring that bleeding bird's neck one day. S'w'elp-me-Bob!' (a soldier's oath).

Starlings are fair mimics and whenever Joe heard Fanny's footsteps descending the stone steps to the kitchen each morning, he would flutter around the mess room squawking something which sounded suspiciously like 'bleeding bird, bleeding bird'.

However, much as we liked him, his forays for food and his lime droppings became a bit too much for us and when the warmer days came round we were obliged to evict him once again. But whether the cold of winter did it, or whether he died of a broken heart through being abandoned, we shall never know, but one morning in April we found him lying on his back in the light-well with his feet sticking straight up. He was dead.

We just couldn't throw his tiny body into the dustbin and decided to give him a proper burial. We placed him in a cigar-box lined with tissues and laid him to rest beneath a chestnut just inside Green Park. When the crew of the RAF barrage balloon located a few yards away witnessed the ceremony and were told what it was all about they said nothing. But the look on their faces was enough to tell us that they thought we were stark, staring mad.

Fanny's catering was aided by two war-time measures which were designed to supplement the official rations. Hyde Park police started a Pig Club, which bought and reared piglets, feeding them on swill scrounged from the kitchens of hotels in Park Lane and Knightsbridge until they were ready for slaughter, and the Arch personnel became members and benefited from occasional legs and ribs of prime pork which did not require the surrender of meat coupons.

The other measure was that we rented an allotment in Hyde Park which we took turns in working to provide us with a steady supply of fresh vegetables. It was hard work cultivating the plot for we discovered that a few inches below the surface were the foundations of the Crystal Palace which was erected on the site in 1851, but the results were good. The soil was enriched with bags of manure from Mounted Branch stables attached to Hyde Park police station.

Finally, in bringing my story to a conclusion I extend my thanks to a serving police officer on the staff of the Royal Household police, PC Alan Graham, and to another Arch colleague, ex PC Ron Pope, who also responded to Alan's appeal with information

Doug Lightwood

Attempted Murder in High Places

Murders of Metropolitan Policemen since 1829 have generally been of Constables, but now this story goes to the other end of the scale and concerns the attempted murder of the Commissioner and two Assistant Commissioners.

Almost since the formation of the Force it was customary to appoint a retired Army Officer as Commissioner, and 1922 saw the appointment of Brigadier-General Sir William Horwood to the post. Perhaps like Earl Mountbatten he did not realise how anyone could possibly want to murder him or perhaps he was not sufficiently aware of the hazards of his occupation.

The General's secretary went into his office one day and found him eating chocolate. He passed the box to her and invited her to take one, saying they had been sent by his daughter Beryl for his birthday. The secretary, fortunately, was somewhat suspicious, but she took one and was about to eat it when she remembered her lunch was on her desk, so she said, 'I won't eat it now as I am going to have my lunch.'

She had also noticed they had been packed in a fancy box which had contained soap, and back in her own office she thought long and hard about the whole incident. The General had cut his chocolate in half and whilst eating the remaining portion he said to his secretary who had now returned with some more papers to sign, 'this tastes funny'. The papers were signed and as she was busy she thought no more of the incident until later that day the Commissioner was violently sick and felt very ill.

They retrieved the wrapper from the waste basket and found the parcel was addressed to 'Brigadier-General Horwood', and he then realised the chocolates were not from his daughter as she would never have addressed him in that way. He then discovered they had been posted from Balham and a Doctor was called. He found the Commissioner very ill with hardly any pulse and in a state of collapse.

The Doctor was then handed three chocolates and he noticed on the bottom of one a bluish tint mixture among the yellow cream. The chocolates were sealed up and sent immediately to Mr Webster at St. Mary's Hospital for analysis and at 8.30pm he rang the Doctor to say the substance in the chocolates was arsenic.

Early next day the Commissioner was removed in a partly conscious condition to St. Thomas's Nursing Home where he remained for a considerable time.

Two days prior to this, two Assistant Commissioners, Major Elliot and the Hon. Trevor Bingham had been sent chocolate eclairs also from Balham, with a note saying, 'A good lunch and a hearty appetite - Molly' - but instead of eating them, they had sent theirs to the Public Analyst's Office thinking it was a Guy Fawkes joke.

When it became known the Commissioner had been poisoned, these eclairs were fetched from the Analyst's office where they were still waiting to be analysed. It was found these also contained arsenic as used in weed killers.

Large numbers of CID officers were called in to investigate, and the fancy box that contained the eclairs gave the first clue. These boxes were only used by a Mr Kierle, a baker and confectioner who had four shops in Balham. The signature 'Molly' on the note with the eclairs caused a great deal of wasted time and a Balham prostitute of that name was under suspicion until she was able to prove her innocence, at least in respect of the poison.

After several false leads Chief Inspector Helden called at 226 Balham High Road where a servant opened the door. A Mr Walter Frank Tatem lived with his parents, who immediately ordered out the investigating officers.

After much hassle and amid threats from the parents, the son drew a sword stick and attempted to use it, but he was disarmed and arrested. On opening the front gate, the prisoner, as a last defiant gesture, kicked the Chief Inspector on the buttock, and he was eventually put in the cells with some difficulty.

On 23 February 1923 he was charged at the Old Bailey but was found unfit to plead and ordered to be detained during His Majesty's pleasure. The Commissioner eventually made a complete recovery from his ordeal.

Geoffrey Taylor, DT7, H

Another Attempted Murder of a Commissioner

Attempts to assassinate Commissioners are not a new phenomenon: it happened on previous occasions by poisoning and by shooting.

Sir Edward Henry took up an appointment with the Indian Civil Service in 1873, and soon became part of the English Establishment in that continent, learning the language and playing polo at which game he became a very good player.

In the Indian Civil Service it was the custom for Indian coolies and servants to sign for their wages on the pay sheets by dipping their fingers in ink and then pressing them on to the wages sheets opposite their names. Almost none could read or write and this was a quick and convenient way of signing for their wages, and the pay sheets when full were held in bundles kept together with a thorn from the thorn bushes. This system was still in use in Deolali in 1944.

After several years Sir Edward was appointed Inspector General of Police in Bengal, at that time a province of India on the eastern side and an area where crime was high and several British Servicemen had been murdered.

After Sir Edward settled in to this new job he began to look again at the system of thumb and finger prints as a means of identification as he had been told by an elderly Indian Civil Servant years before that everyone had different designs on their prints. He became very interested in the subject and put his ideas down into print and wrote a thesis on the subject, and later some research was done on the subject by various Police Forces.

Sir Edward left India in 1898 to take up an appointment as Commissioner of Police in the Transvaal in South Africa, but after three years he left and was appointed Assistant Commissioner at New Scotland Yard. This was a CID position, and with other senior officers he began to take an increasing interest in finger prints, being convinced that his theories were correct.

The Commissioner at the time, Edward Bradford, retired and Sir Edward was promoted to that post, and in the early years of this century some criminals were being convicted with the help of finger prints as evidence.

Alfred Bowes lived in Acton and had applied for a Taxi Licence, but it was refused, and he then bore a grudge against the Police. Bowes harboured resentment which built up into hatred, and he began to find out all he could about the Police and the Commissioner in particular.

He cut out from newspapers many snippets of information about the movements and duties of the Commissioner, and he eventually found out where Sir Edward lived. In those days there was not much need for secrecy as there is today.

On the 27 November 1912, in early evening fog, Sir Edward came back to his home in Kensington by car and walked towards his front door.

Bowes who had been watching and waiting nearby for some time ran up and fired several shots at Sir Edward, but luckily only one bullet struck him, and he stumbled and staggered forward to get to the safety of his home. With great courage and speed his driver and two other workmen raced forward and knocked Bowes to the ground.

Sir Edward's daughter ran out of the house and helped her father inside, while Police officers nearby came running up and arrested Bowes and took him to Kensington Police station where he was charged. He later pleaded guilty at the Old Bailey and was sentenced to 15 years penal servitude, and a newspaper report said the sentence was 'too lenient'.

Bowes was not released until after he had served 10 years, and when Sir Edward heard of Bowes' attempts to get to Canada to find work, he paid for his passage and helped him find work there.

Sir Edward resigned soon after the Police strike of 1918 for more pay, and as a result of this the pay of a Constable was raised from 30 shillings a week to 43 shillings. He died in 1931 at the age of 80 years and there are no records of the shooting damaging his health in any way.

Geoffrey Taylor ex H, DT7, 124166

Bermondsey Ghost

A few months after the formation of Sir Robert Peel's Police Force, reports began of a ghost at the upper window of a house in Grange Road, Bermondsey.

For some days the road had been the scene of much commotion when the ghost was seen wearing a large night cap, dressed in a grotesque fashion and smoking a pipe. The house had previously been occupied by an eccentric person, who was scarcely ever seen by neighbours and who was believed to be mad. Since his death the house had been empty, and soon after he was buried, reports of the ghostly sightings became more frequent until crowds of men, women and children completely blocked the road nightly. Some who had entered the house said they had seen the ghost and other previous occupants vanish up the chimney in a ball of fire.

So much annoyance was now being caused to locals that police help was called, and the Superintendent called out every man on the Division to disperse the crowd of about 2,000 people. Many had come from miles away and were staying all night in the hope of seeing the ghost. An Inspector entered the house but no one was there. It was suggested the story was got up by an interested party to prevent the letting of the house. Orders to the Police were to watch the house and if any person was seen inside acting as a ghost, 'a punishment awaits him which will check his nocturnal wanderings: there is a horse pond in the neighbourhood and a sousing would quickly bring him to his senses.'

Remembering the antics of a Limehouse PC in the 1930s who used to cover himself with a white sheet and dance around the churchyard on a foggy winter's night, I can't help thinking the PC on the beat in Grange Road got bored with shaking padlocks on the night duty.

Geoffrey Taylor 124166 H DT7

The Memoirs of Chief Inspector Monk

This is an extract from the memoirs of Chief Inspector John Monk who
lived 1859 to 1946 and served in the Metropolitan Police force. His
son, John Monk, discovered his father's writings and compiled this fas-
cinating document from them, in 1969. The memoirs are hitherto
unpublished and were sent to London Police Pensioner magazine by
retired Met Police officer Derek Marrable.

We patrolled each night with a different experienced constable. The first
night I accompanied a man who had been in the Force for 24 years and
for some misdemeanour, which I do not recall, had that day been reduced
to third-class rank. His pay had been reduced to that of mine - a mere
recruit - so I did not receive from him a very good impression of the body
I had joined. He was a strong man and walked me round the beat at a
great pace, making me do all the work of trying doors. I went off duty
tired and disgusted. We did not get on at all well together and about the
only thing I learned from this was that I should not make much progress
unless I drank.

I was on duty again at 9am for the lesson in police court procedure
which was to take place at the Worship Street court, about two miles
away. We were expected to walk and were warned that if we rode in a
public vehicle we were to pay our fare. For not doing so there were heavy
penalties.

Having been on my feet all night without much rest, I boarded a tram
and offered my fare. The conductor refused it as he did that of my two
chums who had decided to ride with me. We soon found this to be usual
practice.

The next night I was sent out with a constable named Pooley. We got
on very well together, and although it snowed all the time, I was sorry
when I had to leave him at 2am. He gave me some good advice and
instruction. After I left him he found two men who had broken into the
rear of a house at Clissold Park. He managed to knock them both out and
arrest them. I have always regretted I was not with him at the time.
Pooley received a reward and was recommended for sergeant.

I think the longest night I have ever spent was that Sunday night when
I had to take a beat on my own: 9pm to 6am, and I had to be on parade
for the police court three hours later! I breathed a great sigh of relief when

my fourteen days of police duty instruction was over. Not one word of instruction was given to any of the recruits by an officer. Our only mentors were the constables who showed us round the beats.

I was not a drinking man, and because I would not drink, most of the constables who showed me round were a bit suspicious of me. It was the custom at most public houses to allow the PC on the beat a pint of beer at closing time. The general idea was to ensure his being present when the customers were turned out in case there was trouble!

In March I was again posted to night duty. My beat was not a very popular one. It extended from the top of Stamford Hill, through Tottenham Hale to Tottenham Lock, then along the towing path to Bailey's Lane and back to the starting point. In those days it was a lonely and muddy walk except for the bit along the main road to Tottenham Hale. This beat had to be patrolled three times and worked to time. The sergeant knew just when the constable should arrive at Bailey's Lane and woe betide him if he was not there on time!

The second night I was on this beat, I found a man lying helplessly drunk on the grass beside the road, near the Seven Sisters trees. He could not walk; he could not even stand, and this put me in a quandary. Bear in mind, this was my first experience of its kind on a lonely night beat and I had been warned I must not spring my rattle (whistles had not yet been issued) unless in difficulties. I had also been told that any charge arising on that particular beat must be taken to Tottenham Police Station. I made my decision. I was young, healthy and very strong. Getting his two arms over my shoulders, I picked the man up and carried him to Tottenham station about a mile distant. I never met a soul on the way.

Covered with perspiration, and muddy, I entered the station with my burden, only to be greeted with derisive laughter from the officers on duty. They seemed to think I was a bit of an idiot, but after hearing my reasons for my actions the officer in charge became sympathetic, gave me a cup of tea, charged the man and had him put in a cell.

I was warned to appear in court at Edmonton the following Friday at 10am. My man had been on bail. I found him and told him to wait until his name was called. When this happened he was absent and I was sent to find him. I soon found him in a public house nearby, more than half-drunk. Being in that state his case was put back to the rising of the court. It was 5pm before this occurred as the court was in Licensing Session. My man was eventually fined 7/- or seven days.

I got back to the station at Stoke Newington, tired and hungry, only to be abused by the Inspector who refused to believe my story that the court had sat so long. He told me to parade at 9.45pm for another night on duty. I protested that I had been on duty all the previous night and all that day. He snapped back that policemen had no time off for court work which had to be done in their own time. I replied obstinately 'I managed to get my living before I came into this job and can again. I am going to bed'. Then I stalked out into the mess kitchen and had my supper.

My companions advised me to see the night duty Inspector but I persisted in my intention and went to bed. At 10pm I was awakened by the night duty sergeant. He coaxed me to get up and I went to see the Inspector. I explained to him exactly what had happened and he wired to Tottenham and received confirmation of my story. I was still in no humour to go on duty and was told I might be charged with leaving the force without notice.

Eventually I agreed to go on duty until 12 midnight. When I reported off duty, the Inspector called me into his office. He was very nice to me and as a result of my talk with him, I agreed to carry on.

Chief Inspector Monk, 1859-1946

A Child in the Arbour

An East-End childhood is recorded by Mabel Vaughan, who was living at 26 Arbour Square in 1910. Her grandfather was in the Met 1855-1880, her father 1885-1911 and her late husband 1925-1950. We take up her story in 1910.

My father was a Metropolitan Policeman, with the rank of Station Sergeant. He was stationed at King David Lane, Shadwell (closed many years ago). He wore number 4HR, and his pay was £2.20 per week.

He retired in 1911 after serving 26 years, 3 months and eleven days (he was a very precise man!). His pension was £73.3.1 per annum. A Constable's pay at that time was 17/- per week, and a working man's pay was 12/6 per week.

The hours worked by policemen then were 6am till 2pm, 2pm till 10pm and 10pm till 6am, one month day duty and one month night duty. There was also another duty called 'turn and turn about' which was four hours on, four hours off and then 4 hours on again!

Mr Mulvaney was the 'Super' of H in those days, and he lived in a house on the east side of the Square looked after by his batman, a massive police constable known to us children as 'Mick'. The Police Surgeon was Dr Grant, who lived in the Commercial Road.

Much to the envy of other children, all the policeman's children were allowed to play in the Station yard. We could watch the prisoners being taken in and out of the Black Maria, the prison van which was drawn by two horses. When any unfit horses were brought into the Yard we would watch the Vet poleaxe them and yet it meant nothing to us children as we watched those great dray horses heel over.

My father had many tales to tell of happenings during his police service. In Watney Street, our local market in the Commercial Road, there was a large empty shop in which was installed a machine for making sausages. Father said at night you could see rats running all over the machines picking out the bits of sausage meat. One day father said to the owner 'When you start the machine don't any of the rats get caught up in the machinery?' Said the owner 'I expect they do, Guv, but what's two or three rats in a ton of sausage meat?' (What indeed!)

At the top of Devonport Street, was a narrow alley which led through to Stepney Causeway. This was known to the local police as the 'Khyber Pass' and was always patrolled in 'twos'. The houses were two rooms up and two rooms down and generally two families occupied each house. A 'privy' in the back yard served every 6 houses!

One day father was called to a 'Wake' which had got out of hand. When he and his fellow officer arrived at the house, the mourners were all drunk, the corpse had been tipped out of the coffin and the whole lot of them were laying around in the beer all split on the floor!

In 1911 we had all the excitement of the Sidney Street siege. We would rush up there after school but of course could not get anywhere near the scene. In 1910 when Halley's Comet was due we heard fearsome tales that if the tail of the comet touched the earth we would all be blown into smithereens. We children went to bed in fear and trembling each night until the Comet departed on its way. As it was, it was terrifying to go up to bed with candle light making grotesque shadows on the wall, as there was no gas beyond the first floor. We also heard fearsome tales of 'Jack the Ripper' although, of course, the episode happened many, many years before. However we did use to sing a little ditty which went:

Jack the Ripper stole a kipper
On a Sunday morning

A copper came by and spit in his eye
And made him say 'Good Morning.'

Also we had another little ditty which ran:
Little bits of rabbit pie
Little drops of stout
Puts a bloom on Bobby's nose
And fills his tunic out!

Mrs French (nee Vaughan)

The Real Inspector Bucket

Whilst recuperating from a recent operation, I re-read Charles Dickens' *Bleak House* where I met again the redoubtable 'Inspector Bucket of Scotland Yard'. The novel was the first English Detective novel, in which Bucket was introduced as a 'Detective Officer'. It was written about ten years after the establishment of the CID in 1842, and Dickens based the fictional Bucket on a real-life Detective called Charles Frederick Field.

Field was born about 1805 and joined the newly-formed Metropolitan Police as a sergeant (warrant no 1332) on 21 September 1829. Dickens, whom he later befriended, believed him to have been a Bow Street Runner, but there is no firm evidence for that. Initially Field was posted to Holborn Division, and then on 16 November 1833 he was promoted to Inspector and transferred to Lambeth Division. It was here that he took charge of the investigation into the death of Eliza Grimwood, a 28-year-old prostitute, known as 'the Countess' who, on 26 May 1838 was found at her lodgings at 12 Wellington Terrace, Waterloo Road, with her throat cut - almost to the point of decapitation.

A doctor who was called to the scene originally classified the death as suicide, but later, when Field arrived, he re-called the same doctor, and carefully pointed to a cut at the back of the head and defensive cuts on the hands. The poor doctor confessed that he hadn't noticed them earlier, and decided that it was murder after all.

Field's enquiries lasted several weeks and a full document can still be found at the Public Record Office, and although unfortunately they did not lead to a positive result, they nevertheless remain a record of a classic murder investigation. Small wonder that Field was transferred to the CID about seven years after its formation, replacing an Inspector.

It was about this time that Field met Charles Dickens reputedly at the public execution of Mr & Mrs Manning, who Field and his colleagues had arrested and brought to trial for the murder of Patrick O'Connor in August 1849. It is clear that Field and Dickens struck up a friendship, although the latter was not above using Field's connections and expertise for his journalistic and literary works.

In 1850 Dickens founded a weekly periodical called Household Words. Some of the articles which appeared in it can still be read in his *Reprinted Pieces* (1858). One was called *The Detective Police* written after Dickens had invited the whole Detective force (two Inspectors and six Sergeants) to the office. Except for one Sergeant, all attended, and were seated at a round table, plied with drink and cigars, and encouraged to relate stories from their careers. When the article appeared their names were slightly disguised (Field appears as 'Weild').

Field related in detail part of his investigation of the Eliza Grimwood murder. In the second article *Three Detective Anecdotes* Wield describes how he meticulously traced the owner of a pair of gloves found at the scene of Grimwood's murder.

No longer disguised, Field later appeared in an article in the periodical called On Duty with Inspector Field (1851). In it, Dickens described brilliantly a tour of night duty with Field in which he met all kinds of villains.

Thanks to Dickens and others, we have quite a good description of Field. No photograph is known to exist, but there are contemporary sketches and descriptions in both *Bleak House* and the journalist pieces.

Field did not long remain in the Detective Force, retiring on pension on 6 December 1852, and set up a private enquiry office. This got him into some trouble in the early 1860s when it was alleged that he was using his former position for his own business purposes, and for a while his police pension was taken away, although it was subsequently restored. Field's retirement from the police did not appear to affect his friendship with Dickens, who, up to his death in 1870, continued to visit 'dens of thieves and other haunts of infamy' with Field. Dickens referred to these times affectionately as his 'Field-days'.

Field himself died on 27 September 1874 at his home at 6 Stanley Villas, Chelsea, having suffered from heart disease for some years. He lies buried in Brompton Cemetery.

Arthur Fanning

Redcaps on Madagascar

Many Metropolitan police officers played a proud part in the Dunkirk landing and no doubt mark the anniversary.

But I will be remembering a different anniversary: that of the last sea and land battle in which armed forces of His Britannic Majesty did attack the French army. As a result of this action, the French tricolour, so to speak, was lowered, to be replaced by the union flag of the United Kingdom.

Despite the undoubted accuracy of the French 75mm artillery, which were eventually overrun despite determined opposition, the British force's Commander was pleased to accept the surrender of the French General.

It was a powerful force which carried out this successful campaign. Two battleships, aircraft carriers, cruisers, destroyers, frigates, corvettes, tank landing craft, tankers (oil for the use of) and landing craft, all were involved. The troop-carriers were elegant cruise liners, selected not so much for their comfort as their sailing speed. They were needed to out-distance submarines.

This was Madagascar, May 5 1942.

No need to bore you with the politics of the situation, this was not our concern. When I say 'our' concern, I refer to a small detachment of Military Police, which landed on the beach of northern Madagascar, from a landing craft of the 'second wave', to assist the Beach Masters, to direct traffic away from the water line, to gathering points.

The 5th (Y) Division, Provost company, was made up for the most part by ex-police officers (reservists), AA patrol men, and a few old sweats of the regular army. That was in November 1939, when we left the depot at Mytechett.

Elements of the 5th Division took part in the landing. We, with our trusty Norton and BSA motorcycles were 'invited' along.

Unfortunately, I cannot remember a single name of the ex-Met men in that section,. (There was a PC Fred Sawford, on the island, but he was, I believe, an officer in 36 Div. He was latterly at Windsor Castle, serving alongside me for about 17 years). There must have been some eight to ten ex-Met men in that section. No doubt they will let us know if any are still in the land of the living.

To get back to the sandy beach. The Red Caps were not always looked upon as natural enemies of the fighting soldier. Our tact and diplomacy came to the fore, as we calmly cajoled, booted, pushed, and otherwise persuaded, men and machines off the beaches, and on to the roads.

Our last big stint had been at the end of a pier at Dunkirk, where we had shepherded troops, from a sandy beach. This has been well-documented, but little, if anything, to my knowledge, has been written about the Red Caps on Madagascar. Our section was for the most part made up of Met police.

The battle force which left South Africa in May 1942 was massive. The rumour prevalent in Durban was about a possible attack by the Japanese. I imagine that our leaders thought to prevent any landings in the vicinity. Pure speculation of course.

So, having secured this part of the island, we were to step up security. Town patrols were introduced in Antsarane and a curfew put into force. All the French officers, having given their word of honour, were permitted comparative freedom. The need for a prisoner-of-war camp, with us operating it, we were told, was unnecessary. Apart from the mosquitoes, almost as big as sparrows, and very virulent too, we settled into a quiet routine of policing the area.

All seemed well until, under the cover of darkness, one of the battleships, the *Malaya* I think, anchored in Diego Suarez harbour, was either torpedoed or hit by limpet mines. We never found out. Almost every man-jack of the force was formed into a chain to heave bags of cement, to be used to plug a large hole in the side of the craft. It must have been successful enough for her to sail back to base for permanent repair. Red alert brought long hours of duty. Eventually all was again quiet.

Along with elements of the 5th Division , we sailed for Bombay, and thence for reorganisation to Ranchi and our first experience of the Monsoon. Can you imagine a Red Cap on patrol, carrying an umbrella? Quite true.

Later, with two other ex-police officers, I took up the job of being an instructor at the Military Police training depot at Fyzabad.

I was later to see ex-Mets directing traffic across a one-way bridge at a place, known as Bawli Bazaar. And some two years later, saw more of them, doing the same on The Road to Mandalay.

Didn't they just get everywhere?

Arthur Wood 126615, ex 255K 255G, 617A (Windsor Castle).

Proud Moments: the Met at War

Half a century since the end of the last war in Europe, it is interesting to look back and study the efforts of the Met police who helped to bring about VE day, and shortly after that, VJ. There is an impressive number of policemen who joined the Forces during the last war and who were decorated for bravery. .

I have not yet been able to find out the total number of men who went into other Services, but of those who did, 389 died, including 1 Superintendent, 15 Station Inspectors, 1 Junior Station Inspector, 2 Station Sergeants, 14 Sergeants, and 356 Constables. 31 officers died in the Royal Navy and the Fleet Air Arm, 77 in the Army, and 281 in the Royal Air Force. At first sight it would seem the RAF was the most dangerous arm of all three, and this is probably true, but without knowing how many men entered each Service, it is not possible to say so with any certainty.

At home 208 Regular and Auxiliary Policemen were killed in Air Raids on London, making a total of almost 600 men who gave their lives for Britain.

In the three Services 202 Honours and Awards were given to officers serving in HM Forces, including 88 DFCs, 5 MCs, 4 DSOs, 4 OBEs, 41 awards of the Military Medal, DFM, and Foreign Awards, 60 Mentions in Despatches, and 28 men received more than one award or honour.

On the Home Front, awards in connection with Air Raids totalled 276: 2 OBEs, 82 George Medals, 4 King's Police and Fire Services Medals, 72 BEMs, 115 Commendations by the King, and one Dutch Cross of Merit awarded to a Sergeant.

There were 90 other awards for General Police Service, ranging from the Order of the Bath to the Commissioner, Knighthoods to George Abbiss OBE, and Alker Tripp CBE, 2 CBEs, 5OBEs, 14 MBEs, 4 MVOs and 28 King's Police and Fire Services Medals and 4 Commendations for distinguished service.

Looking at these figures I think the Met can be justifiably proud of it's war time achievements. One colleague with whom I worked on occasions, George Martin, a Traffic Patrol from Bow Garage, achieved a DSO and DFC and Bar. Though not a Pilot but a Flight Engineer, he managed to fly home his crippled bomber to this country and land it safely, even though all his crew were either dead or severely wounded. The episode was broadcast on the BBC radio soon after the war in the programme *In*

Town Tonight. George survived and returned to the Police Service, but six others from Bow garage lost their lives, and their names are now inscribed on an imposing memorial at the garage.

Geoffrey Taylor ex H, DT7, 124166

Bow Garage, Blitz-Style

3 September 1939 saw Britain involved in some very hasty preparations for the oncoming conflict. Bow District Garage had been purchased by the Receiver in 1938 and was at first used as a store for about 30 new Humber cars and a small detachment of one PS and two PCs who acted as caretakers of the property with only a table, two chairs, a telephone and brazier, with coal purloined from Bow station. We were still operating from the station on H and K divisions, and the garage did not operate as such until 10 June 1940.

Each car was equipped with a siren and two Ross .303 rifles and ammunition for expected German paratroopers, but of course none arrived. Perhaps 'Lord Haw-Haw' had told Hitler the Traffic patrols were ready and waiting for them!

We had a little training in the use of rifles from one of the First War veterans, Clary Packman. Our Wolseley cars, Triumph speed twins and BSA twin motor cycles were getting a little old and worn, but later on we also had a supply of 15 khaki clad 500cc motor cycles destined originally for the Belgian Army, but when they were overrun the machines were handed over to the police.

Nearly every day most of us were on Convoy and escort duty, being stretched to the limit during the Dunkirk and Blitz periods. Some large troop movements took much more than a tour of duty as the first vehicle in the convoy had to travel at an average speed of 12.5mph. That seems very slow now but was necessary to prevent breaks in the columns which could easily occur, and as most of the army vehicles were very new and some driven by ATS girls who had never handled a 30cwt or 3 ton truck before. It was hard work to keep the vehicles together with the traffic patrols dashing up and down the column and pushing out the odd private cars that had crept in.

This did not often occur when tanks or Bren-gun carriers were in the column, as no civilian driver seemed willing to get tangled up with the tank tracks and their habit of sliding about sideways.

We helped to move all the Services, huge propellers made in the Isle of Dogs and destined for battleships, unexploded bombs and enormous land mines dropped by parachute, crated aircraft and other very high or wide loads.

With a colleague I helped to escort one of these mines from Essex to the Epsom boundary in an open 30 cwt truck driven by a navy man. The mine only just fitted into the truck and looked like an overgrown tar barrel. It was one of the fastest escort rides I can remember, probably because the truck was flying the red flag. No other traffic came too near - most drivers knew the flag signified unexploded bombs.

At the garage we had a mobile canteen donated for use at incidents and a mobile generator to tow out to any station that had been hit or had lost electricity. All the ground floor ceilings of stations were heavily reinforced with large wooden beams to prevent total collapse in the event of being hit, and brick blast-walls protected the entrances, with ground floor windows covered with heavy wood and metal shutters.

We sometimes worked very long hours, but if I recall correctly, never bothered to claim overtime.

The phoney war ended on 7 September 1940 when a large raid on the London docks resulted in huge areas in the East End being set ablaze and also in the City of London. On an escort duty from Abridge Aerodrome in Essex that day the RAF intimated a large assembly of German planes in France was a build-up for a big raid. These then continued almost every night for some months until Germany invaded Russia and they then slackened considerably.

After a week of incessant aerial bombardment Winston Churchill moved into London all the guns that could be spared, and though I did not see any planes hit, it was gratifying to hear the noise and it cheered up the people who had been clamouring for action.

One really large gun used to travel up and down a railway line near the Garage and made quite a din. It was common to see hasty messages scrawled on damaged shops saying, 'We can take it', and when Churchill toured the worst-hit areas of the East End he received a spontaneous welcome from the cockneys who had suffered great losses in people and homes.

Later on in the war, after I had left the police and was serving in Burma with the 14th Army, we heard rumours of London being bombarded again by pilotless planes and huge rockets, but that is another story that I am not qualified to relate and I hope someone else can continue and refresh our memories.

At Bow we lost one colleague, Wally Stewart, who literally disappeared when a rocket fell very close to him. All that was found of him and the motor cycle was one tunic button and a small piece of the tyre.

Geoffrey Taylor, ex H, DT7, 124166

Evacuating the East End Youngsters

Most of us can of course remember 3 September 1939, the day Chamberlain declared war, but there was little activity in this country until a year later. I believe it was 7 September 1940, a Saturday, when, with another colleague we left Bow Garage at 6am to travel to Abridge Aerodrome in Essex to escort a crated Spitfire to the docks en route for the desert.

On arrival we were somewhat surprised to see the Airfield perimeter ringed with small Ack-Ack guns and Bren carriers, which we had not seen before on any of our previous visits.

After several hours and many excuses from the RAF who were rather reticent about the delay, we were told the aircraft would not be released, and mention was made of a 'big flap on over the water.'

We replenished our tanks from the high octane fuel and returned to Bow almost airborne, booked off duty and I thought no more of it for several hours.

We were just about to sit down to tea when the sirens wailed and with their dying note I heard the unmistakable sound of machine guns. On going outside to get into the shelter I was amazed to see a barrage balloon in flames over Woolwich and many of our Spitfires zooming round what were obviously large German bombers. My amazement was tinged with a sense of disbelief and surprise to think that German bombers could reach so far in broad daylight and still in formation; it had not happened before, and now the full alert at Abridge began to make sense.

In minutes we could see fires everywhere in the Docks area, and the bombing continued almost until dusk when there was a short lull but it all started again about 8pm and continued right through the night. The whole of London seemed to be burning and at 5.15am I left home in Blackheath to cycle to Bow, but the only place in which I could ride was through Blackwall Tunnel - every other road was littered with bricks and masonry. At each end of the tunnel huge concrete gates had been constructed to lower in case the tunnel roof was pierced by bombs, as this would have caused severe flooding in Greenwich.

On arrival at Bow Garage we were all sent to North Woolwich to escort bus loads of frightened children and a few parents and teachers out to Epping Forest where they were left among the trees, some crying for parents, others white-faced and bewildered.

We went back and forth many times until late in the evening and must have moved many hundreds of people, some of them now homeless and their only possessions the clothes they were wearing. It was fortunate the weather was warm and dry.

My last recollection of these children as I rode out of the woods into the setting sun was of two little girls about eight years old and obviously twins, holding hands and crying profusely with large tears falling down their cheeks. I have wondered many times since then what happened to these children - as far as I could see there were no facilities made for them and indeed no time to do so, but I suppose they were evacuated out of London eventually.

A few years ago the Imperial War Museum in Lambeth was organising a project on the theme 'London children during the Blitz', and I helped the keeper with the facts about this hurried dispersal of the victims of the bombing. She was very pleased to get this story about this hitherto-unrecorded episode.

Geoffrey Taylor ex H, DT7, 124166

Waiting for Hitler

I was on early turn at Bow Street on the day we had our first, false air raid alert of the war, and I was posted to Hungerford Bridge, 11 Beat at ED.

This was covered 24 hours a day, why, I never understood; perhaps the higher authorities feared that some felon would attempt to steal the nuts and bolts. However, on a fine day it made a peaceful and pleasant tour of duty, watching the trains go by or the boats passing up and down the river.

On that fateful morning I was fully equipped with tin hat, respirator and anti-gas clothing. I was accompanied by a War Reserve, a chap about 5' 4", who was similarly equipped but in civilian clothes. We must have been an odd looking pair.

We heard that war had been declared and soon afterwards the air raid siren sounded. The effect was immediate pandemonium. Down below, on the Embankment, vehicles were abandoned and people were running from all directions to the shelter of Charing Cross Underground. In the space of a few minutes the streets were swept clear of all humanity. The War Reserve and I were the only living creatures above ground.

We gallantly stood by our post on the bridge, though with some trepidation anxiously scanning the Eastern horizon for sight of the fleet of German bombers which, we were convinced, was on its way to rain death and destruction upon us.

After a while since no sound of falling bombs or gunfire disturbed the cloistered calm, one or two intrepid heroes emerged from the Underground and eventually we heard the 'All Clear'.

The rest of course is history. We were entering the period of the 'Phoney War'. Indeed, I believe there was no serious bombing of London until the 'Blitz' started in earnest a year later, and that was an altogether different story.

Arthur Scougall, Ex PC 529E

First Prisoners of War?

In all the annals of the Metropolitan Police, I doubt if you will find reference to the following story, unless the relevant Occurrence Book at Arbour Square Police Station is still around.

It was on the day that War broke out - September 3, 1939 - at 11am at Arbour Square police station. The Prime Minister, Neville Chamberlain, had hardly finished his 'state of war with Germany' broadcast when the Divisional Police van with half a dozen or so PCs aboard, raced out of the yard at HD.

Their destination was reached in four minutes and was the '600 Cohen' dock at Branch Road, Stepney, at the northern approach to the Rotherhithe Tunnel. In that dock was a German cargo ship laden with scrap metal from Cohens, bound for Germany to fuel the German War machine.

In about 10 minutes, police had boarded the vessel and arrested the crew, just in time to prevent them from scuttling the ship in the dock. They were taken to Arbour Square and detained for a military escort.

Surely they were the first POWs taken in World War 2. While in the

Charge Room at HD, they persisted in arrogantly informing us that the war would be over in a few months when we would be either dead or working for Hitler!

Frank Reynolds ex PC 62311/125197

Fate Deals a Hand

It happened that on 6 November 1940 the old police station at Kilburn was completely demolished by a direct hit from a stick of three high explosive bombs during the first blitz on London. In the number of fatalities, this was the worst incident affecting the police service in the whole of the Second World War.

No one actually in the building at the time survived, but as in all tragedies, fate played some strange tricks. It transpired that I was the only person present at the recent Kilburn re-union who had served at Kilburn pre-war and had any knowledge of what had happened in the bombing. Several of the younger officers present displayed a great interest in the history of their station site and asked me to write up the story. Here it is.

Kilburn was my first station when joining the Force in 1937 but after only a year the sectional station was closed due to a policy of centralisation and all personnel were transferred to Harrow Road. I remember the occasion well - I was a member of X division dance band in those days and, having just finished an engagement at the *Spotted Dog*, Willesden, we decided to pay a visit to Kilburn on the way home to give an impromptu, and perhaps slightly inebriated, musical performance for Station Sergeant Tim Sheehan, 'the King of Kilburn', on his last tour of duty there. What the local population thought of this effort in the early hours of the morning is not clear!

At 6am on 1 March 1938, Kilburn ceased to operate as a police station although the Section House adjoining the main station continued to be used. The imposing porch-way at the junction of Salusbury (sic) Road and Harvist (sic) Road was sealed and converted into a Police Box with the same facilities as the Trenchard boxes of the time, namely a shelf, a stool, a telephone and a useless heater! Its official designation was now No 64 X Box. From that time on there was no operational police station at Kilburn until 1 April 1965.

During the early days of the war the old building at Kilburn was brought back into use as a 'Group Reserve Centre' where a reserve of men could be available to attend local incidents at short notice. The first blitz on London started in early September 1940, with night bombing continuous throughout October, November and December. I was posted to the Kilburn section for night duty during the month of November and had managed to secure a few days annual leave from 3-5 November to travel to Somerset for my engagement party (rather an old fashioned touch that!)

On my return to Harrow Road I was soon made aware of a direct hit on the old Kilburn station and learned that practically all officers were still at Kilburn making efforts to extricate any possible survivors. The rescue work in which I joined was continued throughout the day with the help of teams of the ARP but to no avail. But for those three days leave I would surely have been among the victims.

The officers who paraded for night duty at Kilburn on 5 November 1940 were PC Charlie Summers, a retired regular who had volunteered to re-join for the duration of the war; PC Charles McInnes, a quiet and unassuming young Scot from the Isle of Skye; PCs John Brown, Clifford Davies and Donald Light (initials really T J but always known as Donald) the same Donald Light that many readers will remember as the Assistant Secretary to the MPAA during the 50s and 60s; War Reserve PCs Bert Borham, Gerard Harvey, Llewellyn Davies, George Wallis, Len Bowes, George Smith, Thomas Coe and Tom Craven; and Special Constable Acton. The relief was in the charge of Sergeant Patrick McGee an uncommunicative Irishman who, being a bachelor, resided in Harrow Road Section House.

Of all these named, only Sergeant McGee and Donald Light survived the night, the reason for this being a peculiar quirk of fate. You will note that I have named only 12 victims; the 13th was an elderly civilian (I believe an ex-PC) Bob Boast, the section house cleaner and odd job man who happened to be sleeping on the premises where he felt safer than in his own home!

The system of working was for some of the relief to remain inside the building 'on call' whilst the remainder patrolled the beats with a change over at 2am, ie four hours in and four hours out. This was the basic idea, but of course, it could not be rigidly adhered to due to the blitz. However, of all these men, the only ones with instructions to remain in the Centre for the whole eight hour tour were Sergeant McGee (to direct operations) and Donald Light (to man the telephones and record messages etc).

Charlie Summers, the rejoined reservist, was in his early sixties and had served his last ten or so years before retiring at Portsmouth Dockyard. (The Met policed the Royal Naval Dockyards until 1935). He was a likeable father-figure to us all and his great love was a game of solo. His home was in Southsea and he travelled down there to see his wife on every leave day. We always chided him that he only came back to the Job because of his penchant for a game of cards.

Charlie picked up the 13 cards as they were dealt. No one would ever know if it was a winning hand but it is known that his love of a game of cards cost him his life. Twelve of his colleagues perished with him making the tragic number of thirteen - the number of cards he held in his hand!

At some time around midnight a message was received relating to a bombing incident believed to be an incendiary fire at premises next to the *Mason Arms* close by Kensal Rise Railway Station. This happened to be on the beat allocated to Charlie, but as he was so engrossed in the card school at that particular time, Donald Light offered to attend instead saying, 'a breath of fresh air will do me good, look after the board for me.' Donald left for Kensal Rise accompanied by Special Constable Acton.

After dealing with the incident, the two officers began to make their way back to Kilburn. The blitz, which in the area had been rather light so far, suddenly seemed to intensify and several times during their return journey on foot they had been tempted to throw themselves to the ground when the screech of falling bombs seemed too close.

As they reached the corner of Dudley Road a particularly loud screaming from falling bombs prompted them to fall flat on their faces to take cover. This no doubt saved their lives as the air was rent with an enormous explosion, the shock wave passed over them and large quantities of debris fell on them. Donald described the experience as being 'like millions of red hot coals falling on my back'.

When after a period some of the dust had settled, they looked up at what shortly before had been the old Kilburn Police Station and was now an almost level heap of smoking rubble. Had Donald Light not volunteered to do the old chap a favour he would certainly have met the fate of his colleagues. Had Charlie's love of a game of cards not been so compelling, he might have lived to play for a few more years!

Earlier that night at around 1.45am, Sergeant McGree realised that he had forgotten to provide himself with sustenance for the long night. Thinking that there appeared to be a lull in the Huns' activities, he decided to cycle down to Harrow Road and have a bite to eat. On his return as he rode along Ferndale Roads towards Kilburn, the intensity of the blitz increased. He crossed the junction of Kilburn Lane into Salusbury Road and as he put more pressure on the pedals to climb the slight rise over the bridge at Queens Park Station he also heard the screaming of the bombs, heard and felt the enormous explosion only a few yards away and was thrown off his bike by the blast and hurled against the station wall.

Picking himself up and finding himself relatively unharmed some little time later, he realised that his destination had been completely destroyed. Had he not disobeyed orders (and no one could ever have imagined Sergeant McGee doing that!) he would at that moment have been dead. Later, when the facts were known, a certain senior officer wanted to take disciplinary action against Sgt McGee for leaving his post without permission. Fortunately common sense prevailed. Just as a thought, however, could this perhaps been made an offence under the old Discipline Code - of failing to be killed?

Ironically, Sgt McGee and Donald Light - the only two officers who were scheduled to remain in the Centre all night - were the only ones to survive!

Back at Harrow Road, the first reserve was seated at the old style telephone console - a multiplicity of plugs and leads, holes and tiny lights and small shutters that dropped down to indicate an incoming call. In the main station office Station Sergeant Maurice Churcher sat on his stool at the high desk writing long hand in the Occurrence Book. The time was exactly 2.40am on 6 November when the small light above the indicator of 64 Box flashed. Plugging a lead into the socket, the operator could obtain no answer.

Both he and Maurice Churcher had heard the crunch of bombs, although at least a mile and a half away, at exactly the same time as the light had appeared and concluded that some damage had been caused at or near 64 Box: they sent officers to investigate. It was some time before a message of what had actually occurred was received - all telephones were out of order.

As soon as it was known what had happened every man, on or off duty, was on his way to Kilburn. In the meantime Sgt McGee had met up with Donald Light and SC Acton. Unable to find any means of communication with Harrow Road or the ARP Services they climbed over the rubble trying to find a way of rescuing those they knew to be underneath.

Donald has always declared that at that time he could hear the voice of Charlie Summers calling for help from beneath the rubble. It was two more days before all bodies were recovered.

Colleagues attended all the funerals of the victims. Two particular friends of Charles McInnes escorted him to the Isle of Skye, the home-land that he had left for the first and only time some five years previous-ly. My old friend Stewart Mawer and myself attended Charlie's funeral at Southsea. Soon after the war had ended, a plaque bearing the names of the 13 victims was placed in St Andrews Church in Salusbury Road. I am not certain whether the plaque or even the church is still there.

The fact that Kilburn was destroyed and that 13 men lost their lives is, of course, briefly documented in official records. The Police Orders of the time boldly state under the Roll of Honour that 'the undermentioned officers were killed by a bomb explosion during an enemy air attack.' The names follow, but that is all. Their names are also recorded in the Remembrance Book at Scotland Yard and in the booklet *The Metropolitan Police at War* published by HM Stationery Office in 1947.

This personal account of the events that took place in those few days attempts to fill out the cold official record. Fifty years on I feel that any surviving relatives of the victims will forgive me reviving old sorrows.

Donald Light is now the sole survivor of that Kilburn relief that parad-ed half a century ago. He tells me that the minute details of that night have always been with him and he remembers it as if it was only yesterday.

Don Milburn, 126407, XK, XD, SW, COB8

Bert Mead, Spycatcher

It was during the blitz and we were parading for night duty in Hornsey when the Inspector came out with a memo from the Railway Police at King's Cross which stated that several engine drivers travelling between Hornsey and Harringay during the blackout and air raids had reported that over in Chingford direction they had seen a flashing light which appeared to be someone signalling to the enemy planes. It went on to say that there was a very suitable observation post in Hornsey engine sheds in the shape of a water softening tower.

The Inspector suggested that this was a job for volunteers. As it was something a bit out of the ordinary, I said that I would go. Stan, a Special

Sergeant parading with us. who was pally with me, said he would go with me.

It didn't take long to get there. The sheds were less than half a mile from the nick. We went in the staff entrance and were halted by a uniformed Home Guard complete with rifle and bayonet. He knew nothing of our mission but shouted down the passage and soon the shed foreman arrived and he was expecting us. Lighting the way with a dim, hand-held oil lamp, he led us out of the shed across some ground to the foot of the tower. He said, 'There you are, gents, hope you get the bastard,' and disappeared into the gloom.

In the darkness we couldn't see the top of the tower but I had seen it many times before from the road, in daylight, without knowing its use - from memory I would say it was about the same overall height as the average suburban house.

The ground in this part of Hornsey falls away slightly and in daylight a good view could be obtained from the top of the tower across Harringay, South Tottenham and the Lee Valley to higher ground beyond.

We climbed a narrow stairway that wound round the sides and at the top, by discreet use of our lamps, discovered a narrow metal walkway right round the top protected on the inside by a handrail. The top or the lid of the tower was about two feet below this.

We had hardly settled in, so to speak, and were debating the truth or otherwise of the report when suddenly there it was. Away in the distance (although difficult to estimate the distance in the blackout), a light twinkled away for some seconds, stopped, then gave another burst and there were enemy bombers overhead. We watched intently, and sure enough each time a plane came in from the east, the light flashed away. We really were on to something. Owing to the darkness, we could not see any points of reference such as church towers, etc, to take a line to the light.

At that time, a lot of people in that part of north London firmly believed, and with a certain amount of justification, that the enemy planes were using the Alexandra Palace as a landmark. They appeared to fly in from the east straight to the Palace then turned left towards central London.

I suppose the extensive glass roof would reflect the stars or moonlight. In view of this, we wondered if there was any tie-up with this light.

There was also a silly story doing the rounds about spies driving high vans around London with illuminated signs recessed in the roof.

After a while we became dubious as to whether this was some bloke actually signalling to the enemy. This had been going on for some time according to the drivers, always more or less in the same place and now we were looking at it, in the given direction. We couldn't imagine any spy being daft enough to risk capture by continually doing this in the same place.

The sighting gradually became less frequent and we were getting the lights without the planes, and the planes without the lights. Finally we had to admit, reluctantly, that our first thoughts had been wrong, and what we had seen was pure coincidence.

A chilly wind had sprung up and we were very cold, standing still up the tower. The light appeared much less now with several minutes between showings. We decided that there was no point in stopping any longer that night and were about to start looking for the top of the stairs when a piece of shrapnel whizzed down, hitting the tower. Of course, during the time that we had been up there the blitz was going on as usual, planes flying around, AA guns blazing away, the crunch of bombs and in various places an angry glow in the sky showed where fires were raging. Suddenly we heard the bombs coming down, there was no time to do anything but crouch down on the walkway, clinging to the pillars supporting the handrail. I saw a row of vivid, V-shaped flashes erupt from the ground in the light of which I saw the debris flying, just about far away enough not to affect us.

We scrambled down and back in the shed. I had been working on an idea for something that I could make next day to help us pinpoint this elusive light, so we told the foreman that we would be back the next night, better equipped, then back to Hornsey to report, said what I intended to do and got the ok.

As old colleagues will know, working in metal has been my hobby for years and I had a fair amateur's workshop. Getting up early I went down and turned out my masterpiece. I paraded briefly and we were soon back on top of the tower. I produced the 'Mead Mark 1 Optical Spy Detector'. This was 6" of steel rod with a G clamp, one end of which was fixed to the handrail with the rod standing vertically. On this rod was another clamp with 9" of tube fixed to it. On the 'look through' end was a light shade made from a large tin-lid with a hole in the middle into which the tube was soldered. By slackening the wing nut on the clamp the tube could be swung in any direction. Our friend was still blinking away. I pointed the tube in the direction, crouched down and after several attempts was able to see the light through the tube. We locked it up tight, had a final look to see that we were still on target and went and found the foreman.

I asked him to prevent anyone going up the tower before someone from the nick had been up there the next morning. I went on duty the next night, very anxious to know if my device had done any good. To my great delight, it had. Whoever went up the tower that morning had a look through the tube and saw cars coming over the crest of a hill on a road on the other side of the valley.

So that was it. As cars came over the top in the blackout, distant viewers had a brief flash of their lights through the slots in the headlamp mask. Several close together gave a convincing show of morse signalling. I never found out who went there to check my device - the uniform said the CID, the CID said the uniform - but whoever it was pinched my little spy detector and I never saw it again. I like to think that it was successfully used in some other police activity. If by the remotest chance, someone reading this can tell me of its subsequent history, I would be very pleased. Speak up, all is forgiven after over 50 years.

Bert Mead ex PC 433Y

Walter Haycock's Private War

I was stationed at Hornsey and posted late turn on a beat between Priory Road and the boundary of the 'Ally Pally' grounds, during the last war.

On the section was PC 109Y Walter Haycock, a Great War veteran, always very smart and fussy about his appearance. He was generally an amiable bloke, but like a lot of chaps in the Job at the time had a permanent grievance because he was due to retire (being a 25 year serviceman) just after the war started and had to stop till the end of hostilities.

He showed a fiery temper if upset and was totally unapproachable before 8am when early turn Station Officer. For example, while on reserve at 6.30am one day, we received an unusual message and I wasn't sure what action to take. With some trepidation I took it in to him and said, 'What should I do with this one Sarge?' and he shouted 'Stick it on the bloody wall and dance round it!' - but he was generally amiable.

On the day in question, I was coming out of the back gate after refreshments on my way back to the beat when Walter caught up with me and we walked down the road together. I mentioned in conversation that I was going to Baden Road and he said that he hadn't been there lately and had better come with me.

Now Baden Road was a cul-de-sac where the two bottom houses on the left had been demolished by a bomb with the usual damage to surrounding property. For some unknown reason this particular bomb-site had become the adventure playground for all the kids for streets around. Here they re-enacted the battles of the war with full verbal effects, clouds of dust and showers of stones, causing complete bedlam. This of course led to a flood of complaints at the nick, with one old boy ringing up the Yard every day.

The result, as expected, was that the bloke on the beat had to make frequent visits to abate the nuisance. The action was always the same - when the PC turned the corner, up went the shout 'Copper' and all the kids disappeared through back alleys and gardens or bomb-damaged buildings only to return, so the residents said, as soon as he had gone. Some of us tried hiding in the house next to the site with the object of catching one of the little blighters, taking him round to Mum and pointing out that little Johnny might be injured by falling brickwork. But that didn't work. Their 'obbo' was pretty good.

Walter and I turned the corner and all the kids disappeared or so we thought. Walking down the road to the scene, it became obvious from the noise coming from the upstairs of the adjoining building that some of the little herberts had not heard the warning shout and were playing on, oblivious to approaching retribution.

At the house Walter said, 'We'll put the fear of God into these little buggers - you stop here and I'll go in.' The front door of the house was jammed by the explosion but the upper half had been one big sheet of glass which, with all the windows, had been blown away. One could stand in the porch and look straight into the hall, with the passage to the rear of the house on the right and the stairs straight in front.

Walter went round the back where access was easy through the bomb damage and shortly after he came creeping through the hall and started up the stairs. He was about half way up when there was a sudden noise like a shower of hail or heavy rain and Walter disappeared in a huge cloud of dust which came billowing out, all over me, causing a hasty retreat down the front garden path. Thinking that he had fallen through the stairs I ran round the back and through to the foot of the stairs. The dust had cleared slightly and the stairs were intact but each tread had a pile of plaster and plaster dust on it, and no sign of Walter. I ran upstairs and in the front room saw a sight that I shall never forget.

Two little boys stood there motionless and speechless. Walter crouched over them, his hands opening and shutting convulsively, the veins on his forehead standing out like the rails in Hornsey sidings. His face was purple. He was covered in dust from the top of his helmet to his boots with not a bit of constabulary blue showing anywhere.

This tableau appeared to last some minutes, but it could only have been seconds before Walter screamed 'Get out, get out, I'll see your fathers and get you the biggest bloody hiding you ever had!'

The kids came to life, burst into tears and ran down the stairs and away.

With them gone, I could hold myself no longer and burst out laughing. He rounded on me with a string of profanities that left me speechless. I thought that I knew all the words but this was an education. Perhaps the fact that as a PC he had been round the docks in the East End had something to do with it.

He eventually calmed down and told me what had happened. With the aid of a bit of board the lads had scraped a pile of plaster and dust on the landing which was without banisters and apparently thinking that it was their mates coming up, pushed the lot over the side onto the stairs and Walter. He said that he heard the noise and looked up just in time to see it coming but too late get out of the way.

We then had to get cleaned up. I went to one of the occupied houses and explained to the dear old lady who came to the door that the PS and I were investigating a complaint when there had been a fall of plaster. She lent me a large clothes brush, large towel and a large wet flannel.

It took a hell of a time for us to get reasonably tidy. He shot home nearby for a quick bath and change. His parting words were: 'Not a word about this mind' - an injunction faithfully obeyed, because if Walter heard about it from someone else, I knew my life would be difficult.

He retired when the war ended and if I ever bumped into him he always said, 'Been in any bomb damaged houses lately?' I believe that he eventually went to America where his only daughter had gone. Sadly, he passed on years ago.

Bert Mead ex PC 433Y

German Bomber in Difficulties

I was stationed at Brockley (PK). A message was received about 2am that a German bomber was seen to be in difficulties, that two parachutes were floating towards south London, and that all open spaces were to be searched.

I was on reserve duty and I was ordered by PS 25P Len Taylor to go with him in the GP car driven by PC Leslie Card. Off we went to search Peckham Rye, an open space of over 60 acres. The Rye is normally covered in mist in the early mornings and this was no exception. As we travelled down the east side of the Rye, Sergeant Taylor suddenly said 'Stop the car', pointed to a heavily built figure walking across the Rye and ordered me to challenge him.

As I left the car I picked up a .303 Lee Enfield rifle which the cars then carried, but he prevented me from taking it from the car. I remonstrated that I was going to challenge what was thought to be a fully-armed German parachutist; but to no avail.

So off I went to challenge this burly figure who I noticed as I got nearer was wearing a heavy overcoat and a woolly hat. As I drew near him his right hand went inside the left side of his overcoat. I immediately grabbed his wrist and patted the coat to see if there was a gun there. He pulled out his hand with me still holding his wrist and produced a grubby piece of cardboard on which was written the legend, 'I am a deaf and dumb bus cleaner at Nunhead bus garage'. It could have been so very different.

Albert Kennard, ex PS 45E, 43C, 124956

Feeding the War-Time Coppers

I found an advert among the mountain of papers I had to sort through when my mother died last September. It reads:

> A thousand women are asked to volunteer to help feed London's policemen in the event of war.
> Three hundred have already offered their services.
> They would form a new organisation to assist the Metropolitan Police Canteen Board during war-time. The work will be paid for.
> It is estimated that a week's requirements would include 94 tons of meat, 17,000 gallons of milk, 185 tons of potatoes and 70,000 loaves

of bread.

This advert was in the national press early in 1939, and my mother volunteered her services. As we were not on the telephone then, there follows a series of 1d stamped postcards giving details of when and where to meet for the next instruction course.

On 9 August 1939 a telegram was received advising her to listen to the 6 o'clock news.

My mother was stationed at Stoke Newington (fortunately quite close to our home) and carried out her duties throughout the war. Because our surname was Matthews, all the 'lads' called her Jessie.

Kate Fuller

The Making of a WAPC

It was a dark and dreary morning on 1 January 1945 (made more so by the blackout which was still in force) when I walked up the steps of Tottenham Police Station. I was a WAPC about to start on a Job of National Importance. This was a must in those days of hostilities.

In case you are wondering what a WAPC was, for there are none in existence now, the initials stood for Woman Auxiliary Police Constable, With this honourable title went a navy-blue skirt, black tie, navy-blue jacket, airforce-blue shirt, black shoes and stockings and a rather heavy-looking cloth cap. We wore no Divisional number, but a light blue flash on the sleeve. Very smart - a WAPC was kitted out.

I gazed around as I entered the charge room. Not a glimmer of light entered from the outside for the windows were heavily sandbagged. One long table or rather bench, and a high desk, were the only furniture.

On the walls were rows of hooks from which hung large lamps, which I learned afterwards were carried by the Night Duty. Woe betide any PC who failed to hand in this piece of archaic appointment to the checking E/T Sergeant at the completion of the tour of duty. To enter the Communication or Comms Room as it was called, I had to walk through the Station Office, skirting as I did so, a fireplace in which burned a beautiful coal fire. The fire place boasted a fine set of heavy steel Victorian fire-irons. (The clatter of one of these being hurled through the communicating door often led the reserve officer to realise that the Station officer was busy and needed help or a cuppa - other tactics are used today).

The Comms Room was again a blacked-out department. Huge wooden beams were placed strategically to shore up the ceiling and protect the switchboard. This piece of furniture dominated the room, looking like a monstrous Wurlitzer organ 8ft high and 5ft wide. To operate it one had to mount a high swivel chair. The woodwork of this monster was scratched and marked by a succession of doodlers. It had been there since 1906. Attached to both sides was the mechanism for the Police Boxes. It sometimes took an hour or more to contact a PC for an assignment by this method. It was hoped that a foot-sore Bobby would spot the light being operated on the top of those Blue Boxes.

Having taken all this in, I looked across at a table in the corner of the Comms Room. There a portly gentleman Reserve Constable in a hot looking buttoned-up-to-the-neck tunic with Divisional number on his collar and a striped arm-ban on his left sleeve, sat with phone in hand. Conversation over, he stood up to greet me. How old he looked, this first of my many friends.

I was made welcome. All the station staff seemed to find business in the Comms Room just then. I was being appraised. It was practically a new venture to admit women into the Admin Dept of the Met Police. A Woman Police Constable was bad enough but the offices? No good would come of it, was the opinion of some die-hards.

However, I must have passed inspection, for the Station Officer (three stripes and a crown) offered to take me on a tour of inspection of the rest of the premises and to the canteen for a cuppa. It was downstairs for the latter. As we approached I heard much talking and laughter. Some of the men were having their refreshments, playing 'chips', dominoes in other words, or just chipping the lovely young girl behind the counter - Rosie I think her name was. I often wonder where she might be now. Like me, very much older.

The canteen was not a very inviting place. Wooden tables and benches - no cloths or modern plastics. It was gloomy and rather smoky. Smoking was taboo in all parts of the establishment. The grill-type windows were at street level but the tea was good at 1d a cup. Mind you, the sugar bowl was kept under the counter. War-time sausages had little to recommend them but not much else was available except spam or macon, a war time ersatz meat concoction. I well remember the large stone jar of pippy jam which was watered down to make it go further, and the thin rashers of bacon served very seldom.

I grew to know that canteen very well. Some years after that first introduction, it had to be abandoned as it flooded every time it rained heavily. The drains could not cope. Rats became the only customers then. The new upstairs accommodation was much better for all.

My next port of call was upstairs to the Section House to see the single men's abode. By today's standards the cubicles were very inadequate but the boys were a happy bunch on the whole. Humour, leg-pulling, practical jokes and good fellowship helped them to forget home comforts. The Section sergeant saw to that and also dealt personally with any defaulters as regards the 'Nights Out' book. No climbing over the wall after time if one hadn't signed on the dotted line in this book.

Now for the I job I had come to do. The reserve man did his best to initiate me into the routine. Many and varied were the calls. As it was still war time the Army and Navy liaised with Police about AWOL personnel. The station cyclist was kept busy with these - the large sum of 3d a week was his reward for using his own cycle.

Air raid fatalities were still coming in. This meant that relatives had to be informed, not a very pleasant task. People still lost their dogs and even their goats. Many people kept the latter to help out the milk problem. Accidents occurred although not many cars were on the roads, but the blackout was a godsend to thieves and robbers.

Every hour, on the hour, broadcasts were made from Divisional Stations. These had to be relayed orally to Sectional Stations. No teleprinter to ease the telephonists in those days. When they were at last installed in Sub-Div stations they proved a mixed blessing and even at times a menace, as it took one longer to contact some stations that way. Every out-going emergency call had to be phoned to IR for transmission to the Area Cars - at first morse code operated. No wonder that some of the operators went deaf eventually.

Each day various returns had to be sent to Div stations. One day Sick Returns, Prostitute Returns, another day, lists of dogs, accidents, etc.

My first presiding officer was a very helpful soul. 'I'll show you how the station works,' said he. So all the books with their entries he explained. I learnt in time of HORTs 1 and 2, Forms 963s, 728s, Warrant Books and Charge Books. I was allowed access to all as he vowed it would be more interesting for me and helpful to him. 'You will know what is required and be of greater assistance to the public.' I've always been grateful to him for making the telephonist's job much more than a 'plugging-in of plugs'.

Wednesday was pay day. Everyone except those on beds of sickness were expected to attend the station. A multi-coloured cell blanket was placed on the Charge room table. At precisely 2pm the Section sergeant walked in from the bank with his bag of swag, accompanied by the Sub's clerk. In those days, the Sub Div Officer was in charge of the Sub division, not, as now, the Chief Superintendent. His clerk, an elderly PC dealt with all the admin of the Station.

He was a mine of information and was held in great respect. Placing all the money on the table and consulting the clerk's list, the sergeant doled out the pay. If in uniform one saluted, if not one just said 'Thanks'. My share each week was £2.10s for a six day week, eight hours a day, and minus National Insurance and a 1d deduction for something or other - Orphan Fund I think. I did get a rise after a time - just a few shillings.

At times my work was varied by other calls on my services, such as a call from the Sub's flat above the station, to babysit for an hour or two while wife went out shopping; to search female prisoners when the WPC was on leave (just one WPC worked the whole division in those days); to escort female prisoners to Holloway or young girls to Remand Homes. It was an interesting time.

But the tempo changed. Suddenly one realised everything was speeding up. Men returned from active service and many young probationers joined the force. Some stayed while others transferred. Many I remember but others I have forgotten, although I worked so closely with them all.

Some of the 'young ones', now no longer young, have gone ahead in the Job, for one occasionally hears of them or sees them through the media or the national press or on TV. It is strange to think that at one time they relied on me to teach them the rudiments of the switch board and other Comms duties.

Cars gradually took the place of cycles, nearly every station was equipped with a teleprinter, no longer morse code on the area cars and we, the WAPCs, were divested our our uniform and relegated to the ranks of the Civil Service. Over the years systems and modern equipment took over. Gone were the over-large switch boards, the Police boxes and old fashioned teleprinters.

Walk into any police station and what meets the eye? the same organised confusion at times and the same overflowing waste paper bins, but to help fight crime there are computers, VDU machines, small button switch boards and personal radios. (Immediate response is expected from the latter.) So much has changed since that New Year's Day 1945 when I was a raw Rookie walking up those steps into 'the Lion's Den'.

Now it is just a memory, albeit a very pleasant one, just about fifty years on. I often wish that I could go back and meet the many with whom I worked. I wonder where they all are now?

Kathleen Farringdon

Canadian Soldiers Murder Epsom Policeman

There will not be many pensioners who can remember the occasion when a Station Sergeant was killed by a mob of drunken Canadian soldiers in the station at Epsom in 1919.

Soon after the First World War a number of Canadian soldiers were convalescing in a camp at Woodcote Park, Epsom. On the evening of 17 June 1919, the licensee of the *Rifleman* Public House in the High Street called two PCs to eject some Canadians who had been causing trouble.

The officers ejected the trouble-makers but one Private began using obscene language and wanted to fight, so, naturally he was arrested. On the way to the the station Inspector Pawley and PS Durham and APS Shirley followed the detained soldier as most of the ejected men were following the prisoner and using threatening language. One of the party, James Connors, also had to be arrested for disorderly conduct and both prisoners were lodged in the cells. At this point all the remaining soldiers returned noisily to their camp.

As everything then appeared to settle down, Inspector Pawley dismissed the late turn relief, but wisely held the night duty men at the station. Soon afterwards a bugle call was heard coming from the camp, and the Inspector immediately telephoned all the surrounding stations for urgent assistance as it was obvious from the shouting and bugle calls that a large body of rioting soldiers were on their way to the station. Major Ross from the camp had been contacted, and he and the Inspector tried to reason with the mob as they arrived at the station entrance, but they could not be heard above the shouting and tumult.

A concerted rush by the mob soon overpowered the small number of policemen present; all the windows were broken, the doors were battered down, and the surrounding fences were used as cudgels. Inspector Pawley and the defenders, all with truncheons drawn, had to retreat inside and guard the window openings and the door space and they at first succeeded in keeping the mob at bay until some of them went round the back and battered their way into the cell passage.

SPS Thomas Green had just arrived at the station from his home where he had been off duty. He had 24 years service, was 51 years of age, and had been at Epsom for the last eight years. When the call came for help he immediately put on his uniform and cycled to the station. Sergeant Green suggested to the Inspector that they should make a charge and disperse the rioters, and this they did, driving them all out into the road. In that charge Inspector Pawley and Sergeant Green were both knocked unconscious but after the Inspector recovered they were again overpowered by the mob and driven back to the interior rooms.

The Inspector was then told that Sergeant Green had been severely injured and had been carried to a house on the other side of the road.

The station and surrounding area looked like a slaughter house with blood all over the wall and serious injuries on both sides. When it is considered the defenders were out-numbered by more than ten to one, it seems they gave a good account of themselves.

Inspector Pawley then discovered that one prisoner had been released from the cells with the aid of a jemmy, and with Major Ross assisting, he then released the other prisoner and the soldiers marched back to their camp in a body, shouting, blowing bugles, and trying to stem the flow of blood from their very considerable wounds.

The Inspector, four PSs and eight PCs were seriously injured and SPS Green died soon afterwards from multiple injuries and a fractured skull. All the railings, gates, doors and windows of the station were smashed and some of the 400 soldiers attempted to set fire to the station.

Soon after the fighting ended Superintendent Boxall from Wandsworth arrived in a car together with about 100 PCs all on bicycles from as far afield as Wimbledon, Malden, Surbition and Wandsworth. Inspector Pawley later asked for a Service subscription through the Force to be limited to a two pence a man, and this resulted in a total sum of £139.17.4 being collected. A further small collection was made in V Division to bring the total up to £155.04 - just 14/4d more than the cost of the Celtic Cross erected to the Sergeant's memory in Epsom cemetery.

Winston Churchill expressed the greatest sympathy on behalf of the Government, and the Canadian Red Cross voted a sum of £200 to be given to Mrs Green and her family of two teenage daughters. At what must have been one of the most distressing functions in the history of the police, in the same building in the defence of which her late husband had given his life, Mrs Green was handed the small change, and as might be expected she was asked to sign a receipt, witnessed by the indomitable Inspector Pawley.

In Epsom Police station there is an old group photograph of local Policemen, including Inspector Pawley, SPS Green, PC Hinton and others who had made the original arrest, and there is also a picture of the wrecked station with the cell bars wrenched off, the broken windows and metal railings, and standing in front are two PCs and an Army Lance Corporal wearing puttees; I imagine the latter must surely be a Royal Artillery man.

The photograph of Sergeant Green's gravestone clearly shows the words: *In memory of SPS Thomas Green who found death in the path of duty. He was killed in defending the Epsom Police Station against a riotous mob.* There is also a cutting from a paper which reads: 'Souvenir in Commemoration of the Presentation by Lord Rosebery to the brave Epsom Policemen. As a sequel to the attack on Epsom Police station by several hundred Canadian soldiers last June, Inspector Pawley and 23 Sergeants and Constables will each receive a gold watch or gold chain in recognition of the bravery displayed during the attack. 20 of the men have selected watches and the others chains. Lord Rosebery will make the presentation on January 14 1920. A fund amounting to £567 was raised on the appeal of Lord Rosebery for the purpose of recognising the men's conduct against overwhelming odds. God save the King.'

The old ivy covered station in Ashley Avenue, the scene of the fighting, has been demolished. Its roof was badly damaged by a bomb during the last war, it was then temporarily used as a store and later pulled down, but the Public House in the High Street, the Rifleman, is still there, showing the same name. Eight soldiers were charged with manslaughter and five were convicted and sent to prison for 12 months, a rather lenient punishment for such a crime.

Whilst on a visit to the station I learned that one of Sergeant Green's daughters is still alive and living in Canada and she sends a Christmas card to the 'Officers of Epsom Police Station' each year. I have since had the pleasure of making contact with her.

Geoffrey Taylor

The Hand Ambulance

When I joined the Metropolitan Police in 1929 I was posted to Paddington FD. A story going round the station was as follows:

A young recruit at the station was called to Maida Vale where a badly decomposed body of a man had been pulled from the canal. He collected the Hand Ambulance and with a little help put the body of the man on it. Whilst pushing it to the Mortuary, some distance away, an arm fell off into the street. He put it back on to the ambulance and continued his journey. After depositing it at the Mortuary he went into the station and promptly put in his resignation. Obviously the Police Force was not his cup of tea.

I cannot swear that the story is correct, but the following story is true.

About three years later I was transferred from Portsmouth Dockyard, No 2 division, to Bow Street. While on night duty in the Aldwych, I was called to a woman who was very drunk and unable to stand, making a lot of noise. A Hand Ambulance was sited on Waterloo Bridge junction of the Strand, quite near. Knowing that the woman was not going to run away, I went and collected the Ambulance and returned to the woman who was still making a lot of noise.

She was a very large person, about 15 stone I should think, and with the assistance of another PC we managed to get her on the ambulance. Theatres in the vicinity were just finishing the evening performance and Aldwych was crowded with people, all of whom wanted to see what was happening. As we moved off the woman was still making a lot of noise but we did not take too much notice until we saw that she had caught her arm in the wheel.

However we got her to Bow Street station without too much damage.

Incidentally, I wonder if there are many ex Portsmouth Dockyard Police still about?

Eric Oddy ex Insp 119031

Give Him a Hand

It was on a Saturday afternoon in 1932 and I was on the beat around Great Marlborough Street Station when I entered the station for a quick cuppa. Inspector Pitt who was the Station Officer saw me enter and as I passed through the Charge Room shouted 'Land, come in here'. I thought I was in for a ticking off for leaving my beat.

As I entered the office he said 'When you were at Peel House, did you visit the Horseferry Road Mortuary?' 'Yes Sir, its in Horseferry Road.' 'Right, you know where it is - go to Charing Cross Road Section House, collect the hand ambulance, and bring it back here.'

Off I went and arrived at SF Section House. First I had to ask for Sergeant Fox and sign the book for the hand ambulance. Then I had to unlock the padlock on the pavement basement door where it was stored. All the equipment had to be brought up by hand onto the pavement where it was all assembled onto the frame. The frame had to be pulled by rope up a ramp.

This was impossible for one person to do by himself so I asked in the Mess Room if anybody would give me a hand. Not a murmur or movement.

Into the PS office I went and asked how I was going to get the frame up the ramp as it was too heavy. 'Right lad,' he said, 'Leave it to me,' and into the Mess Room he goes. 'Right, who wants two hours time off for helping with a hand ambulance?' There was a sudden stampede to help. One chap was chosen and helped me to put it all together and away I went back to CM (the station).

After about an hour a dead body was loaded onto the Ambulance. Inspector Pitt instructed me to keep to main roads and not get lost - this meant Charing Cross Road, Whitehall, Victoria Street and Horseferry Road.

I crossed Soho avoiding the busy theatre area near Piccadilly Circus and came to Cambridge Circus, passing by the Section House. As I approached the junction of Charing Cross and Cranbourn Street I saw that PC Mick Husted who lived in the Section House with me was on Point Duty.

I thought to myself, 'Good, he will see me cross over without stopping.' But no! as I reached the junction, up goes his hand to stop the traffic and me. He was laughing at me and it seemed ages before he let the traffic and me go. Whilst waiting, folks were raising their hats and I could see Mick quite enjoying my embarrassment.

Away I went but as I passed him he sprang to attention, gave me a smart salute and called out 'Bring Out Your Dead!'

The return journey was uneventful and after reaching the Section House I had to take the ambulance apart and carry it all back into the basement; but when I came to the frame I again went into the PS office to seek help. This time an acting PS was on duty and was not entitled to give anybody time off for helping. So nobody in the Mess Room would help me. I had to lower it into the basement, down into the ramp by myself. I managed to start it sliding down but it was falling too fast so I had to let go before I fell with it. Fortunately it only fell about three feet before it hit the floor. A quick inspection did not reveal any damage so after signing the book I booked off duty to CM from the Section House.

Tom Land, Ex PC 179C 121496

On Yer Bike

'Cycle patrols were paid 6d a day extra'; for their pains, according to a colleague of mine, but as I remember things, it was a bit more complicated than that.

Firstly you had to become an 'Authorised Cyclist' which involved presenting one's bike for inspection by the Sergeant whose responsibilities included this task. He would ensure that its appearance was appropriate, that it was mechanically sound, had effective brakes and sported a working front lamp, a bell or instrument of warning and a red rear reflector. Once passed as suitable one's name and number were entered in the Cycle book. As one bike in those days could look very much like another, the PS concerned must sometimes have wondered whether he was authorising the same bike for different Section House inmates. Perish the thought!

Once registered it was a case of waiting until a monthly posting came your way for a Cycle Patrol, or possibly a Beat in outer divisions, or as Station Cyclist or 3rd Reserve. The latter's duties involved - apart that is from making tea and cooking the Station Officer's and Inspector's breakfasts and teas - delivering messages, answering emergency calls received locally, often beating the van and the area car to the scene into the bargain, and, in the case of Sectional Stations, taking and collecting correspondence and despatches to and from the Sub-Divisional Station. Remember the leather satchel one slung over the right shoulder before mounting the trusty steed?

Only when one had completed an eight hour tour of cycle duty was one entitled to be marked up in the Cycle Book for a 'ride' and the 6d allowance and it was your responsibility to see that the Station Officer or Section Sergeant did so. If only four hours or less were completed or if, as 2nd Reserve one got sent out urgently, the duty Cyclist being else-where, this qualified only as a 'half-ride' earning the princely sum of 3d!

At the end of the month the 'Cycle' Sergeant or Station Officer totalled up all the whole and half rides against each name and submitted a return. In due course the allowance was paid and the recipient signed the Cycle Book as having received it. Not quite the same thing as 'six-pence a day extra'.

At the end of a 'four-week' month, allowing for leave days, this might amount to twelve shillings. This was intended to compensate for wear and tear maintenance, puncture repair kit, new tyres and inner tubes, oil, acetylene or paraffin for your lamp (batteries if you were really with it) and replacements for the red rear reflector which somehow always seemed to be getting broken. The initial outlay on the machine was your own responsibility - after all you could use it off duty and/or between home and the Station! Those were the days - or were they? Much the same procedure probably operates today except that it is all logged on the computer and it is £6 a ride rather than 6d!

Pat Moorhead 123398

Service in the Saddle

During my probationary service whilst serving at Dagenham KG, I was posted to my very first cycle beat which in the Fifties were rather large.

Being young and keen, I was determined that there would be no break-ins that night on my beat.

Round and round I cycled - every street was silently visited over and over again. After three hours of this, carried out at considerable speed, I eventually came to, lying in the gutter.

I had dropped off to sleep from sheer exhaustion and collided with a lamp post. Having previously served at sea and in the Army I was very ashamed.

Looking around to make sure no person of the night had witnessed the incident I brushed myself down, remounted and rode majestically into the night, helmet slightly askew, to book in for a well-earned refreshment.

How keen we were - no crimes committed that night! Now older and,

I suppose wiser, I see the funny side of it all.

Ron Marke 331K KG

Watch Out

The telephone box system was due to come into operation on the Richmond sub-division. The boxes had been erected at strategic points, telephones installed and each officer issued with a key.

At last the great day arrived. My relief was night duty. We paraded in two ranks in the parade room at 9.45pm and, after being posted to our beats etc, the Inspector arrived and addressed the troops as follows: 'Well men, as you know, today sees the commencement of the telephone box system. It is imperative that your watches are synchronised to correspond to the station clock.'

He then noticed that 11 officers, with the exception of one, checked their watches. Addressing the officer, whose nickname was 'Cinema Joe', he said: 'Does your watch agree with the station clock?'

Jones retorted: 'There is nothing in General Orders to say that I should carry a watch. If I can't tell the time by the clocks in the town, then to hell with the Box system!' The Inspector, no doubt unsure as to whether there was anything in GO relating to the carrying of watches on duty, huffed and puffed and said: 'Parade, 'shun! Left turn, quick march.'

The following night, the procedure was as before except that the Inspector failed to tell us the time and when he started to call us to attention, Joe, from the rear rank shouted, 'And what about the time then, Sir?' The Inspector, taken aback, said, 'Two minutes to ten o'clock.'

Joe, groping beneath his greatcoat and at the same time barging into the man on his left and then the man on his right, produced an enormous alarm clock and holding it aloft, he said, 'Yes, you're just about right, Sir.' Chuckles all round, except from the Inspector.

E. R. Boast, ex PS 58T and PC127V Wt no 118335

The Accident that Never Was

I well remember being on duty with Bill Tilbury (my usual colleague John Woodward being on leave) driving the Daimler Dart. We had had grub, went to Greenwich Court, changed over and Bill was now driving to Tower Bridge Courts, so that we could give evidence in more cases.

It was raining hard at the time, and Bill was pressing on up Deptford High Street, under the railway bridge, when suddenly I saw a young man running hard across the pavement on my left, obviously intent on crossing the road and not getting too wet while he was about it.

As I shouted I felt the brakes go on very firmly. Everything seemed to happen in slow motion from then on; the lad bounding into the air in graceful long leaps, the bonnet of the Dart sliding under him, he flat on his belly sliding up the bonnet until his startled face was pressed against the windscreen, nose flattened, two inches from mine, a graceful slow, slide back down the soaking wet bonnet and as the four wheel disc brakes did their job and stopped us, the lad fell off the front of the car.

We were now stationary. He leapt to his feet and, with amazing acceleration, disappeared onto the crowded pavement on our right. We got out, searched around and were approached by two of Deptford's finest who were sheltering near the railway bridge and had seem the whole episode.

No trace was ever found of the young man, not a mark on the highly polished glass fibre bodywork of the Daimler Dart and if it hadn't been for the two lads from Deptford I might not have believed the whole incident. Also while at DT8 I remember we had the Sunbeam Tiger for speed chases as well as the Dart. It had a massive 5 litre engine and very good brakes; it accelerated as if it was jet-propelled, ideal for catching, checking and stopping the Brands Hatch Herberts on their way to race meetings in Kent. Happy days.

Ken 'Dinger' Bell DT7, DT8, TDR.

Macmillan was Right!

We said 'All correct Sergeant' several times a day
We saluted Inspectors and above nearly as often
We shared one large frying pan between 6 or more in our half hour
Fish, eggs, bacon, sausages, in different coArners of the pan
We sat on a long form at a scrubbed table
With floors of bare wood swept up with old tea leaves
We gave away 15 minutes every day to the Service
We worked clockwise Monday, anti-clockwise Tuesday, and so on
We polished buttons and belts and our toe-caps daily, with spittal, and
Paid 8 shillings and 6 pence for our week's mess bill

We wrote down the numbers of stolen cars and read Information
We pinned and whaleboned the banks and jewellers and
If the yobs blocked the footway they moved on our approach
We asked permission to marry and to draw Rent Aid, and
Sir Oswald Mosley stopped all our Sunday leave for months
We often worked 12 hours a day in 1940 for no extra pay, and
If we broke something we promised 'to be more careful in future'.
With pay on Wednesdays, we were broke on Tuesday
So it was a Warrant Card stand at the Queens Theatre or
A six-hour ride on the trams for 6 pence
We slept in large 'Cupboards' about 8 feet by 5 feet and were
Only allowed one suitcase not more than 21 inches
We had to be in by the midnight hour no matter what age we were
AND WE'RE STILL HERE WITHOUT COUNSELLING
Adolf, Musso, and Tojo caused many problems, but they, and we,
Long suffering on £3.00 per week
Certainly improved the Police Force, thank God
Yes you're quite right Mac, they've never had it so good.

Geoffrey Taylor HH, DT7, DT3, 124166 Met police 1935-1960

Retirement

Is work the only meaning life provides?
For four and thirty years my weeks have sped
Structured in time and place with much besides -
Letters, meetings, offices and rules. Fed
By ambition, it cannot be denied
That rank dependency has sapped and bred,
Mining and ramparts, worming the firm flesh.
Now scaffolding fails, the trap door closes,
Future, friendships, fall into emptiness.
No audience to applaud or judge the poses.
Work has provided challenge, hope, success -
But oft a bed of nails and not of roses.
Now - I can do anything, turn a new page -
Life after work will be more than old age.

Lady Jennifer Hilton, ex Met police officer.

After Sheehy

The Policeman stood at the Golden Gate
his head was bent and low,
He meekly asked the Man of Fate
which way he had to go,
'What have you done,' St. Peter asked,
'to gain admission here?'
'I've kept the peace on earth,' said he
"for many and many a year.'
St. Peter opened wide the gate
and beamed on him as well.
'Come in,' he said, 'and choose a harp
You've had your share of Hell.'

Anon

Mobile Column

I joined the Met police in 1956 and very shortly after, was invited to join the Met police Mobile Column.

During the late 1950s, with the threat of nuclear war always hanging over us, the idea was for police, fire and ambulance columns to be set up, and situated outside the major cities, to be called in after a nuclear attack.

The police column consisted of the familiar 'green goddess' carriers (recently used for the fire and ambulance strikes), to carry 1 PS and 10 PCs. There was also a water dowser, food lorries, a Queen Mary carrier, various other vehicles and a large number of motor cycle out-riders for escort. We were a completely self-contained unit.

Having recently completed my National Service in the RAF as a wireless operator conversant with the Morse Code, I joined the column as a radio operator. That was as close as I got to actually being a wireless operator - general dogsbody more like it, helping with general duties whilst in camp.

The Mobile Column course in London was two weeks. The first week we were based at Hendon, and made use of Hendon runway, embarking and disembarking from moving vehicles, until we could do it very quickly and efficiently. The second week we were based at the former Polish prisoner-of-war camp, now Helicopter Support, at Lippitts Hill, Essex.

The local inn, The Owl, was immediately placed out of bounds to us until the last night.

We were housed in E block at the camp, and there we waited until the alarm went, day or night, informing us that a nuclear attack had taken place. We then boarded the carriers, and moved out in convoy through London to deal with whatever crisis we had been allocated.

On one occasion we did a late night/early morning sweep of Wimbledon Common rounding up everybody, including courting couples, who were then taken to a compound set up near the famous windmill, where they were processed. These were fifth columnists. Another time we picked up an unexploded H-bomb on the Queen Mary, and did a fast run back to Lippitts Hill.

We also dealt with a mass exodus of refugees out of London, travelling from Marble Arch up the Edgware Road. These last two incidents used all we had learned in the first week of our training. A PC was dropped from a moving carrier at every junction as it travelled along. The officer's job was to stop all side traffic entering and allow the main traffic (the refugees) to leave without hindrance. The backlog of traffic in the centre of London caused by this had to be seen to be believed. It was absolute chaos.

We were also sent to Hampstead to do duty, with steel helmets and gas masks on. The locals were not a bit impressed. Come to that, neither were we. Nobody knew the area, and giving directions caused a few headaches.

All in all it was fun, and we learned a little of what we might be called on to deal with in a real situation.

One of the courses was involved in a search, in the Dagenham area I believe, for a missing child. Another focussed on an incident in Bedfordshire. Apparently the group was invited by the local police to a 'do'. This was vetoed because the group was on a 'war footing'. The next day all the group's vehicles had notices attached with the words 'This vehicle has been destroyed' on it. The locals had raided the mobile column, who had not posted a sentry though they were on a war footing.

The Met police column moved elsewhere, on leaving us. Each area had the column for a set number of weeks before it moved on.

Luckily the nuclear threat waned and the mobile columns went into hibernation - never to be heard of again.

Adrian Collins ex Met Police 120A & 175A

Ever Onwards

I was a member of that Mobile Column involved in the search of the Dagenham area, and our search area involved such delights as the slagheap of Beckton power station and a sewage works, and it was there that we enjoyed one of the funniest incidents of the whole two weeks.

On our column we had a rather elderly PC, of Welsh extraction, who was always looking for 'the easy option'. At the sewage works we were told to keep strictly to the footpaths, and not to stray therefrom, but Taffy decided to take it upon himself to take a short cut across the tarmac.

Unfortunately for him, it was not tarmac, just a rather fragile crust over the sewage and no way was it going to support the weight of a grown man. Talk about B.O!

We were searching the area for a young lad who had gone missing. Unfortunately his body was eventually found hidden in a cupboard somewhere. He had been murdered.

The local inhabitants were very appreciative of our efforts and kept us all well refreshed. We had a lot of fun during our search; what a pity it had such a tragic conclusion.

I got the impression that some of your correspondents were not over-impressed with the Mobile Column. For my part, I had a whale of a time, a really enjoyable two weeks with a smashing crowd of blokes, both from the Met and the City of London Police.

We were fortunate to have had such a good governor in charge, Supt Richardson, and a Chief Inspector from the City who was a real stickler and somewhat short of a sense of humour. I cannot remember his name but I know that sometime later he became quite well-known for doing an excellent job at the Moorgate underground disaster.

Thinking of him brings to mind another hilarious episode of this particular Column. One evening we were all despatched (I believe to the Wood Green area) to where a whole row of houses had been demolished for some development scheme. There we met up with the local Civil Defence people who had hidden various 'bodies' around the site for us to find and rescue.

The whole area looked as though it had been well and truly blitzed, and to give some air of realism to it all our Ch Insp started a small bonfire in one of the derelict houses. It certainly gave realism, as the fire got bigger.

Fortunately, the local fire station was just around the corner, and it was a very red-faced Ch Insp who, around 2am, had to knock on their door and asked them, nicely, if they would be kind enough to pop round the corner and put our fire out. They were not amused.

By this time there had been so many complaints from locals of the noise and disturbances we were making that the exercise was called off, and we all went home to bed, which was at Lippits Hill.

Another fascinating exercise that all these Columns enjoyed was that of 'leap-frogging'. Normally what happened when the Column was on the move was that our motorcycle outriders raced ahead and closed off any side roads, junctions etc until the Column had gone through.

They then had to race like stink to get ahead of us before the next junction, and we weren't hanging about either.

I well remember driving across the Stamford Hill junction one evening in excess of 60 mph, with my 'troops' in the back shouting encouragement. (We were on our way to the City of London to search for hidden nuclear weapons!)

Anyway, this leapfrogging idea was to achieve the same result at junctions but without the use of the motorcyclists.

The theory was that one personnel carrier would set off ahead of the main Column and at each junction would drop off one of the troop to close the junction off when the rest of the Column approached. Having dropped all his troops, the driver would then park and await the arrival of the Column. Then, when it had safely passed, he would set off and collect the men from the various junctions along the route.

This was done by each carrier in turn, thus the term 'leapfrogging'. Well, that at least was the theory.

Many hours later, long after the exercise had officially ended, 'some of our troops are missing' was the cry from carrier after carrier.

They were scattered far and wide around the countryside where some of them had spent long lonely hours at the end of some muddy country lane, no doubt cursing and swearing as their supposed pick-up carrier went hurtling by. Eventually all were safely gathered in.

In cold print that leapfrogging might not seem much, but boy! had you seen it, it was impressive, and believe me, it had to be seen to be believed. It must be the closest that the Met and the City of London Police ever came to taking over from the Keystone Kops.

Another of our exercises almost ended up with a hanging! We were all sent off on a secret mission. We had no idea where we were off to as we were under sealed orders - all we knew was that we would be staying overnight somewhere. Eventually we ended up at some army barracks in the Aldershot area, a Junior Leaders depot, I believe.

After sorting out our billets etc, we were sent off to some very very wild scrubland to search for, find, and interrogate some spies, who were in fact TA SAS members, many of them coppers.

Their instructions were not to get caught, but if caught not to be deliberately obstructive but at the same time to be as uncooperative as was decent. Also they were to try and 'blow up' our transports.

All the drivers were expected to join in with the searching but we did not think this was a very good idea so we went on strike. We pleaded that we should be allowed to stay behind both to protect our vehicles and at the same time carry out routine maintenance.

Our pleas were granted. We formed all the vehicles up in a circle, in real Wild West fashion, without a second's thought for our colleagues out there, being torn apart in all that wild scrub.

It was not too long before one group returned triumphant with a spy. He looked just too good to be true, scruffy, unkempt and wheeling an old tradesman's pedal cycle, with the front carrier filled with old newspapers. He declined all knowledge of our exercise and refused to answer any questions. Inside the personnel carriers was a bench down the centre of the vehicle which opened out into a table.

Our spy was promptly hoisted into the back of a carrier and tied down to the table. He still refused to co-operate.

In desperation someone found a length of rope, formed a noose, stuck it over his head and he was then marched to the nearest tree. It was only at the last moment, when the rope was slung over a sturdy branch, and the poor man started screaming, that we eventually decided that perhaps he wasn't a part of our game after all!

He went storming off to complain to the Supt but was given very short shrift. The governor told him in no uncertain terms that it was all his own fault for being on land that was barred to all civilians, and to think himself lucky he was not going to be prosecuted for trespassing. As I said, a good governor!For me the Mobile Column was two weeks of sheer pleasure with a smashing crowd of blokes.

Fred (Chalky) White ex 204J/214G 138105

Always Remember your Brake Test

In 1935 the Metropolitan Police Driving School opened. In 1936, Sir Phillip Game, the Commissioner, decided a higher standard of police driving was required, and he requested a friend, Lord Cottenham, a noted racing car enthusiast, to assist him.

The Peer accordingly set up a course, based on racing and rallying techniques, which he called the Advanced Course, and introduced the Class 1 and Class 2 driver. To train drivers at this level the noble lord conducted tests with the existing instructors, and he selected six. He also prevailed upon some of his wealthy friends to donate fast, expensive cars to the new course.

In 1939 the Metropolitan Police Driving School shut down for the duration of the war.

In 1945/6 the school re-opened, and three of those original six advanced course instructors were still available, and amazingly, almost the entire fleet of Advanced Course vehicles had survived. The Bentley, Lagonda, Alvis, Railton, Chevrolet and the Citroens Light 15 and Big 6, were under covers in the converted hanger at Hendon, and all were found to be serviceable.

My story concerns one of those instructors, and one of those cars, the vintage Bentley in fact.

The day commenced in the usual way, with three students occupying the rear and front passenger seats of the beautiful car. The instructor left the school and commenced his demonstration drive. He pointed out that although the mileage was enormous, there was still considerable power under the bonnet.

Over the years however, the lack of spares had meant that certain replacements could not be made. The brake drums for instance were original and had become elliptical. This meant that when applying the rod-operated brakes, the foot tended to ride a little on the pedal. The brakes were very efficient, but pressure should be applied gently and with a gradual firmness.

After 20-minutes demonstration the instructor pulled into a lay-by and transferred to the front passenger seat, whilst the driver's seat was occupied by the first student, a PC from the East End, all of 6'3", 15 stone and exuding a fine sweat!

The sergeant settled back comfortably, placed his tin of tobacco and his papers in his lap and began a roll, whilst he instructed the driver to pull out when he was ready and at the first opportunity, to carry out a brake test.

The driver moved gently forward at what he no doubt felt was about 15 miles per hour, but in the Bentley was closer to 30mph. He realised he was going too fast to join the flow of traffic and braked. This, not being a brake test, caused him to panic as his foot rode the pedal, giving the impression that the brakes were not answering.

He reacted positively and stamped hard on the pedal. The result was, to say the least, spectacular! The Bentley practically stood up and begged, whilst the sergeant, cap, tin and makings, disappeared under the dashboard. The two students from the back came over into the front and settled comfortably on the driver and the sergeant.

The two passengers were the first to extricate themselves, and busied themselves helping the sergeant out from under the dashboard. He stood speechless whilst they dusted him down and carefully brushed up his tobacco from the floor. They climbed back in the rear, whilst the instructor gazed at the driver, who stared miserably out through the windscreen.

The sergeant was noted for a remarkable knowledge of the English language, albeit with a Scots flavour. He went for a short walk along the lay-by, gazing at the weather, and finally returned to the car. He talked to the driver for ten minutes and never repeated himself. For years his remarks were recalled with genuine awe and respect.

An incident such as described would have been regarded as sure passport to failure but in fact the lad from the East End passed out with a Class 1!

Terry Butcher 130142

Black Rats

One of our jobs as a Trafpol Black Rat was escorting unusual loads through the MPD. This normally occurred in the evenings after the rush hour had finished. On this particular evening there were two ships' propellers to be escorted from Stones at Charlton to the West India Docks, a short run over Tower Bridge. After the loads were dropped it was up to Limehouse nick for a cup of tea before returning to the garage to book off.

There were three officers to each load. The first three set off via

Rotherhithe Tunnel to get to the south side of the river. Whilst tearing through the Tunnel, they came across the night maintenance crew washing down the walls of the tunnel. Acting with one accord they pressed the earthing buttons on their 'Speed Twins', always guaranteed to create a terrific explosive noise when the fuel was released, and 'dropped their bombs' creating a terrible din in the tunnel.

About ten minutes later the second trio set forth over the same route. This time the maintenance crew were ready for them and before they had a chance to drop their bombs, the crew turned their hoses on them, soaking them to the skin. Oh well, the fortunes of war I suppose!

John Back, ex Trafpol

Salute to Bow Street

Having recently applied for and received my ticket for the Bow Street reunion to mark the closing down of Bow Street Police Station, (1992) memories of my ten years served there came flooding back.

On joining the Met Police at the latter end of 1946, the greater part of the intake at Peel House were ex-servicemen. But on passing out and being posted to Division we suddenly found ourselves in the minority, and Bow Street was no exception.

We soon found out which canteen tables we could sit at, or more important the ones we couldn't. The beats and patrols were open to all, but traffic points had their priorities. We probationers, about ten in total, were allowed to cut our teeth on the three in the Strand outside Charing Cross Railway Station, the one in St Martins Lane at the junction with Trafalgar Square, and in the Strand outside the Savoy Hotel. The latter caused some confusion to begin with as traffic entering and leaving the front of the hotel drove on the right side of the road leading to the main entrance.

After a few months service we were allowed to work the manual traffic lights at the Strand junction with Waterloo Bridge. This consisted of a tarpaulin-covered 'sentry box' with a threeway handle. Green for the Strand, an all red phase for pedestrians to cross, then green for Waterloo Bridge traffic. When selecting the all red phase, large groups of pedestrians would swarm across and not a few would stop and ask directions. After three or four hours of this and particularly if plied with several questions by visitors to London, you could easily forget which line of traffic you had last let run. If you mistakenly gave the Strand a 'double run' you would be certain to invite the wrath of disgruntled taxi drivers waiting impatiently at the stop line at Waterloo Bridge!

After you had passed your probation you were then allowed to work the 'senior' traffic point at the Victoria Embankment junction with Savoy Hill. These traffic lights also controlled the trams entering and leaving the tunnel under Waterloo Bridge. You were privileged to sit inside a wooden box with windows all round and controlled the lights with a small wheel. On one occasion when a certain young PC was on this posting a woman driver stopped, got out of her car, walked over to the box and asked the way to Surrey Street. The PC leaned out of the box and pointing towards the City said 'It's first on the left'. After thanking him, she got back into her car and started off; and then to the PC's horror she promptly turned left into the tramway tunnel. He alleges he closed his eyes and prayed, but it was the motorist's lucky day, there were no trams travelling in that part of the tunnel at the moment. It was later learnt that the woman drove all the way to the Aldwych station, where she was waved down by an ashen-faced tram Ticket Inspector who then escorted her back out of the tunnel.

The traffic along the Victoria Embankment was considerably less in those days and speeding was a problem. Frequently a police trap was set, consisting of a sergeant and a PC in plain clothes with stop watches, and further along a uniformed PC acting as the 'stopper'. On this occasion a motorist travelling at almost 60mph entered the trap and when this was confirmed by the sergeant's stop watch he turned and waved his arm as a signal for the uniformed PC to stop the offender. Unfortunately on this occasion in his haste, the sergeant used the hand holding the stop watch which promptly left his hand and sailed gracefully over the embankment parapet into the Thames. This was one lucky motorist, for half of the evidence was now lying on the river bed. At the end of the session it was the practice to write up our notes in the small canteen on the Waterloo Bridge floating station, so it's possible some retired Thames Division officer will remember this incident.

All stations had their old time 'characters' and Bow Street had its full share. PC Taffy Thomas for one, a man of generous girth and PC Adams of similar stature, at refreshment time on night duty would regularly with the aid of fellow conspirators get a certain PC who hailed from north of the border, to demonstrate how, with the aid of a billiard cue, the caber was tossed at the Highland Games. They would feign disbelief in its feasibility which would invite many repeat performances.

At that time we worked a four week rota, and periodically during the month before night duty some of us would be brought out 9am-5pm on accident prevention. We worked in pairs, usually one experienced officer with a probationer. My partner and mentor was frequently PC Billy Britten a most knowledgeable and likeable chap. We were issued with Process Books about an inch thick containing some 20-25 traffic reports. After the tour you could have anything up to a hundred summonses pending. The Court staff, aware of this, would arrange for an officer's cases to be heard in one batch so that there was less traffic to and from the witness box. In those days all cases had to be proved personally by the officer concerned regardless of the plea.

On this occasion PC Britten had some eight summonses spread over four of these thick books, with several pieces of paper inserted in the appropriate places as markers. He entered the witness box and placed all four books on the front ledge of the box. He then took hold of the holy testament and in raising it above his head to take the oath promptly knocked all four books off the shelf into the well of the court with the all important markers scattered far and wide. After a pregnant silence the Chief Magistrate Sir Laurence Dunne, in his usual unflappable manner said 'I think we will put your cases back Mr Britten so that you can replace your markers.' Sir Laurence knew all the regular attending police officers by name.

On another occasion PC Anderson, known as Chelsea because of his support for that team, had just given his evidence, when the defending solicitor said 'Are you sure you are telling the truth officer?' PC Anderson drew himself up to his full 6ft 1in height and with his right index finger pointing straight at the advocate said 'There's more truth told on this side of the court than there is ever told on your side.' 'That will do Mr Anderson,' said the Chief Magistrate reprovingly, but Chelsea had won his case.

The 'Subs' Clerk in those early days spent all Wednesday morning counting out the weekly pay and placing it in small envelopes ready for pay parade at 2pm. As a matter of economy the envelopes were left unsealed so that they could be used again.

At about 1.45pm on this particular Wednesday the Clerk came out of his office on the first floor carrying the tray containing about 300 full envelopes and on reaching the top of the stairs missed his footing and the entire station's pay was scattered over three flights of stairs as far down as the basement. Needless to say pay parade was late that day.

Whilst memories remain, time marches steadily on. First the Stoll Theatre disappeared, then the Tivoli, followed by the closure of the Lyceum Ballroom. Covent Garden fruit and vegetable market and Charing Cross Hospital have moved away, and now Bow Street Police Station itself is closed.

Alan Webster ex Ch Insp 129291 E, J, N, Y

Learning the Ropes, Commercial Street Way

It has to be something of a Metropolitan Police record that at the beginning of 1954, five newly promoted Sergeants were posted to Commercial Street: John, Reg, Danny Brennan, myself and another, whose name the old grey matter refuses to divulge. Talk about the blind leading the blind! Lesser mortals than Supt Reg Owen (the Panda) would have thrown in the towel.

However, we all reckoned without the calibre of the seasoned Inspectors and mature Sergeants there. They quickly showed us the ropes of real coppering. Shortly, even Panda beamed on us fledglings.

Where does anyone begin to recount memories of that marvellous mad-house which was Commercial Street GC in the Fifties? Like when the night relief quietly moved all the barrows to one end of Spitalfields Market, leaving the wheels at the other, to the consternation of the early turn porters.

Danny Brennan, proudly showing us new duty boots he had bought in Cheshire Street. When he booked off, they had disappeared, to be found later tied to the highest rafter.

PC Edgar Spencer, just before Christmas, cycling home with a Christmas tree tied to his back, the top wavering just below the trolley bus wires. Edgar had been involved in a bomb incident which had affected his balance. He would carry a tray of teas to the reserve room with more spilled in the tray than left in the cups.

Who could ever forget the Panda standing in the Station yard, looking up to his flat and calling out to his wife, 'Win', in a voice discernable at Aldgate Pump? I stepped out on foot patrol one afternoon and he joined me, resplendent in his uniform. A major film company had been granted authority to shoot scenes in a street between the markets, provided they 'caused no obstruction'. On rounding a corner to the site, the Panda let out a roar. Traffic was at a standstill, because hundreds of sightseers were watching the filming. In no uncertain terms, Reg told those responsible to pack up filming for the day. The Producer came over saying, 'Don't you dare shout at me, Superintendent'. Reg replied 'I am not shouting'. Turning to me he said, 'This is my normal voice isn't it sergeant?' I had to agree, although the audience visibly flinched as Reg spoke.

By midnight Saturday, every cell would hold a drunk. Usually no fixed abode, but still bailed next morning, Sunday, by the early relief. One such occasion included a 'toff' who had a lot of money. Apparently, it was decided to bail him last. As preparation was made, a disaster unfolded. It was revealed that an already-bailed drunk had been inadvertently handed the toff's money. The entire early turn tore out of the nick in search of this drunk who was soon found, already inebriated, in 'Itchy Park'. He still had most of the cash, the balance being made up by our relief whip round.

The toff was duly bailed and handed the correct money, oblivious of the incident. What's more, the matter was squared up without involving a single Senior Officer. The Station Officer responsible was a very relieved man and subsequently became one of our highest ranking Force Officers.

The atmosphere in the Job then had much to do with the fact we were nearly all recently discharged from Armed Forces War Service.

I sometimes look at present day coppers and wonder if they have the characters, the comradeship and above all the leadership we enjoyed. For their sake and that of the general public, I sincerely hope so.

Eddie Twitchings, Ex Insp H,G,J,K,TDJ

To Mother, with Love

The mention of Gilmour House, where I spent seven happy years, awakens nostalgia. Scottie, having enjoyed a few drinks, going to bed, dragging behind him a huge haddock. As Hugh Penny, another Scot, said: 'Scottie, Drunk in Charge of a Haddock.' I could go on and on. Think I had better not.

Finally to record first impressions of a Section House, I enclose a letter found amongst my late mother's possessions - one dated 2 May 1950, that I wrote to her on my return to Gilmour House following the week's leave after initial training at TS:

> 'You should see my room. Floor, bed, and bed rug. Easy chair and chair for desk in a lovely pale green. Velvet cushions on easy chair, and green leather pad on desk chair. You know what I mean. Other parts of chairs stained wood of course. The rest of my room is a pale lemon colour.
>
> Two lights, one in centre of room, one jutting out over my head in bed for reading. Constant hot and cold water in sink which is in corner of room. Towel rack under sink. Above sink, small cabinet for shaving requisites. A large mirror as part of door of cabinet for shaving.
>
> A wardrobe seven feet high in wall, rack on top, five drawers inside and two trays. Also, above wardrobe, a cupboard for empty cases. A radiator switch for heat, and even a little catch on door which slides and says whether we are in or not, so that cleaners do not disturb us. And of course desk. The wardrobe and desk lock.
>
> It is a pretty room and as you know, rooms don't interest me, but this is a lovely room. Even green curtains to match. We are allowed to have a wireless in our rooms too, if we get permission.'

John Primeau

Gray's Inn Road

Gray's Inn Road Police Station (EG) had that well-known street Hatton Garden on the patch, famous for jewellers and diamond merchants. It was policed by a regular Shop Patrol for 24 hours.

PCs were posted to the patrol for the month (in my day that meant four weeks but was later reduced to three weeks). Needless to say, the night duty patrol was dreaded by all, but there was no escape and should you report sick on that posting, it would be waiting for you whenever you resumed.

Continuity was assured by Sergeant (Piggy) Chandler, the duty sergeant and Inspector George Parsons who arranged the monthly postings. The night man paraded at 11pm, one hour after his mates, and if you were unfortunate to have an 'old sweat' on the adjoining beat, you would have little human contact except when you were relieved for refreshments at an appointed hour. This was taken at Macnaghton Section House.

'Willie Hood' was the sub-divisional Inspector, one of the old school who walked the ground in uniform and, as he lived in married quarters at Charles Rowan house nearby, he could and frequently did appear at any hour of night. It went without saying that you did not leave your patrol without being properly relieved. A discipline indictment would be the inevitable consequence and as the starting pay for a PC was £5 per week (gross), fines would be a real hardship.

To my horror, my night duty posting arrived during the winter of 1949. Although not remembered for heavy snow, it had a fair share of hard frosts and biting north-easterly winds that blew right through you. I was fortunate in having a couple of youngsters (like myself) on the adjacent beats; named PC Harry Hodgkinson and PC Cook.

I settled into the routine in the first week, getting to know every door handle and padlock at the front and rear of all the premises. I even got used to the sickly smell of tobacco from Lloyds Tobacco factory at Clerkenwell Road and the acrid fumes from the Johnson Mathay bullion works, halfway down the road.

There would be the occasional brief chat with the very tall City of London coppers at the boundary at Holborn Circus, but they, like all other living creatures, seemed to disappear soon after midnight leaving you alone in the cold and gloom.

The one crumb of comfort in an otherwise drab existence was the stationers shop near Holborn Circus. It had a deep doorway and every night after closing, the proprietor placed an empty wooden milk crate outside his door for the patrol man to sit and take the weight off his feet.

Provided you kept your eye open for the reflected light of the Police Post when it was flashed or got to your feet smartly on the approach of the Section Sergeant to report 'All Correct', the Powers-that-be appeared to turn a blind eye to this little privilege.

In the early hours of one morning, sitting on the crate like a hermit crab in my heavy overcoat and oil-skin cape, with frost bite getting to my ears, toes and fingers and contemplating putting my papers in the next morning, Harry arrived on his rounds. After discussion, we decided that we just had to devise some scheme for bringing a little warmth into our lives besides the flask of coffee that we shared.

At the junction of Hatton Garden and Cross Street stood the shell of a bombed church, a relic of the war years. It was partly roofed, and access was obtained by sliding a loose plank fixed to the front door. In a corner at the rear and out of sight of the street, we set up a small oil drum, suitably punctured to provide air and filled with coke scrounged from the huge pile in the yard at the back of EG. We very soon had a glowing brazier as snug as any night watchman. Frequent, careful visits to the scene enabled us to keep our fire glowing and the rest of that night passed comfortably. On subsequent nights, parade would be followed by a visit to the back yard to fill a paper bag with small quantities of coke to replenish our stock and the first man on the site would start the fire.

This routine continued successfully until one morning towards the end of the month. At about 5am, I spotted the approach of Section Sergeant Parlett, near Clerkenwell Road, and after the formal exchanges I accompanied him to the Circus where he phoned in. I watched his departure past Gamages Store, heading (I thought) in the direction of the nick at EG.

After my final check of my doors, I joined Harry at our 'snug' where he was sitting on an old stool we had acquired along the way. He was having his last drag before going up to book off when the silence was broken by the sound of heavy footsteps approaching along the nave of the church.

'Is that you Cookie?' Harry called out. 'No,' was the stern reply - 'this is Sergeant Parlett here!' He unceremoniously kicked over our oil drum and sent us packing with a few chosen expletives.

What had given us away? With hindsight I can only assume that when the sergeant first saw me, I did not look frozen enough to be natural, causing him to double back.

We were not asked to leave 728s and no further action was taken other than the fact that the milk crate disappeared for the remainder of my posting, only to reappear when taken up by a new bloke on the next.

Cliff (Taffy) Sankey, Wt no 132719. PC 293 E/124, B/PS 90V

The Wapping Nightingale

I was aged 22 when I left Peel House with four others to join Shadwell in November 1920.

Since there was no room for us, we were lodged with the 'Water Rats' at Wapping, where we stayed for two years or more.

Having finished the usual lessons, I was posted night duty at, of all places, Pennington Street. On my ground was also the notorious Prospect of Whitby Public House.

It was a pea-souper fog all night, and my beat only took a few minutes round all the warehouses. I could hear the Thames running but I could not see the flow for fog. I did not see a soul all night and at 6am I eventually found my way to the station.

The people of Wapping were mostly of Irish descent and would never admit a Jew to their district. The working women wore lace-up boots and leather cuffs and bought snuff every morning before they began work at Alexander Tingle Jacobs warehouse where they picked and sorted rags. The men were mostly dockers and at that time unemployment was rife.

They would assemble each morning for work at Middletons Wharf where the chief stevedore would pick just a few of them. Joe's horses and carts would arrive there early every morning in order to get the first load for market. Some of the horses would lie down in the road and sleep.

This wharf had a private policeman named Joe, and carters would leave him a tip in the pub opposite, where the coins mounted up in a pint glass. One day, two old coppers called at the pub and asked for a drink out of Joe's glass. They got it.

We would see the woman knocker-up, paid to give people the early morning call with her long cane, tapping on the windows.

At weekends the Sunday lunch was cooked at the bakers. Each Sunday, you could see the women seated outside the pubs shelling peas for the West End Hotels. One woman - I think her name was Mary Barrot, was a problem when she got drunk and would fight anybody. Placing her on the barrow was an effort. She came from Watts Street but in the end she met a younger woman who gave her a dusting.

George Warner the baker and Jack Hartman with his straw boater and white apron, were real characters. There was the priest Father Wainwright - a small man who arrived at Wapping quite wealthy. He would help the poor and visit the sick in St George's Hospital. On one occasion he took off his shirt to give to a patient ready for discharge, as he hadn't one. He would attend Thames Police Court if one of his flock got into trouble, and normally paid the fine.

Fighting at weekends was common and if the police were unable to stop it, Father would arrive and peace was restored. When he died, 25,000 people lined the route, and it was said he died broke.

There was a young school girl named Rose, 14 years old, and she and her friend both lived in Wapping but Rose had the most wonderful voice. During the light evenings they would sit on Wapping Old Steps near the *Tower of Ramsgate* public house and sing *Charmaine* and other songs.

Her voice would float across the Thames and people on the Rotherhithe side would applaud her. It was said that agents were eager to book her but being adopted marred her success. She was known as the Wapping Nightingale.

It was in 1922 when I became a member of the coxed four boat from Shadwell Station. We kept our boat at Thames Station and one evening the remainder of the crew turned up to go out training. Now it was flood tide. I had to warn them it was too dangerous to go out, but the cox suggested I was windy and became obstinate. I agreed to go and we rowed up the Thames past Tower and London bridges, dodging ships on our way.

On the way back, the tide was in full flood and we were proceeding under London Bridge when we got caught in a strong eddy around the buttress. We were in peril and I shouted to the crew to sit tight as I breasted my oar against the brickwork. We then got clear and proceeded down river to Limehouse where we had to take shelter behind an anchored ship to avoid being run down.

We then crossed over to the Surrey Docks side where we rested and met up with the Thames police who warned me it was too dangerous to be out. I agreed with them, and asked if they would stay with us. They replied, 'We must go to Erith,' and left us.

It was then I noticed we were taking in water. I suggested that if we kept baling out, we might be lucky. We then took off for Wapping station. Half way across came a big ship which swamped us and down we went. We could hear the kids from Shadwell Pier Head shouting, 'The coppers boat has gone down!'

Smith the stoke swam away to a lighter, as did Wixen the bow, but Brooker, the number 2, a fine swimmer, was treading water and keeping his eye on myself and the cox Richmond, as we were waterlogged. The tug Eclipse rescued us and towed us back to Wapping Station. I had learned my rowing in the Royal Navy during the Great War where I served three years.

The children of Wapping were the usual cockney kids but they had never seen Tower Bridge, a few minutes walk away. They played devilish tricks and one afternoon I was patrolling the back streets when I came across eight to ten excited boys and girls with a 36 gallon cask of beer.

It was on its head and they had house bricks trying to bash it in. Of course they bolted and a cyclist stopped to see what was going on. I told him to guard it with his life whilst I went off to ascertain whence it came.

I found it had come from a pub by the bridge in Old Gravel Lane some 300 yards away. I knocked up the landlord and saw other full barrels outside. The charge hand and his mate got a shock, I can tell you, as they had to roll it back up hill.

Van dragging was another trick of theirs. With knives they would slit the bags of molasses etc and then nip off with their gains. Another trick was picking locks, and we had complaints abouts horses being loose. I kept watch and saw two boys aged about 11 with a small wooden barrel containing several miniature tools trying a lock on a stable door. I took charge of the tools and took them to their parents.

About this time, a dock strike was on and all the men assembled at Wapping to march to Tilbury for their support. We police were caught napping but we managed to march with them to Barking where we were relieved. I recall that most of the women accompanied them and some had never seen parts beyond the boundary of Wapping.

I confess that the people of Wapping were the salt of the earth. I felt so sorry for them recently when the printers fought their case.

George Ludlow ex PC 601T also H and X divs

Sweet Memories of M

I served on M District and later P District from 1947 until 1972. I joined MR the same day as Paddy Grogan. He was a character and was frequently to be heard whilst on night duty playing his fiddle on the top floor at MR (which used to be the Sergeant's quarters).

Many of my era will recall George Cooper and Jimmy Ash, when one day on the RT car they arrested a 'Totter' in Rotherhithe Street, and George took the prisoner back to MR and Jimmy at his flamboyant best, drove the Totter's horse and cart at breakneck speed to the station. A heated argument then took place in the charge room as to whose arrest it was! Jim was a natural thief catcher.

When I first joined the nick I was shown round the beats by 'Uncle'

Tom Bergin, one of the old school. On night duty it was not unusual to call at the pubs on the beat and Tom would put his head through the door and make his presence known, then he would visit the external toilet, saying to me 'You don't drink boy, do you?' more a statement of fact than question. On a shelf he would then recover two pints of the best to set him up for the next eight hours!

I later saw duty on M2, the area car covering MF, MR & MT. The crew (three, one plain clothes) was drawn from the three stations, and those who experienced the posting will recall 'Steve' Stevens, early turn, who was one of the greatest. A breakfast supplied by Steve was one to be remembered (if you could consume it all)! He was also in charge of the local Sea Cadet Corps - their boat the Jacaranda was moored in Surrey Docks. Often a trip was arranged for officers, either fishing or a run across to France. I heard tell that was some experience, the officers being the crew and it was no small boat; and those victualling runs before a trip, what memories!

Another of the R/T drivers was Yorky Blanchard whom you could say had a musical talent! Those who knew him will known what I mean. Alas, he came to grief one day.

Bill Moore will recall, as will others, that when taking refreshment on night duty at MF it was frequently necessary to run the gauntlet through the yard into the station to avoid being bombed with paper bags full of water, the culprits being those already inside standing on the flat roof of the cells! Bill may also recall a service I rendered his wife once when driving M1, for she had become locked in at her office.

I recall service on bookmakers on the Division, as will many others. On Kennington's ground in West Square there used to be a man, with two walking sticks, who stood outside his house on a corner. It was almost an impossibility to catch him, he may have had sticks but he was indoors like greased lighting. I did succeed once, took the slips and cash from him and he made his way under his own steam to MK (then part of Gilmour House) arriving about 45 minutes later!

Another pitch off Waterloo Road was due to be done. On approaching the centre of the block of flats the call went out and the look-out ran for his life. Catching him some 200 yards further on he stated that he had a bad heart but needed to make it look good - fortunately his heart held out. Phew! Three weeks on bookies.

Most at Deptford in my time will recall Deptford market, in the arches: many's the time we spent watching the blacksmith shoeing the traders' horses, and the dogs waiting for the trimmings from the hoof as the shoe was fitted. At Rotherhithe, where the old terraced houses were in and off Silwood Street, one used to see the old ladies peeling onions or whatever on their doorsteps for the pickle factory in Silwood Street. If any like me went inside and saw what went into their pickles and sauces, one never touched the stuff afterwards!

Many will remember the arches which were rented by Youngs of Southwark Park Road, and the stench; how on night duty we would go in with our lanterns in one hand, stick in the other, switch on and see how may of the rats we could hit! I wonder to this day how they made gelatine, so pure, from those rotten animal carcasses. Recalling gelatine: anyone for a Perry's ice cream? They don't make it like that any more!

John Livett , ex M, P

Tottenham Court Road

I often think about an incident that happened before my time at Tottenham Court Road, in 1926, which was still being spoken about when I joined the Met and worked there 1930-38.

It referred to PC Joe Hearn, a great big 6'4" stern-looking man.

He was on annual leave at Plymouth, staying with relatives, when the General Strike broke out. He received a telegram from Tottenham Court Road to return at once. All transport had stopped, and he could not ride a bicycle, so he had to walk. His relatives packed him off with two cold chickens and two loaves of bread.

He walked during the day and slept in the local police stations at night. At 9am every morning, he sent the following message to Tottenham Court Road SD Inspector: 'PC 568C Hearn passing through the village of .... enroute for Tottenham Court Road. All correct.'

He walked all the way back and needless to say, the strike was practically over by the time he arrived.

Another incident I recall was night duty around 1935. A little old lady came down the steps into the parade shed at about 9.45pm. She said to the Inspector: 'Excuse me, sir, I have lost my cat. I have not seen it for about a week. It's a tom and it looks a bit like me, so I wonder if your officers would have a look for it?'

She lived in a basement flat in Howland Street, W1 and said she would leave the front room window unlocked, and if any policeman saw her cat, to capture it and pop it through the front window.

There were dozens of cats around Howland Street at night-time. The Inspector turned to us and said, 'Now don't forget lads, if you see a cat that looks like this lady, catch it and pop it through her front room window.'

When we came off duty at 6am, the subject of the cats was brought up, and we found everybody on the relief had caught at least two cats. We reckoned we had put at least a hundred cats in that front room. We never heard anything more from the old lady, so we assumed she had found her cat. We were always ready to give people a helping hand in those days.

I was in the Section House at Tottenham Court Road during my first two years in the Job, and we all slept in cubicles. When we were on early turn, I remember old PC Topper Brown coming along to wake up the ones who were early turn, and he spoke very quietly like this: 'Wakey wakey wakey, shakey shakey shakey, peep bo, peep bo.' You would hear a voice from the other end of the corridor, from someone who apparently was not early turn: 'Xxxx off, Bo Peep!'

I was in business for 28 years after I retired from the Job, and last March was the first time I was able to attend the C division reunion. My son who is in the Job accompanied me. I did not see anyone who was at Tottenham Court Road during the thirties.

My son remarked that perhaps I had outlived them all.

Percy Ledger, ex PC 528C and 188T

Adventures at Norwood Green

The ground at Norwood Green was vast. I transferred there in 1938 after eight years at Tottenham Court Road. We were on Ealing Sub-division and had four cycle beats. They started at No 16 which took in half of Southall. Fifty years ago, Southall was a lovely little country town. Number 17 beat took part of Heston and all Osterley. Number 19 Beat was part of Heston, the whole of Osterley Park, and right down the Great West Road to Firstone Bridge at Brentford.

I missed the hustle and bustle of the West End very much. I felt like transferring back after the first month, it was so quiet. The only thing that kept me there was my house in Fern Lane, Heston. The rent was 12/9d a week and the rates 4/6d a week. It was a medium size semi-detached. The rent allowance those days was 17/6d.

A few incidents come to mind which I often think about.

I had only been there about two months, and I was on parade night duty when the Sergeant said, 'PC 188, you have got gypos on your beat, on the footpath north side of Heston Airport: get rid of them. Complaints have been received from residents in that vicinity about losing poultry and rabbits from their back gardens. It's obvious who is having them.' As I left the station, PC Fred Cracknell, one of the older PCs, said to me, 'It's no use asking them to go, they won't take any notice. Would you like me to help?' I said, 'Yes please.'

We arranged to meet at midnight, at the entrance to the footpath in North Hyde Lane. It was very dark as all the street lights went out in those days just after 10.30pm when the pubs closed. PC Cracknell arrived at midnight. He was carrying a small parcel of meat which he said was to keep the dogs quiet. I stayed there and he disappeared into the darkness.

About half-an-hour later he appeared leading a large horse, and was followed by about 12 other horses. When he got on to the road he took a flying leap onto the horse's back and as he landed, I gave the horse a swipe with my rolled cape on the rear as we had previously arranged.

The horse stood up on its hind legs and as it came down, it shot off like a rocket up North Hyde Lane with all the other 12 horses following in a single line. I brought up the rear riding my bicycle with my left hand and wheeling PC Cracknell's bicycle with my right. The horses galloped over the canal bridge, down Regina Road, through King Street, Southall, over the Great Western railway bridge and down South Road. They turned right at Uxbridge Road then right again in Southall Market and were handed over to the greenyard keeper.

Next morning all the gypos were at Norwood Green police station to report losing their horses. They were told it would cost them 25 shillings each for their horses' food and lodging for the night, and that they would be summonsed for allowing their horses to stray on the highway. They collected their horses and were away like the wind, and were never seen again.

At Heston Airport before the War was a pilot named Captain Baker, who used to take a plane with passengers to Jersey and return about 1.30pm. If you were on duty and happened to pop in to their canteen for a cup of tea, he always came over for a chat. He used to say: 'You can have a run over to Jersey with me if you like. I'll get you back in time to book off at 2pm.' I always refused. Too risky for me.

I was on 18 beat early turn, when the SD Inspector came along and told me to follow him to Heston Airport. When I arrived he said that he had received information from Jersey, that a Metropolitan Police officer in uniform was on the 1.30 plane.

The plane landed, and after all the passengers had got off, out came the man on 17 beat, PC (Darkly) Gunton. He must have nearly collapsed when he saw the SD Inspector waiting for him. He came straight across and came to attention, gave him a Guardsman's salute and said, 'Just been testing the brakes, sir.' The SD Inspector never said a word for about two minutes. I think he nearly exploded, and by that time, Capt. Baker was arriving on the scene. The SD Insp. shouted very loud, 'Get out of my sight you horrible man.' We both made ourselves scarce. PC Gunton was on tenterhooks for a week, but nothing happened.

We had a lady named Mrs Sweet who resided in Heston. She was forever ringing up the station at all times of day and night, and making trivial complaints. No foundation in any of them. She became a nuisance to us. I went round to her house once. It was at the junction of New Heston Road and Vicarage Farm Road. There was a very high wall round her house, and I noticed her large garden was like a wilderness. Nothing had been done to it for years. It was during the War when I was on night duty on 17 beat. It was dark and about 5am I heard an unusual noise coming along Cranford Lane. I flashed my torch and discovered a herd of cows coming towards me. They, no doubt, had been disturbed by the bombs dropped in the vicinity of their farm in Cranford.

I stood in front of them and tried to turn them back, but they just came towards me and in the end I had to jump out of the way to prevent them from walking over me. I shone my torch and I noticed they tended to follow the beam of my light. I thought to myself, I could not take them to the station which was just over a mile away, because PC Cracknell had an allotment at the rear, and they would have ruined all his vegetables.

I did not fancy walking right round Heston Airport, as it would be after 7am before I booked off duty. So I turned them into Vicarage Farm Road, then cycled ahead of them, opened Mrs Sweet's garden gate and shone my light into her garden. They all walked in. I closed the gate and booked off duty. All correct, Sergeant? Nothing to report.

I heard afterwards Mrs Sweet rang up the station just after 6am to report she had a herd of cows in her garden. The reserve man did not believe her and said 'Don't worry, I've got a herd of elephants in mine.' When the farmer rang up afterwards, they soon discovered the cows.

It was just after the War, and I was night duty Station Officer. It was about 10pm and everyone had left the station. A little old lady came in with her grand-daughter. She had lost her dog. We had a couple of stray dogs in the kennel at the back of the station. I took them out and they recognised one as their own.

They came back into the station and I commenced to take particulars. I asked the old lady if she had her dog licence with her. She said, 'I haven't got one.' I deliberately went into a fit of coughing and when I had finished I said, 'I didn't quite catch what you said. Did you say it was under six months old? Because if you did, you do not need a licence.'

She was just going to say something when her grand-daughter aged about nine or ten, nudged her with her elbow and said, 'Yes, that's right.' I told them to get a dog licence and that I would come round to their house and take particulars when I came back on day duty. As they were leaving the station, I heard the girl say to her grandma, 'He reminds me of Wilfred Pickles.'

We had a Sergeant George Kelland on the section. He had retired before the War, and had come back for the duration. He had a voice like a fog-horn and when he got upset his language was unprintable.

I purposely left the Dogs' Register open on the counter and when he came in he said, 'I see you have got rid of one of your dogs.' He glanced at the book, his face went red, and he said in a loud voice; 'What's this? Puppy under six months old!' I said, 'that's what the lady said, Sergeant.' I thought he was going to explode and he shouted, 'Let me tell you - that dog had a beard and side whiskers and was the grandfather of all grand-fathers!' There were peals of laughter from the PCs who had come in from their refreshments and were waiting in the next room to hear him blow his top.

I have a noteworthy connection with the Force. My brother-in-law James Rintoul served in the Met at the same time as myself 1930-55. My nephew Robert Rintoul retired this year after 30 years in S division. My nephew's son Sergeant Andrew Rintoul is at present attached to Wembley. My son, Chief Superintendent John Ledger retired from Chingford J Division not long ago,, after 30 years service.

Percy Ledger Ex PC 199T and 528

Tottenham Court Road in the Thirties

I slept in the Section House above Tottenham Court Road police station when I first joined the Met in 1930.

They were a fine crowd of fellows there. PC Bob Mumby was the caterer and we paid him 13 shillings a week, which included bed and cooked dinner every night. We provided our own breakfasts and teas.

PC Roger Casely was the Rip Van Winkle of the Section House. We finished night duty at 6am one Monday morning. I said to him: 'See you at 10 tonight,' but he replied, 'No, I'm on leave tonight, see you at 10 Tuesday.' He did not turn up for night duty on Tuesday and I was sent to find him - he was asleep in bed.

He insisted, when I woke him, that he was on leave that night but when I convinced him it was Tuesday night, he realised he had slept all day Monday, Monday night, all day Tuesday. Just over 40 hours.

PC Pocock was the best dressed man in the Section House. We had to be in by midnight and he had been cautioned by the night duty Inspector for coming in late. A couple of weeks later, he was late again. Instead of coming in by the front door and risking being caught again, he decided to climb over the back gate which was about 6ft 4in high with iron spikes on the top.

He had a brand new suit on and it got torn very badly on the iron spikes. The order was that the back gate be closed at midnight and locked with a large padlock. If we knew anyone was out, we used to just close the gate but not lock it until they were in.

I arrived at the scene just as he had freed himself off the spikes. He smelt like a brewery and when I pointed out to him that the gate was not locked, and he could have turned the handle and walked in, his language was unrepeatable.

Then there was PC Reggie Wray. We nicknamed him Beano because of his love for Heinz baked beans. It was the first really sweltering hot day since we arrived at Tottenham Court Road, having been on late turn. We joined the Job at the same time. I had been in bed for a short time when I woke up.

There was a horrible smell coming along the corridor outside my cubicle, like a decomposed body. Eventually I had to get up because of the smell. I went outside my cubicle and joined a number of other fellows who were opening doors and sniffing outside. We tracked down the smell to PC Wray's cubicle. It was his socks. He had horrible stinking feet in hot weather. He agreed to place his socks outside on the window ledge during hot weather.

A number of us in the Section House were very proud of our appetites. A couple of rashers of bacon, two fried eggs, tomatoes and fried bread was our usual breakfast. PC Mortimer (nicknamed Rudolf) was the undisputed champion with the largest appetite and he was very proud of it.

I had just cooked my breakfast one morning when he came into the kitchen and asked: 'Finished, Yorkie?' I said I had. This was just as well because he needed the whole range to cook his breakfast. He said, 'I feel real peckish this morning'. I'll never forget what he then cooked and ate for his breakfast. PC Bob Mumby was there and we both sat and watched with our mouths open.

He ate nine rashers of bacon, one tin of baked beans, half a pound of sausages, one tin of tomatoes, fried bread and a trimming of nine fried eggs all round the edge of his plate. He had been in the cook's kitchen and she had given him a large amount of bubble and squeak which he fried up and had on another large plate.

He was just sitting down to eat these two large platefuls when in walked the Deputy Assistant Commissioner. We all stood up and he said to PC Mortimer, 'Is that your dinner?' 'No sir, this is my breakfast,' he replied. Said the DAC, 'There's nothing wrong with your appetite, is there?' 'No, Sir,' said PC Mortimer, 'I have a good appetite.' 'I thought you had,' said the DAC, and walked out.

PC Mortimer polished off all that food, then finished off with a large tin of peaches. Needless to say, when he got married his wife stopped all those capers.

PC Walden was a great big fellow about 6ft 5in or more and on one occasion he was on point duty at Tottenham Court Road junction with Goodge Street. A man came up to him, height about 5ft 5in and said, 'I'm your Chief Constable.' PC Walden said, 'And I'm the King of Denmark, now bugger off, I'm busy.' The man in fact was the Chief Constable, Lt. Col. Carter. He got the SD Inspector out, who took PC Walden off the point and gave him a dressing down.

I can still hear PC Walden saying, 'How was I to know he was a policeman, he wasn't big enough. I thought he was a nutter!'

I was on night duty in Percy Street, a turning off Tottenham Court

Road, and it was about 4am. A man came along and said, 'There's an elephant on your beat in Tottenham Court Road.' He smelt of alcohol. I said, 'Is it a pink one?' and he said, 'No, it's a real one.' I walked him towards Tottenham Court Road and when I got to the junction, I nearly collided with the largest elephant I had seen in my life. He was walking along the pavement northwards all on his own. I could hardly believe my eyes.

We had learnt at training school how to stop a runaway horse but we hadn't done elephants. I don't mind admitting I was a bit scared to go near it. I started to follow it and I thought when I got level with the police station, I would nip inside and get them to ring the zoo at Regent's Park and try to get the elephant keeper down here.

Before I got to the station, PC Bill Gooding appeared on the other side of the road. He shouted, 'What you got, Yorkie?' and when I told him, he asked if I wanted a hand. 'Not half,' I said.

He was a very old policeman and had bad feet, so he had a job to catch up with the elephant. To my amazement, he caught hold of the elephant by its left ear and said, 'This way boy.'

He led it along Goodge Street, Charlotte Street, Rathbone Place, and into a large stable. The big doors which always had a large padlock had been pushed off their hinges and were lying on the ground. We put the doors back and we wedged them shut.

On another occasion I was on late turn Oxford Street patrol. I arrived at Oxford Circus the same time as the man on the beat, PC Darky Garnham. We passed the time of day and he suddenly spotted an old boy who, he told me, had a hobby of walking round the West End of London shaking hands with policemen, and when he let go of their hand, he always left half-a-crown there.

Darky said, 'I'll see him first at Regent Street, then you go on to Great Portland Street and wait until he arrives there. Keep him talking to enable me to walk up Regent Street and along Eastcastle Street and down to the corner of Winsley Street and I'll see him again. Then I'll keep him talking to enable you to see him at Wells Street and I'll see him at Berners Street and you'll see him at Newman Street.'

The old fellow arrived at Newman Street, very well dressed and all smiles. He shook hands with me again for the third time and I collected my third half-crown. He said, 'I've never felt so secure in all my life. A policeman on every street corner since I left Oxford Circus! You know, you boys all look alike to me.'

I never saw him again. When I told the chaps at the station, they all agreed that it was typical of old Darky Garnham.

Percy Ledger Ex PC 199T and 528

Private Schwartz, H Division

I recall in the 50s a young man by the name of Benny Schwartz, who lived with his parents on the borders of West Ham and Forest Gate. Mr Schwartz Senior owned residential property in that area, and being a good handyman was fully employed with the running repairs to these properties. Their house was a large, double-fronted detached affair on a corner, the back garden of which Mr Schwartz kept as a builder's yard.

Benny had always been interested in repairing and tinkering with radios. As a consequence, when he got his calling-up papers in the later stages of the war, he went into the Royal Corps of Signals. Now Benny's mind had always been on a bit of a knife edge and the rough and tumble of service life proved too much for him and he was in due course discharged as 'mentally unfit'.

He was unemployable, unless perhaps his father used him as his assistant in doing odd jobs. From time to time if Benny got too much for his parents he would go to Goodmayes Mental hospital as a voluntary patient. During his time on our patch he would call at either KW or KF with odd snippets of 'information' about suspicious persons or vehicles. There must be hundreds of such 'informants' scattered about the Metropolitan Police District at any one time. In the course of time Benny came to look upon himself as an 'undercover agent', code-name 'Private Schwartz of H Division'.

One afternoon when I was the observer on the area car 5K we had a call to the Schwartz household. Benny, in a fit of pique had taken a swing at his mother with a kitchen chair, missed, and chipped the enamel of the oven. This was the last straw for Mrs Schwartz, who wanted a break from his tantrums, if only for a week or two, so that she could recharge her batteries.

Benny showed us a radio that he was converting into a TV by cutting a rectangular hole in the front. He also proudly showed us his shoe box full of oddments: a comb, a fork, a pencil and an atom bomb, which to us looked more like a radio valve.

While the R/T driver was on the telephone getting the GP and the Mental Health Officer, Benny took me to the side wall of the garden where building material was stacked. This, according to Benny, constituted a dangerous structure since it caused the wall to bow slightly over the pavement and could fall on pedestrians. There was also a brick missing in the wall and he feared that persons could be sucked through.

When the doctor and the Mental Health Officer arrived they decided that Benny was to be taken to Goodmayes Hospital and an ambulance was called. Now on the last occasion that Benny had been forcibly taken to hospital, it had taken six men to get him into the ambulance. We did not want a repeat of that, so a hurried police conference was held to review the possibilities. Benny had also complained that he was due back-pay from the Commissioner.

In due course the ambulance arrived and Benny climbed gratefully into the back to be taken by 'undercover police ambulance' to Scotland Yard to get his back-pay. The ambulance attendants had of course been put in the picture and we later heard that by the time he arrived at the hospital all thoughts of back-pay had gone. The sight of old friends from his previous visits made him feel at home and he thanked the ambulance attendants.

Some little time after this incident I was transferred on promotion and did not have any further news of Benny.

John (Jan) Fillery, KW, JB

A Spot of Bother in the Rotherhithe Cells

Joe Rolfe spent the last few years of his service at the old Rotherhithe Police Station in Paradise Street, Rotherhithe.

It was an ideal situation for a Police Station, being where nobody could find it, midway between Jamaica Road and the Thames, where the Station Officer led a peaceful existence especially as very few of the locals drove cars so he was not pestered by drivers producing documents or reporting accidents.

The incident I have in mind concerned Joe one peaceful Sunday morning in early spring. It was one of those days when the office fire was still lit even though it was turning out to be a warm day.

Joe was dozing with his feet up on his desk in the tiny cubbyhole known by the grand title of 'The Front Office'. The sun streamed in through the open window and Joe's only worry was if his relief was going to be on time or not.

His reverie was rudely shattered by the entrance of a very indignant, well spoken customer. We got them occasionally at Rotherhithe when some West End toff liked to show his smart friends how well he knew London by taking them for lunch at the Angel or some other riverside pub.

To say this gent was indignant was understating it somewhat: he was livid.

'I think it's disgraceful. I've heard of such things but didn't believe it of the Metropolitan Police. I shall be contacting my MP and will inform the National newspapers. You should be ashamed of yourselves.'

Joe came down to earth with a bump. 'Hang on, Hang on, what are you going on about?'

'What am I going on about?' said the gent. 'I'm going on about that poor man in your cells being beaten up by your thugs. They are beating him unmercifully.'

Joe was bemused. He didn't know anyone was down in the cells let alone beating up prisoners. Agreed, if anything happened in the cell area, the public would hear it as they passed down the side of the station and the cell passage windows, which were open in view of the warm day, adjoined the footway in Paradise Street; but the cell keys were still on their hook on the key board above the fireplace.

Our indignant gent was in the meantime leaving the station muttering something about not hearing the last of this, etc.

Joe came to abruptly, he grabbed the keys off the hook with one hand, the gent by the scruff of his neck with the other, and propelled him across the entrance hall to the Charge Room saying 'Oh no you don't, you're coming with me to see for yourself.' 'No no no, I don't want to see it, the sight of blood makes me faint.'

Joe unlocked the cell passage door and it was immediately apparent that some dastardly deed was taking place. The sound of blows and screams of agony echoed down the passage.

Joe went pale. He belatedly tried to get rid of the complainant saying 'Leave this to me sir, I'll sort it out'. But chummy was having nothing of it and before Joe could do anything he had ducked under his arm and dashed down the passage 'Now I've come this far, I'll see it out.'

There were two prisoners in the cells. Young seamen arrested the

Saturday night for Drunk and Disorderly, and if the truth was known, Joe had probably forgotten about them.

They must have been bored to tears languishing down there all morning, so one had his mattress up against the cell door and was thumping hell out of it. 'Take that you B.... '(wallop) 'and that, and that.' (Bang, bang, bang). His mate in the next cell was crying out for mercy. 'Don't hit me any more, I can't take it, I confess, I confess.'

After a rather embarrassed gentleman (let's face it, his heart was in the right place) had slunk away from the station and Joe had bailed the seamen, it occurred to him that he should have got the man's name and address as there was no knowing how many other members of the public had heard it all. As it happened there were no repercussions but one can see how stories of police brutality could get started.

Bryan Billings, M, P, R

On the Plank

Those at Cannon Row (AD) police station during the Fifties performed duty at the official residence of the Foreign Secretary. At the time it was 17 protection post.

It was one of several armed posts at AD at that time. We carried a Berretta automatic in a shoulder holster.

Many famous people have lived there over the years, before it became the official residence of the Foreign Secretary. Lord Kitchener resided there before his death in the 1914/18 war.

We were posted at the door, and around the railings as far as the King George VI statue overlooking The Mall. In fact we kept our vigil from just inside the front door, to the left. We sat on a plank of wood, laid across a sink, with our feet on a chair. It meant having to twist the body left to peer down Carlton House Terrace. Uncomfortable it was, but dry and warm.

When the Foreign Secretary was about to leave, or arrive, we stood at the door. Most duty officers and Sergeants walked up from Waterloo Place, so we had time to get out and meet them. Nobody bothered so long as you were seen to be alert.

One Inspector at AD at the time was Insp Barchard, a sagacious chap and well liked. He would arrive, and the following exchange usually took place. A salute, and 'All correct Sir'. His reply without fail was 'Alright old boy', a brief chat and he was away.

The Foreign Secretary had a flat within the building. The reception rooms and furniture were very fine, befitting the Foreign Secretary's residence. When a reception was to be held there, we hoped some 'fare' might be put our way. The only culinary delight I ever had was a bag of Smiths crisps and a glass of neat gin. It was handed to me by a uniformed flunkey, with almost regal ceremony.

On night duty, Ron or Ginger would retire into the building to study the Wall St Journal or some such reading matter. We perched on the plank, and gazed down the gas-lit road. As the night dragged on the lamps seemed to start moving. Time for a stroll around the railings.

The Savage Club was nearby. It was frequented by actors and theatrical people. Charlie Burgess was called away from the post to eject a very tipsy thespian causing trouble in the Club. The Foreign Secretary was abroad, so why not?

He was taken to the top floor by Committee members, and the drunken member was pointed out. It seemed he was a Donald Woolfit character, and didn't warm to Charlie. After the usual proceedings had been taken care of, he was asked to leave. No, he wouldn't. Charlie took hold of his arm. In a voice that had been heard in theatres nationwide he boomed out 'Release me at once Sir.'

Then started the long journey down flights of stairs; and as Charlie related, on each landing, a clutch of members stood, each with glasses of whisky and cigars. As he struggled past, comments like 'Disgraceful!' 'Scandalous!' 'Bounder!' and 'It's Glasgow Empire that's done this to him.' At intervals punctuated by lines of Shakespeare and 'My Solicitor knows the Commissioner,' the descent was made.

On the final landing, a voice called 'Lock him in the ladies lavatory to cool off.' With that the drunk eased his struggle, drew himself up and said 'How dare you, Sir.' He then calmly walked down the stairs and out of the Club. A cab drew up and he was away. The thespian was off the stage.

As I mentioned, it was an armed post, and at that time we had a number of armed posts at AD. Also we had some 'accidental discharges'. The firearms training then was indeed basic, and the handling of weapons poor. I had been a small-arms instructor for part of my Army service, and saw the shortcomings. Training did however improve greatly through the Sixties, as I continued to attend firearms courses.

One night a PC fired off a round accidentally near the 'plank'.

Remarkably, the bullet went through a four inch gap, where the viewing window was open at the top, and carried on skyward. Ginger was 'resting' and leapt out of his chair with fright, rushed out and saw the smoking gun.

The Duty Officer was sent for, and Insp Barchard was soon at the scene. He listened most intently to the PCs explanation, then he pursed his lips and declared 'Alright old boy, a few lines in the OB but do be more careful.'

Next day, late turn, I was sitting on the 'plank' and saw Ginger walking along Carlton House Terrace. As he drew near, he took out a white handkerchief, and proceeded to wave it slowly above his head. I almost fell off my perch with laughter. Those tourists nearby who stared never knew.

A Jackson, AD, AH, CTS, LK, TDM, TDP, TDR, B10

Swifting them in

I have often wondered if I hold the UK and World record for the number of arrests in ten minutes: 11.

In the 1930s the Fascists (black shirts) and the Communists (red shirts), inflamed by the Spanish Civil War, were deadly enemies and the cause of much trouble to us, not only because of the frequency of their meetings, but also because of their rowdyism.

Now it so happened a meeting of the Communists had been sanctioned by police in Comyn Road, at the junction with St John's Road, Clapham Junction and a meeting of the Fascists in Comyn Road at the junction with Spencer Park, only about 400 yards apart; and whilst most of the late turn relief had been posted to control the Fascists, I was the only uniform policeman deputed to the Red Shirts.

This meeting was reasonably orderly until one of the yobbos in the crowd recognised PC Honnicut who was in civvies to note potential trouble-makers, who had once been arrested by him for some offence. This miscreant set about Honnicut, ably assisted by friends, so I waded to his rescue, knocked off the trouble-maker and proceeded to march him along St Johns Road and up Lavender Hill to the nick, carefully keeping to the tram-lines and followed by a goodly mob, as the Black Shirts had by now joined in the fun. It was quite an unruly mob and I heard many queries about the validity of my parents' marriage, subtle suggestions that I might beautify the local cemetery and many things that I did not know, and did not want to know. I had to walk some 800 yards clutching my prisoner, followed by the motley crowd and I was able to note the faces of the most aggressive yobs.

The news of my coming had gone ahead of me and the doors of the nick were half shut (there were two doors) so I was able to throw my prisoner into the nick, then turn around and grab the two nearest yobs, invite them to enter the portals of the nick then turn and get another two and so on until there were no more volunteers. I was somewhat shocked that I had arrested 11 yobs in total, but luckily three of my mates from Battersea Section House coming on for night duty agreed to take two each whilst I had five allocated to me, a more reasonable amount to present to the Magistrate at South Western court the next morning.

Luckily, they all pleaded guilty, justice was meted out in the time honoured way and that was that. I often wonder what would happen today under similar circumstances. I reckon I would still be breaking rocks in Dartmoor.

Happy days! For me the traditional method of nicking the blokes doing all the shouting always paid off. But in those days the copper on the beat was always right, and it's a great pity that things have now changed so that the copper is nearly always wrong, and to make matters worse, often police from a Force antagonistic to the Met are chosen to make enquiries.

Dick Brown

The Hackney Elephant

In 1952 there was a PC at Hackney by the name of Joe Archer, quite a character, I assure you. The number of stories concerning this PC, and some of the antics he got up to, are legion - and many unprintable!

It was a nice bright sunny Sunday morning when A relief paraded for early turn, then having been duly posted to our respective beats, off we went. I don't know what beat Joe had but he set off down the 'Narrow Way' of Mare Street when, coming up towards him (against the one-way system) was a man leading some elephants.

Now Joe was a very shrewd copper and he knew that elephants were not a common sight on the streets of Hackney on a Sunday morning. So he decided to investigate. Hardly a Secion. 66 'Stop', but well worth looking into. And it appeared that these elephants were part of an act appearing at the Hackney Empire, and amongst the herd, flock or what-ever a collection of elephants were called, was a cute little baby; but even a baby elephant is difficult to pick up and cuddle.

Joe chatted the handler up and it was agreed that Joe could 'borrow' this baby, and off they went, round to the back yard which was literally just around the corner. Quite what he did with it when he got back into the station yard I don't know as I wasn't there at that time. Having parked his charge Joe went into the front office and approached SPS Peggie (who could be quite liverish at times, but then, couldn't we all at the end of two weeks early turn!) and, after a cursory 'All correct Sarge' asked if there was any string he could have, and was told he would find it in its usual place, the bottom drawer of the desk, Joe took the ball of fluffy parcel string, went out into the charge room and tied one end of it around the elephant's trunk.

Casually strolling back into the front office with the other end of the string in his hand, and with another 'All correct Sarge' he announced that he had found a stray animal. There is no doubt in my mind that Bill would have told him, pointedly and very firmly, just what he could do with his 'stray' and probably himself too! Not to be put off, Joe explained that had it been a horse, ass, mule or goat, he would have known what to do, but he insisted: 'Sarge, on the end of this string, I've got an elephant.'

Quite how the conversation went from there I don't know but Joe must have been sufficiently insistent that Bill got out of his chair, fol-lowed the piece of string into the Charge Room and, lo and behold, there was this grey, wrinkly-skinned real live genuine elephant, not of the giant economy size but very genuine.

About that time the old bush telegraph must have worked (no personal radios in those days), as within a few minutes the whole of the relief was back in the station. Then followed the 'photocall' with the elephant being 'charged', to be followed by the station officer being 'charged' by the elephant, wearing the appropriate headgear.

Fred White 138105, 204J/214G

Pink Elephants

It was an autumn Sunday in the late 1950s. The Territorial Army were holding a parade in Croydon when medals were to be presented by the Lord Lieutenant of the County. PC William (Mac) McIlwain and I were sent as motorcycle escorts from DT4 to the TA depot where the Ld. Lieutenant was being entertained to lunch.

On arrival, we were informed that the guest of honour had lunched too well and was three parts to the wind. He appeared, just able to stand, and insisted he would drive himself. My colleague and I debated whether to let him do so, and were persuaded to let him drive.

We set off at tremendous speed, the ADC in a small car behind unable to keep up. The escort had turned into a pursuit.

Now, the day before this event, a circus had arrived at Mitcham, and that afternoon they were holding a parade of the elephants. Old colleagues will know that, as one approaches Mitcham railway station there is a complete 90 degree left turn. As the car turned the corner, the driver was confronted by a line of elephants - and his face had to be seen to be believed. I'm not sure whether it was the 'Pink Elephant' syndrome or a 'road to Damascus' conversion but the escort continued to Croydon at a steady 30mph, where we arrived over half an hour late, but without further incidents.

Dennis Picco, 131210 W, DT4, CTS, TD8, CO

Life in the Saddle

I had a good laugh reading about a colleague's attempts at rope climbing in a back issue of *London Police Pensioner* magazine because I had exactly the same problem on an Army course, and it also reminded me of my pathetic attempts at horse riding - pathetic and strange because my father and others in the family were at home with horses and loved them.

In India during the war prior to going into Burma I was sent on a jungle training course in the Central Provinces and anyone wishing to learn to ride could put their names down. It was part of a mule management course, and I thought it would be useful later on.

Running about the camp loose were a number of local ponies, all skin and bone like most Indian animals, and I thought riding them would be a simple matter. In the local gharries (horse taxis) it was difficult to get them to walk, let alone to trot, they were so starved. I discussed it with a friend, a PC from Glasgow, who said there was nothing to it, and so my name went down.

On the next Monday morning we fools fell in and marched away for quite a mile; I was getting a little puzzled and suspicious, when we rounded a clump of bamboo and there before my eyes stood eight of the biggest and fattest animals I had seen for a long time. My heart sank when the bow-legged ex-cavalry Captain came on the scene and gave us a five minute talk. 'Right, get mounted,' was the order, and I moved to my allotted horse.

I am sure mine was limbering up for the Grand National, because as soon as I took hold of the reins it moved away sideways, and we ended up going round in circles.

The beast was showing the whites of its eyes, and had already made up its mind we were not going to get on together. Eventually I did manage to get one foot in the stirrup and tried very hard to get on its back, and after several attempts with a terrific heave I did get up and promptly fell off on the other side. 'Bow-legs' helped me up, and I knew what he was thinking, 'We've got a right one here.' All the others had by then mounted and were waiting and watching.

I felt as if I was sitting on a huge barrel of energy. I could feel the power of the beast beneath me, but I tried not to show my fear, and soon realised how high off the ground I was.

We moved off walking in line astern round this stockade, and I was pleased to see the timbers were eight feet high. Every time 'Bow-legs' told me to hold the reins with both hands and leave the pommel alone I felt like falling, and I could read the thoughts of the beast beneath me: 'I'll soon get this idiot off'.

My animal was so well fed and full of energy that it soon got fed up with walking in a line and began to close up on the horse in front and as it did so this horse swished its tail across the face of mine, which threw it's head back smartly and I fell off the hind quarters and landed under the head of the next horse which thankfully stopped. Everybody laughed except 'Bow-legs' and me. How I finished the next hour is just a blank in my memory.

The next lesson was with the mules, quite large animals from the Argentine, and thankfully we did not have to ride them. I suppose that would have been impossible even for 'Bow-legs'. Mules have to be handled with great care, because, unlike horses, they kick with front and back legs.

One lesson was to harness the animal with a special saddle to carry two large metal water tanks, one each side. We got this saddle on after about 20 minutes' struggle, and we began to gently lift the full water tank on to the animal on one side, with two of us holding the reins.

As soon as some of the water spilled out on to the animal's side, it charged off, galloping round and round until it had dislodged the water tank. In the afternoon we had to learn how to lead the laden mules along narrow tracks and the beast I had would persist in clipping the heel of my boots, and I would walk a little faster, and then it would happen all over again.

I tried one more morning at horse riding, but when one animal threw its rider and dragged him along with one foot trapped in the stirrup I decided horse riding was not for me and reluctantly came to the obvious conclusion that horses are not my favourite animal. Miraculously, the trainee dragged along was only bruised.

Geoffrey Taylor, H, DT7

A Dignified Retreat

I was sent as aid to A District, near Parliament Square, on the occasion of Princess Margaret's wedding.

We had been lining the route since about 5.30am and the hour of the procession was fast approaching when round the corner came Commander 'Cods Eyes' Osborne on his sorely-tried nag. He was accompanied by a young apprehensive-looking mounted PC to whom he was heard to remark, 'Ere, cop 'old of the bleedin' orse. I gotter get down, me piles is killin' me.'

The PC dutifully took the reins and Cods Eyes dismounted with a grunt of relief. At a loss for something to do, he decided to re-arrange the spacing between all the officers standing at the kerb. In so doing he shifted me three paces to the right in from two diminutive cockney women who had spent the whole night on the pavement in order to secure a front row view of the procession.

One immediately screamed, 'Oi, wassergame mate, we've been here all night, Ow d'yer fink we can see through this great lummox?' She promptly made a lunge at the great man with her rolled umbrella, which caught him a glancing blow before she could be restrained.

'Orlright,' said Cods Eyes, 'Put 'im back where 'e was, missus,' and retired from the scene, deciding that discretion was the better part of valour. He tried to make a dignified retreat but the ferule of his dress sword striking sparks on the road surface at every step was hardly conducive to that end.

I am sure that Cods Eyes Osborne will be long remembered as one of the brightest characters in the annals of the Met Police.

Bill Knapp

The Sport of Kings

'Cods Eyes Osborne, yes, he was a good man. I was on duty in town on some ceremonial occasion and standing in a group when the Commander came bobbing up, with the plume shaking in his helmet, dismounted (practically falling off), asking, 'Anybody got a fag paper?' I obliged. I have never seen such a figure on horseback - and the names he called that poor horse!

On the subject of street book makers, a pitch was usually situated in an alley with a 'look out' at each end to give the warning 'heads up' on the approach of any stranger. The bookie would then dive into any house whose front door faced the alley. I remember one ploy to catch a difficult one - George Bucknole dressed up as a priest complete with dog collar! Also, the Superintendent of M Division would take a short cut through this alley to have his lunch at a restaurant and he was always in plain clothes. The 'heads up' was given at first but after several days they assumed that he was an ordinary business man until his hand felt their shoulders. I remember the SPS saying, when he was charged, 'You should be honoured to be arrested by somebody so high up.'

On another occasion, I saw some men giving a woman something in the busy Borough Market. As I walked down the Market they all dispersed quietly but the woman, who was 30 years old, very attractive and well-spoken, was very distressed when I said I was arresting her for Street Betting. There were cries from the porters of 'Leave her alone Guvnor'. But I told her I would not hold her arm if she just walked ahead of me. On passing the public toilets she asked if she could use them but I refused because all the slips would have gone down the pan. When searched by Matron, all the slips were down her bloomers. She told me at Court this was her first week on the pitch as her father the book maker was ill and she had taken two weeks holiday from nursing.

I now reflect how harmless it was, working men having a bet - those better off could have an account without risk of arrest. The time given to curbing street betting was more than that given to crime. These days one wonders what it was all about, as I and no doubt many more, enjoy watching racing on TV, after having placed my bet legally with William Hill.

Jack Sadler, PC 778, M ,T.

Mad Dogs & Brockleymen

We have all experienced the first time we took action in one form or another: the first arrest; the first accident, etc. My story is of my experience when as a rookie I was ordered to bring to Brockley station an allegedly mad dog.

I had never handled a dog in my life. My only experience of dogs were of those who nipped at my ankles as I roller-skated to school in the East End of London. Off I went, suitably equipped with leather gauntlets and a pole with a string loop with which to lasso the dog.

On my arrival at the location I found a very angry mongrel cornered in a front garden with his hackles well up, lips curled back over menacing teeth, and growling. While reviewing the situation, as Fagin would have said, and wondering how I was going to get near enough to the dog to put the said lasso over its head without getting bitten, a soft voice behind me said: 'Leave this to me, chum.'

By coincidence the Battersea Dogs Home van was passing and the driver had sized up my dilemma and had stopped. He went into action and stooped down in front of the dog saying very softly to it, 'Come on mate,' all the time getting nearer and nearer. Then suddenly his right hand went over the dog's head and grabbed him by the hackles. He lifted the dog bodily and, twisting it round, placed it between his legs where he gripped it. He then struck it smartly across the snout.

The dog became very calm and the driver dropped it to the ground and said, 'Come on mate,' whereupon the dog followed the driver into the back of the dog van. I thanked the driver who left me flabbergasted. That was in 1937 and I had learned a valuable lesson. When dealing with a dog, show it who is master.

Bert Kennard

The Horse in the Fulham Charge Room

Dave Dellar was not the only one in the Job at that time who had a certificate of sanity - we had one Inspector Meek at Walham Green who had a similar certificate. This is a tale told to me by an old Sergeant and he assured me that it was true: Ted Scott, (Uncle Ted to us young PCs at Walham Green Police Station immediately after the war) told me about the night before the war at the old North Fulham nick, long since demolished and replaced by a block of flats.

It was night duty when a PC came into the office and told the Station Officer he had found a horse wandering along Lillie Road, not an unusual happening as most of the North End Road traders lived in the area, in little streets like Lillie Walk, and most had a horse and cart to get to and from Brentford Market.

The horse was tied up in the Station Yard, details entered in the book and the PC returned to his beat. Some time later the owner of the horse came into the office and said that his horse had left its stable and soon identified the one in the yard as his.

He paid the 'Greenyard Fee' of one shilling (5p) and went to lead the horse out but the Station Officer discovered that the gates were locked and the keys were missing. The station was searched but no keys to fit the lock were found and by this time the trader was getting upset because he would be late getting to the market, so it was decided to take the horse out through the Charge Room and through the front door.

The steps up to the Charge Room were the first obstacle and once inside the Charge Room, like all prisoners, the horse didn't like it and started to kick out. The charge desk, one of the old high ones, was kicked over, and a bit chipped out of the walls. Fire buckets were overturned and some floor boards damaged. So much noise woke the resident Inspector who appeared in pyjamas, uniform jacket and cap demanding to know what all the fuss was about (he soon found out on seeing the mess).

The horse was finally lead out through the front door, after causing more minor damage on the way. By this time the early turn were arriving and seemed to be enjoying the joke, and the night duty started to return to be paraded off. The PC who found the horse was asked if he had anything in his pockets and of course the missing keys were pulled out of the depths.

A hurried talk between the Inspector, the night duty Station Officer and the early turn Duty Officer and Station Officer was held before the Night duty were dismissed and the early turn posted. Both reliefs were paraded and told that the damage had to be made good before the Sub Divisional Inspector made his usual visit during the morning.

Both reliefs were sent home and told to return at once with saws, wood, plaster and paint, while some remained and started clearing up the mess in the charge room and the passage. For the next two hours the nick resounded to the efforts of the PCs while the repairs were carried out, which according to Ted were expertly done, even to staining the floor and charge desk with sundry ink blots etc.

Nothing was said when the Sub paid his visit and nothing was ever recorded other than 'One horse found wandering, One shilling fee paid.'

Reg Humphries, BW, DT5

The Downfall of Flannel Foot

Among some old papers, I have found a cutting from the *Daily Telegraph* in December 1987, recalling a report 50 years earlier (Dec 1937) of the trial at Middlesex Sessions of a man claiming to be the legendary 'Flannel Foot' who for some five years had plagued the public - and particularly the Met Police - by his almost weekly depredations as house breaker or burglar in the outer London suburbs.

The eventual arrest and prosecution of this man was the result of a concerted exercise by a team of detectives set up purely for this purpose. At the time some details of the team and its operation were leaked in the Force but I believe that a true and detailed description of the exercise and the officers involved, without the aid of modern electronic or telephone communications, makes very interesting reading.

'Flannel Foot' had become a thorn in the flesh of the force. For months PCs in some number were detached from night duty at inner stations and transported to newly-built outer suburbs to give added cover in the supposed danger areas, but with no result. The eventual arrest and prosecution was the result of a concerted effort by a team of detectives set up purely for that purpose. The leaders, I believe were DI Duncan and DS Roberts, from C Dept, with an unspecified numbers of DCs.

After much probing they at last came up with a suspect and learned that on a certain date he was expected to enter London - I think by coach - and pay a visit to a lady friend. The suspect was seen to arrive at the bus station and was followed to an address in Royal Crescent, Notting Hill. From there he was under full surveillance. With the lady friend he was followed to a greyhound racing track where he bet and appeared to lose - fairly heavily, suggesting a possible shortage of funds and possibly an inducement to house breaking to recoup.

Full surveillance was maintained. Suspect was seen to leave his address and was followed to the Underground where he caught a very late train to Eastcote, being followed at different distances by the several appointed officers. He left Eastcote station and headed into a quiet residential area - now around midnight, with 'tails' in attendance, but due to a sudden heavy fog he was lost.

The officers concerned then all retreated to the vicinity of the underground station keeping watch all night, and shortly before the time for the first train into London the suspect loomed out of the fog and was immediately detained and subsequently charged with being found by night in possession of house breaking implements etc.

The newspaper cutting gives details of his trial and sentence. Henry Vickers, 49, of Holland Park pleaded guilty to six housebreaking charges and was sentenced to five years penal servitude.

Prosecuting, Mr Christmas Humphreys said that the accused had never used violence nor frightened a single person.

My interest in the matter, and reason for keeping the newspaper cutting was just slightly more than 'general'. In November '37 I was doing a turn as Sergeant on the T Division Q car.

On parading at Ealing at 9am, I was informed that Flannel Foot was in custody and due to appear at 10am at Uxbridge court. I considered it sufficiently important to take my team out of the Division just to get a sighting of this notorious character. So we drove to Uxbridge court, and pulled into the rear car park just as the prison van arrived.

We saw the prisoner marched from the van to the rear door of the court but were then informed by a court officer that, on strict orders from Scotland Yard, only officers having cases were to attend the court. But I was left with the impression that this terrible criminal looked like a quite respectable middle-aged member of the public, maybe a plumber or similar craftsman, whose very appearance might have diverted the suspicion of any patrolling PC.

Roland Swanborough

Getting at the Creep

During my years at West End Central as a Detective Constable, I was involved in a case of prostitutes stealing client's wallets; a crime known as 'getting at the creep'.

In 1943 we were getting a spate of these offences. The victim's clothing was always strategically placed on a chair near the door for the attention of the second girl or creeper. Very often pieces of newspaper cut to the size of bank notes would be put back into the wallet with a genuine note on top and at the bottom, in case chummy had a quick look after the fun and games.

In the event of his discovering the theft, the girl responsible had of course left the premises, while the first one was full of concern and commiseration: 'Whoever could have done such a thing darling?'

Invariably the victim was unable to locate the premises, being a stranger to London, but they did describe a wooden flight of stairs to a first floor room. The room had no electric light, but several candles on the mantelpiece and a washstand. The victims came from all walks of life, businessmen from Wales and the Midlands, there was even a Polish priest who lost £200 - he was on his way to a Mission in Africa!

I was working with DC (son of a clergyman) Pierce Butler, and we set out to try and find this room by systematic door-to-door enquiries in Soho. On the second day - Eureka! - we found a wooden flight of stairs and on the first floor was the room with the candles, washstand and an old double bed, No 70 Berwick Street. Adjoining was a second empty room with a communicating door into the first, hinges nicely oiled for quiet opening, and on a shelf above was a stack of newspapers cut to the size of bank notes.

We had the stage, now we awaited the players. That night at 10pm we concealed ourselves in the basement, after having bored a hole in the door of the back room. Shortly after 11 o'clock we heard the sounds of approaching footsteps, and in came two girls and two men, into the room upstairs.

About three minutes later, in came the third girl, the 'creeper', up the stairs on tiptoe into the back room. We removed our shoes and crept up after her. Laughter and other noises were coming from the front room, an eye to the hole bored in the door revealed the 'creeper' opening the communicating door into the front room.

We gave her a few seconds and then quietly entered, unheard and unobserved. There were the two men and two girls performing acrobatics on the double bed, while the third was busy extracting notes from a wallet! She suddenly looked up and her mouth fell open with astonishment, and she stood there petrified.

Fun and games were still going on with the other players, so I called out 'Right, break it up, the law has arrived.' It was like a video still, deathly silence, then a hurried un-tangling of limbs. The two men were asked to inspect their wallets, and much to their surprise found their wages were missing. The money was recovered from the 'creeper' and when the men were told we were arresting the girls and they would all have to accompany us to West End Central they were aghast at the prospect of going to Court. They were in fact two young reporters employed by a well-known tabloid newspaper!

My suggestion that they now had a wonderful first-hand story for their next edition was not favourably received.

Off the record, the three girls admitted they had had a good run, and remembered the £200 they got from the Polish priest, but they declined to have any of the previous thefts taken into consideration when they pleaded guilty the following morning before Mr Sanbach at Marlborough

Street Court, and were each sentenced to two months imprisonment.

It was not often that arrests would be made for this type of offence, for various reasons, and I would imagine this must be a unique occasion when two police officers stood and actually watched the performance. In those days I remember there were four squads of CID officers at West End Central, under the direction of DS Cyril Green, DS Bert Sparks, DS Harry Miller and DS Alfie 'Iron Duke' Hymus. Happy days, exciting days!

Deryck Stanley

Your Sins will Find you Out

One morning in 1943, when stationed at West End Central, I had a case at Bow Street, and on my arrival there I learned my case was to be heard in Court No 1. When I entered this Court I saw two rather attractive young women sitting in the Dock, and a male civilian was just entering the Witness Box. He read the oath in a strong American accent after which he was told by the Magistrate to give his evidence in his own words, and as far as I can remember it went like this - 'About 9 o'clock last night your worship I came out of the Regent Palace Hotel into the blackout and I stood on the pavement a couple of minutes to let my eyes get used to the darkness. Almost immediately I was approached by prisoner No 1, who said to me, 'Hello dearie, would you like a nice time?' I said, 'Sure. Why not?' She took me by the arm and led me round a couple of blocks and then into an apartment on the first floor of a building in what I now know to be Old Compton Street.

'She took me into a bedroom where she told me to take off my clothes and placed them on a chair by the door. She also undressed and got into the bed where I joined her. No sooner were we laid down then she pulled the clothes over my head, so I pushed them back, but she pulled them over me again. When I pushed them back again I noticed prisoner No 2 taking my wallet from my jacket pocket. I shouted, 'You bastard. You've stolen my wallet' and I jumped out of bed and chased her down the stairs into the street, shouting, 'Stop thief.' Some distance along the street she was stopped by a police officer and I caught up with them. I then told the Officer what had happened, and during this time a number of people had collected round us. I then became aware of some tittering going on amongst them and it was then that I realised I had no clothes on.'

The case was remanded, but I later learned that the two women were convicted and received prison sentences.

Cyril G. Green

The Incredible Adventure of Moby Dick

I joined MD in April 1935 and as my previous occupation was deep sea fisherman, as a whalerman I was immediately called 'Moby Dick', usually just 'Moby'. The Section House at Long Lane was full and we were sent to private digs.

On Derby Day in June I was late turn, it was very hot, and I passed by our alley in Great Dover Street. After about five minutes, a man approached holding a hand of bananas and said to me 'What do you fancy for the big one?' I said, 'I don't know anything about horses but I did hear my landlady say she was going to do such-and-such a horse.' He then held the bananas into my view with a 10/- note between the bunch and said, 'I will put that on for you.' Before I could reply, he walked quickly away.

I saw the reason why on the approach of the late turn; Inspector, a Mr Dean, who said to me, 'Do you know who that man was?' I replied that I didn't. He then told me that he was a Bookies Runner and I was standing near the pitch and no business would be transacted, since no punter would go near a policeman. He then told me this had happened to him when he was a young PC and if another supervisory officer had seen the two of us talking, it was possible that I would have been sacked.

I should point out that at that time, bookies received higher police priority than street crime. The parade sheet displayed a large map of their patches, with flags to denote their last arrest. No uniform could get past the look-outs, so two old PCs were employed in plain clothes to keep the flags up to date.

The fines were then £10 first arrest, to £50, then six months inside. Even two pounds was a lot of money in those days, with beer 4d a pint and cigarettes 10 for 4d.

However, returning to my encounter in Great Dover Street, I was furious to think this man could have got me the sack, for what I considered to be such a triviality. At my home town of Great Yarmouth, placing bets was openly done, the Mayor was the William Hill and even as a boy my mother would give one a piece of paper with a win inside (6d each way) on the Grand National and Derby, which I would take to the Public House and give to the landlord. Two or three men were then employed to collect all the bets from cafes and pubs. Thus I had no doubt skipped the Street Betting Act of 1906 in the Information Book.

The sack in those days entailed unemployment (no Social Security) and after the struggle I had to enter the Force, having no education, I was furious and as I walked down Great Dover Street towards the junction, I had an idea.

Pickfords had a depot nearby and large vans arriving from the direction of the Old Kent Road had to slow down. As one did so, I jumped and held onto the tail board, which was folded up. My feet would then have been about two feet from the ground. Those heavy vans didn't travel very fast in those days. I then dropped off and had a momentary glimpse of a crowd of men handing bets to a man in a long overcoat (this was in June). The punters walked away quickly in all directions and as 'overcoat' did the same, I put my hand on his shoulder and told him he was being arrested for street bookmaking. He was appalled, saying, 'The Guvnor is not going to like this.' The station officer, when I told him the charge, left and returned with the SD Inspector Mr Taylor. For this particular offence, the person had to be charged before he could be searched. I knew he was loaded with silver, from the jangle in the raincoat pockets. (I should add that officers from the Yard's Special squad were on the ground. I was amazed one day when I saw a training school Inspector dressed as a butcher on a butcher's bicycle).

The search revealed numerous betting slips and money. I could then see the Inspector was really puzzled and he said to me, 'Go back to the Section House, get into plain clothes and try to arrest the man who takes up his pitch.' I duly obliged.

I was a good runner in those days and had no difficulty in running on the blind side of a van and saw that once again among the crowd, the previous lookout was now taking the bets. In their minds, the police already had their body. My next prisoner was amazed: 'You cant do this, Guvnor the uniform man has just taken Bill.'

The next morning at Tower Bridge Court, the look of amazement when they both realised that I was the same officer! The first was fined £20 and the other on his fifth time £50. A big man, no doubt the boss, threatened me with violence, saying, 'They don't keep you in the Force on crutches,' I was very wary after that, while off duty.

Nearing the end of my probationary period, I had to attend DAC 4 District Office to be confirmed. He was amazed that I had seven arrests of street bookmakers while in uniform and asked why and how. He said if I were to keep up the good work I would go far - little did he know that this would not be possible.

There was never a dull moment with all the characters there at the time at the Borough: Norman the Butcher, Micky Dave, Barney Saunders and many more. There was Barclays Brewers, entrance Park Street, three knocks on the gate at any time and the Lodge keeper would slide the panel back and say either 'No' or 'Yes'. If 'Yes', then one went in for a pint of beer at any time in the 24 hours, if 'No', one wandered off for about 10 minutes knowing that the Inspector or Sergeant was within. The procedure was that one drank the pint or two straight down and then went out of the entrance at Southwark Bridge Road, so never the twain met.

It was said that this was the result of an incident many years before when one of the Barclay's lives had been saved by a policeman when he had been attacked by footpads at Bankside. And this Barclay had left in his will the proviso that a tankard of their best beer would always be available to the policemen. How true this was I do not know, but I do know that four or five of the harder drinkers would be there about 6am, then board the coach for our patch, half cut. Those same characters would come off night duty and wait for the canteen to open, usually about 6.15am. What a life poor Alfie the canteen steward endured, he most likely had not left until about 11pm the previous night. They would then play darts and drink beer until about 10am, dusty night duty uniform showing clearly in the sunshine.

No doubt many remember what a job it was to get a cup of tea out of the canteen, especially at race meetings or any function which they attended - it was all pints, and if somebody did ask for a cup of tea, there was hush and heads turned, especially the steward who had to get the urn going.

Ginger Cooper, said to be a veterinary surgeon who had failed his final exam, and who then joined the police, every other day had a horse cruelty charge, especially Railway horses. The horse was brought to the station, tethered in the Yard, then they had to get one of the lads from the Section House to walk it to the Green Yards at Tower Bridge.

Millwall Football Ground about 1936. The Wall versus Derby County - they were then in the Third Division and Derby in the First. In this semi-final of the FA Cup, Millwall won. the pitch was invaded and all of us at the side of the pitch were swept to the middle. After the enthusiasm had died down, 12 police helmets were found to have been stolen. To my knowledge, no violence or arrest. Just a report to make us pay for them.

I also recall Mother White's doss house for the dregs of the prostitutes from the West End who mostly worked the boys up from the country at Borough market which opened at midnight, near the grounds of Southwark Cathedral.

Young officers would usually be at court every day off after night duty, mostly with drunks, especially from a drink called Red Biddy. Things got so bad that the Magistrate at Tower Bridge advocated its being banned, which happened shortly afterwards.

Mr Campion was the Magistrate, and woe betide anyone brought before him who had even touched an officer - he always referred to us as 'my officers.' In those days, officers could sit in the Court in all domestic cases and I remember one afternoon a young fellow on a paternity order was in Court and the Magistrate wanted to know from the mother where the child was conceived. She said, 'On an empty costermonger's barrow in the railway arch at the end of Waterloo Station. I am not the only one. I know of two others like me.' Mr Campion jumped up from his seat and shouted out to the defendant, 'You beast, you animal! I find this case proved, put him below until we find out about those other unfortunate girls.'

There was a religious station sergeant called Bill Guiney and a station joker, a PC called 'Sailor'. Bill was Station Duty and Sailor arrested Elsie Manners, a prostitute with very large 'boobs'. Bill entered the Charge Room and asked what he had got, then went into the front office to write the Charge Sheet out. In the meantime, Sailor kidded Elsie to strip off as he thought the SPS would love to see her beautiful body. She duty obliged.

Enter Bill, who saw this naked woman before him and covered his eyes with his hands saying, 'Get a horse blanket to cover that woman.' When covered and being charged, she produced one of those large breasts saying, 'Go on, have a feel Bill.' This was too much - he left the Charge Room and the business was completed by a PS.

Pay Parade was a ritual: SD Inspector at his desk flanked by his clerk, a PS at another desk to see the pay-sheet was signed correctly. No biros in those days, and few had a fountain pen, so one dipped the pen in the ink. As I was about to sign, a blob of ink fell on the pay-sheet across other names. The PS blotted it up and implying I had committed some terrible crime, told me to fill in the dreaded 728. I did not how to word the form, but an educated PC, Taffy Morris, who later became a Chief Constable in Wales, helped me out and the report read thus: In May 1935 at 2pm at Southwark Police Station, while signing the Pay Sheet, I inadvertently blotted same. I express my regret and promise to be more careful in the future. Result: an official caution. Unofficial: my next application for a change of leave was not approved.

Jack Sadler 5917

A Magnanimous Gesture

Once upon at time, not so many years ago, PCs patrolled singly, and stood the risk of being placed on the report if they were found by the PS or Inspector in the company of another PC without reasonable excuse. This was before the introduction of Panda cars, personal radios and community policing and when the only means of calling for help was three short sharp blasts on the whistle, or by phone from a newly-introduced Police Box. These were days when the copper was treated with respect by the man in the street who always addressed him as Sir and who was the first to fly to his assistance in times of strife - when the public were always happy that a PC was patrolling the High Street and when 'The Fuzz' and 'The Filth' were words only used by hardened villains and before the import of drugs. During these times there occurred the following incident for which I must first of all set the scene.

Imagine if you will, a quiet rural Station on the outskirts of the busy Metropolis. It is 1.30am on a hot summer night and the main body of the night duty relief are wending their way towards the Station for their respective refreshment periods. The hero of the forthcoming event is a young PC who, having passed the necessary tests, has been issued with a motor cycle, an innovation recently introduced, and on which he was expected to cover the whole Section, report frequently from police boxes and generally act as dogsbody for the Station officer.

Having been delayed by a ringing burglar alarm and a tardy key holder, he is winging his way back towards the Station and an overdue refreshment period. With his mind occupied by the forthcoming promotion examination, he suddenly realises that he has just passed a man carrying on his head two large boxes.

At this stage I should perhaps point out that this particular Section was liberally dotted with large greenhouses used for the production of tomatoes and cucumbers. Feeling that here was a 'stop' well worth pursuing, our hero did a smart right turn on his motorbike, regained admission to the High Street and found that his quarry had meanwhile disappeared down a side street.

Rapidly searching the area he at last came upon the suspect. Pulling into the kerb, he naturally asked Chummy what he was carrying on his head at this time of night. The suspect at once realised the futility of trying to bluff it out and readily admitted that he was carrying a box of tomatoes and a box of cucumbers which he had just stolen from his place of work at a nearby greenhouse.

Can you imagine the dilemma in which our hero now finds himself? Here he was, in the middle of the night, with a cumbersome motorbike, two large boxes of greenhouse produce, a self-confessed prisoner and with the nearest police box a long way away.

Pondering the problem, he alighted from the bike which he intended to prop against the kerb. The suspect meanwhile, seeing that the officer was fully occupied with his motorcycle, carefully placed both boxes on the ground and made off at some speed, with our hero in hot pursuit, on foot.

Saving his puff for the chase and realising anyway that most of the night duty relief were now in the canteen, he did not blow his whistle as per Peel House instruction. Alas, eventually, our hero came to the conclusion that the suspect was much quicker on foot than he, and he then pondered the problem posed by two large boxes of abandoned greenhouse produce and a lost prisoner.

He carefully hid the boxes in a nearby garden and wended his way to the nearest Police Box where he found, much to his pleasure, that he had not been missed by the Station Officer to whom he reported. He then, with information from the reserve man, wrote down all the addresses of the early turn relief who would shortly be parading for duty.

Deciding to forego his refreshment period, he returned to the garden where he left the produce, carefully made it all up into five packages of one cucumber to two pounds of tomatoes and set off on his motor cycle, depositing each package on the doorsteps of each of the early turn relief (one PS and four PCs). Having carried out this chore he wended his way back to the Station, chuckling to himself at the surprises due to each member of the forthcoming relief when they found the packages.

At about 4am he found himself back at the Station where all hell had apparently broken loose. 'Where the hell have you been Smith, I've had all the lights up on the boxes for you for the past hour, you must have seen them!' 'Yes Sarge, I saw them but as I was coming back to the Station anyway I didn't bother to stop. Why, what's happened? I've only just got rid of the key holder at the shop premises.'

Much to our hero's dismay, the Station Officer announced: 'Don't you come that old milarky with me, my lad. In the detention room you will find a chappie who states that he was knocked off by you earlier in the shift for nicking some stuff from his place of work. I understand that you lost him but after he got home he had an attack of conscience and came in to give himself up. Where the hell is the stuff he is supposed to have nicked?'

Mumbling some excuse about not being able to manage it on his bike, the officer had visions of the said property distributed on a number of doorsteps around the Section. 'I'll get the van from Division to go and fetch it if you will tell him where to find it,' said the Station Officer. Oh, Dear! Should he make a clean breast of it all, or was there still a chance?

Carefully explaining to the PS that he had hidden it so carefully that the van driver would never find it, he arranged to go with the van to fetch it.

By the grace of God the van driver was an old sweat and when the situation was explained to him, he at once agreed to help out by collecting it all from the various doorsteps, carefully putting it all back into the boxes from whence it came and taking it all back to the Nick, to be met by a Station Officer who wondered just why it was all taking so long.

In due course the early turn paraded, all of them innocent of the fact that Father Christmas had visited them all during the night, but had had second thoughts about it.

Did it really happen? Yes, you have assurance that it did, but where and to whom? Ah! that would be telling. I can assure you, however, that the PCs name was not Smith.

Ben Hogg, N District

Police Discretion

The Police, like the rest of the community, must move with the times while at the same time retaining their traditional role in society on which their reputation, occasionally tarnished but basically sound, reflects their ability over the years to cope with the problems that affect the daily lives of the public they serve.

Such a reputation has been built up by the combination of common sense and a shrewd appraisal of the situation that confronts them, a faculty that can only be developed by experience, formerly gained by that journalist cliche of 'pounding the beat'.

A recent report in the press stated that the Metropolitan police were to establish a 'battered wives register', presumably on the lines of the 'children at risk' record operated by the Health Authority. The register would record instances where connubial bliss had deteriorated to the extent that police were involved and by a computerised system of totting up, it would indicate the degree to which a battered wife was entitled, or likely, to call on the police in any legal proceedings.

This is a reversal of the attitude that prevailed 60 years ago in regard to domestic disputes. An instruction book in the I.B. advised police not to interfere unless action was clearly necessary. Few marriages endure without an occasional hiccup, fewer still qualify for the Dunmow Flitch. Experience teaches that often what is said in quarrel in the heat of the moment is retracted in the cold light of dawn or the precincts of a law court, leaving the police officer in the case without his main witness.

At the time when the I.B. instruction was formulated, the sanctity of marriage was regarded in a far different light to what it is today and usually carried the blessing of clergy to whom a 'battered' spouse could appeal for advice.

When I joined the police in 1929 the inherent risk of a hasty arrest was avoided by exchanging names and addresses of the parties concerned, and leaving, having advised the complainant as to her legal remedy, but passing the initiative to her to take out a summons when the police would give their version of events. By this means a cooling off period ensued, resulting in no irretrievable step being taken and the marriage usually resumed its normal atmosphere.

During my two years at Wandsworth VD, which took in part of Battersea, the neighbourhood of the fixed 'point' at the junction of Jews

Row and York Road, housing many costers, was notorious for domestic strife, but I never heard of any sequel or protest at this method of dealing with what was only too common.

Two instances involving PC Jack Nelmes, posted to this point during my first month of night duty, are worthy examples of when, and when not, to hasten. About 11pm one night in York Road, I was stopped by a boy about 12 years old who told me his father was fighting with another man and, presumably, getting the worst of it, hence the need for police action.

Turning back we were halted by a shrill whistle from Jack whose measured approach did not reflect my feelings of urgency. The boy, after answering questions from Jack as to his father's name, occupation, reason for fighting, etc, was told to report back to the combatants that 'the coppers were coming.'

I started to follow but was restrained by Jack with the following advice, the culmination of his 20 years experience: 'Always let 'em let a little blood, lad, and honour is satisfied.' Noticing my frustration, he added, 'If you had interfered too soon you would have got a thick ear from both and no thanks.' After a while we proceeded to Wardley Street - and no sign of the pugilists.

The second occasion revealed Jack in a totally different role. Later in the month at about the same time we were in conversation at the 'point' when a distressed female rushed up with the information that 'Mr Penworthy had gone again' which meant that he had been on the booze and was then suffering from DTs. Mr P was well known to Jack whose immediate response was to start running towards Mr P's house in Jews Row, accompanied by me. Our speed was regulated by the necessity to retain our helmets which invariably fell off in anything faster than a jog. Lowering the bottom jaw to tighten the chin strap helps to retain it but gives the wearer an expression that he is about to bite someone.

Relishing the anticipation that something exciting might happen, a small group at the front door offered no impediment to our entry where Mrs Penworthy's hysterical outburst directed us to a bedroom on the first floor. A blowsy individual of middle age, she pointed to the words, 'Curse You', written in blood on the wall over the headboard and immediately had recourse to the contents of a large milk jug containing gin. At this stage our informant joined us having found the pace we set too fast for her staying power. She indicated Mr Penworthy's presence in the sitting room, then shared what remained in the milk jug with Mrs P.

We found the villain of the proceedings, a small insignificant man, in no mood for a conciliatory approach. Standing with one foot on a sofa and brandishing a wicked looking carving knife he challenged 'the whole of Scotland Yard to come on'. Without more ado, a full-blooded left hook from Jack caught him neatly on the chin and he fell over the back of the sofa becoming wedged between it and the wall, dropping the knife. Giving him time to recover, we then hauled him to his feet and walked him back to the point. He was there given the option of keeping away from his house until midnight, or going for a walk 'down the road', ie being charged with an offence whose precise nature I was not clear about. He was released on his promise to keep walking for an hour to clear his senses. With customary brevity Jack reported in time-honoured fashion: 'Mrs P requests attention to her husband Mr P from whom she fears violence. Attention promised by PC John Nelmes.'

In due course I found myself posted to the 'point' at the junction of Granville Road and Merton Road, Wandsworth, on the 72 bus route, and had cause to bless the Instructor in Peel House who impressed on the class that while power of arrest existed for non- paying passengers on trams, under the Light Railways Act, no such power existed for the same offence on buses. Anticipating a warm drink before going to bed in the Section House I was about to start walking to the nick when the conductor of the last bus to Southfields Railway Station hailed me and complained he had a passenger on the bus who had boarded it at Clapham, taken a 3d ticket to Wandsworth and now exceeded the fare stage by 1d (penny), which he refused to pay on the grounds that the conductor should have told him when to get off which the conductor contended was not his responsibility.

Disputes over fares usually involved a passenger the worse for drink and the matter would be resolved by him, or her, throwing the fare on the floor with rude observations on the parentage of all policemen. Slouched in a corner seat with his overcoat collar pulled up around his face, I was unable to 'size up' the disputant and faced with an impasse, intimated he was risking 'going down the road'. Offering me his arm he challenged me to arrest him causing me to hastily add, 'if you don't give me your name and address'.

He then gave me his card showing him to be a barrister with an address at Earls Court, I have forgotten his name. He then left the bus.

The point at issue was of the greatest importance to the L.P.T.B and he was subpoenaed to attend the High Court. Reporting for duty on the due date I was told a phone message had just been received cancelling my attendance, the barrister having had second thoughts at the last moment and paid up. Bluff has its limitations.

Bert Blake, V District

Gipsy Hill in the Twenties

Seven recruits, including myself, were conveyed to Gipsy Hill SD station complete with uniforms and Peel House haircuts on 21 September 1925.

The station then was a large double-fronted converted early Victorian house. On one side of the entrance door was the station office and charge room. On the opposite side was the single men's mess room. The first floor was the SD Inspector's office and the single men's leisure area.

The upper floors were divided into ten cubicles, the single men's sleeping quarters. The flagstones floor basement was the kitchen, uniform room and ablutions; long slate trough with tin basin and a four inch stoneware bath. The water could be near boiling point and the posterior would be near freezing. The coach house was converted into cells and the stables became the CID office and store room.

Events that culminated in the first world war had halted the transition from ancient to modern conditions. No hotel-type section houses or saloon cars to patrol beats then. It was just one shilling per week boot allowance.

But as always, the Job involved an element of risk and robust activity from time to time. I remember my dear old friend DS Tom Cullen telling me that he was sitting at his office table solving crime one warm summer day. He left the door open for a bit of fresh air. An enormous dog came in and cocked his leg against the leg of the table. Tom said, 'It scared the wits out of me. I though it was going to kick me'.

Access to the station yard was from Westow Hill, the shopping street. All the night relief beats and patrols began near Westow Hill. I was on night duty and at 5.55am the relief was waiting to march in to 'book off' when we heard a rhythmic clatter coming from the direction of Anerly Hill. It got louder and eventually two un-manned hansom cart horses came in sight, walking shoulder to shoulder.

The whole relief had to help pushing, cajoling and nudging the beasts along Westow Hill towards the station yard. They had gone AWOL from a brewery delivery depot in Penge. I never did learn whether due to human carelessness or mischief.

J Coxhead 114476.

Constables and Cubicles

Giving my address in the 1950s as: Verandah Lodge, Hyde Park, people would remark 'that sounds posh'. Little did they know, I was in a cubicle measuring about 10 feet by 5 feet. The view was overlooking the stables at Hyde Park (AH).

Being a resident in any section house, meant you lived in a Police environment. When you lived 'over the shop' so to speak, you were totally immersed. In a cubicle, privacy was almost nil. It needed only the effort to stand on the bed, and you looked into the next cubicle.

By all accounts, there were also some austere conditions further along the building in the Guvnors flat. A PC told me he was asked to go along to the flat as the Guvnor wished to see him. The wife came to the door, and he was shown into a room, and invited to sit down while she informed her husband.

Looking around, the only seating was two assembled deck chairs. He flopped into one of them. When he looked at the canvas back on the adjoining chair he saw 'Royal Parks' was stamped thereon. When the Guvnor entered the room, he struggled to get out of the chair (he was a big heavy chap) and in doing so he fell out the chair and at the Chief Inspector's feet. It then appeared the two chairs were a perk that went with the Job.

I had started my police service at the section house over Paddington Green (DP), again as a cubicle dweller. The view from my cell was a brick wall. As there was little natural light, it required lights on, day or night. It did intrigue me how this architectural phenomenon came about. I've looked for clues when watching the film *The Blue Lamp* which was shot mainly at DP, but without success.

My cubicle was above the Charge Room. Night and day, somebody was being charged. Many of them came from a pub along Harrow Road, The Cider House. I looked in there one day and it was like a scene from

Hogarth's London. Whatever that cider was, it sure fired them up.

I understood overtime was for immediate payment at DP then. This explained why a fellow shaver, who was standing next to me in the wash-room, on hearing a commotion in the street below, went rushing to the window. It was a drunk and disorderly.

He rushed out and I saw him appear in the road still in his Y fronts only, seize the drunk who was then swiftly taken back in the station. A stray from The Cider House no doubt! Welcome to Paddington! This was my first week from Peel House. AD was tame compared to that place.

My next cubicle was at Carter Street. The film West-Side Story had been released. The occupant several cubicles along played the LP most evenings around 5pm. After a few weeks I was word perfect for 'Maria' 'Officer Krupke' and 'I wanna be in America'.

This time the washroom was eye level to the railway into London Bridge. If trains stopped at a certain signal, it was possible to be at a wash-basin and speak to commuters on the 8.05am!

In the summer when the windows were open, it was interesting to see a newspaper reader glance out of the train window, and see us shaving just feet away.

There was just enough space between the building and the railway, for the station van to enter and leave the yard. We had a residents canteen, above the canteen cooking area. A dumb waiter system operated by pulley. One Christmas Day lunch time, I walked into the residents canteen to have a couple of sandwiches before going on late turn. There was only one person in there. He was in civvies, and sat at a corner table. The canteen staff were having the day off.

I nodded to him, and made some comment, probably about the state of the place. The floor was ankle-deep in papers, cartons, and rubbish. A half-deflated balloon hanging limp from the ceiling was all the Christmas decoration to be seen.

Despite this hall of doom, he donned a paper hat, and began eating sandwiches, then he produced a cracker and with difficulty pulled it. He retrieved the 'joke' read it, and smiled. Then in a total outburst of festive spirit, he blew a 'toot' on a toy whistle. I sat at the table opposite watching all this with a certain incredulity.

Then I was posted to number 2 Protection outside 10 Downing Street. I felt I could face anything after that humorous Christmas lunch time.

Eventually I was sent to Ambrosden House in Victoria. Though built around 1900, we had our own rooms. My room was on the top floor. Along the corridor, Joe Chadburn, the Guvnors Officer, had his room. He was a Health Secretary's greatest nightmare. He had a frying pan that ice-shows could have been performed in. He fried every part of a pig, drank pints of beer, smoked a pipe, and for exercise he walked slowly around the snooker table. A great fellow!

There was a wonderful atmosphere about the place, and some excellent raconteurs. I occasionally walk past the place when up in London. It's still functioning as a hostel of some kind.

Alan Jackson, AD, AH, CTS, LK, TDM, TDP, TDR, B10

In the Bleak Mid-winter...

As a probationer, I was first sent to Arbour Square in the summer of 1946. Those who can recall the first three months of 1947 will remember the atrocious weather. I have never seen so much snow fall on London or lie on the ground so long.

Foot duty was eight weeks on early and late, then four weeks nights. To combat snow at night we wore a greatcoat, waterproof leggings, rubber galoshes and the old black oilskin cape. This was rounded off with a leather belt and the heavy wooten lamp. The total weight carried was such that after wearing this lot for a month of nights, you either had lumbago or were very fit.

The grub break was a bare half hour. However, when parading at 10pm, if the outdoor temperature was below freezing point, we had a two hour break as an 'indulgence'. Either midnight until two or two until four. My night duty fell in March and we had indulgence on every occasion.

Having the early break one night, I left the nick at 2am to find it snowing harder than ever and lying a good six inches in the streets.

I was posted to a cycle beat for which we received the magnificent sum of six old pence per tour. It was impossible to ride, but I was determined to take the machine and claim the treasured allowance.

I pushed the bike along the middle of Ben Johnson Road, passed the Gas Works and was shattered by the time I reached the crest of Canal Bridge. I paused, leaning back to catch my breath.

Then it happened. My helmet was violently thrust up from the rear covering my eyes and I could see nothing. In that instant, I cringed anticipating a cosh on the back of my head from some villain. Nothing happened. I spun round - and - not a soul in sight. Then, as realisation dawned in the quiet of that night, my laugh must have been heard for hundreds of yards. Snow and ice had literally frozen the back of my cape to a solid board. As I leaned back, the bottom rested on the saddle, pushing the top up and tilting the helmet. Simple - but what a relief!

The second incident occurred about two years later when I was a Traffic Patrol PC at the wonderful old Bow District Garage. During my service, I experienced many different Police Units, but never one with such a bunch of natural comedians as then served at DT7.

The garage entrance in Wellington Way was opposite blocks of flats owned by the Railway Authority and housing their employees. Around midday every Saturday, a simple-minded old chap we called Fred used to wheel a barrel-organ to the entrance of the flats, then give a tune while holding his cap out for coppers. About that time, some of us would be coming into the garage for scheduled vehicle cleaning.

For a lark one Saturday, some of the lads got Fred to quietly push his barrel-organ into the garage, stopping outside the main office. He then gave us a tune and we gave him our whip round. For an encore, we persuaded him to give an impromptu on-the-spot-dance whilst playing another tune. He obliged and received a further collection.

The garage strength was then under the charge of an Inspector - the one and only Arthur Pitcher. He was known to us as The Rural Dean of Bow for his ability to deliver a 'powerful sermon' as a dressing down. Arthur entered into the spirit of things and personally took the hat round for a third time.

I can see old Fred now, wheeling his barrel-organ out of the garage, grinning from ear to ear and delighted with his financial reward. Those were very happy days.

Eddie Twitchings, H, G, J, K, TDJ

No Justice in This World

Let me explain how I was fined four days pay. I was about six months a constable patrolling Clapham High Street and I came to a turning which I found was the only way in and out of Whites Square which was full of slovenly women gossiping with one another. Suddenly it went silent. I thought 'Now what? The bookmaker I expect.'

I came to a pub. I entered the urinal to relieve myself when suddenly a man came in, stood next to me and said 'Cop hold,' and I saw he held a half-crown in his open hand.

I struck his hand and the half crown flew into the air. I said 'If that is for bribery you have picked the wrong person. Clear off and thank the Lord that I am not arresting you for bribery.'

It would appear there was a bookmaker working bets so I hung around to stop him. After about 45 minutes a civvy stood next to me and said 'What are you doing hanging around here?' I said 'What's that to do with you?' He replied 'Don't you know me, I'm Sgt Beasley, the bookmaker Sergeant.' I asked to see his warrant card and he did not like being challenged.

He then said 'You get on round your beat and keep out of Whites Square.' The Supt. decided apparently I had to be taught a lesson. So Sgt Beasley came back to normal police duty. I of course was night duty and was posted to 1 and some of 10 beat.

On the whole beat there was only the taxi garage where I could go to the loo. Sgt Beasley hid up in the front garden of the house opposite the taxi garage - the spider in the web. I entered the garage to use the loo, came out to find Beasley waiting. 'I was using the loo.' I said. Beasley replied 'Oh no you're not, you were sitting on the bench with your helmet off reading this newspaper. When you come off duty at 6am you will be given an indictment to that effect.' I denied this all in my statement.

Next night on duty again I went to the taxi cab garage, saw the cleaner and told him what had happened. He agreed to come to the hearing and give evidence to the effect that I had been to the loo and was not sitting on the bench when Sergeant Beasley came in.

The hearing was held next evening before Supt Clark. When Sgt Beasley gave his evidence as indicated, Supt Clark asked if I had any witnesses to call. I called the taxi cab cleaner. Sgt Beasley went out and called the names out loudly for my benefit. No reply. 'Very well, I find this case proven. I fine you four day's pay.'

The indictment read something like this:- For that you were off your beat found sitting on a bench in the taxi cab garage with your helmet off and placed on the floor and reading a newspaper. It not being your refreshment half hour.'

Donald Bond, ex PC 155W, Insp at Chelsea

A Dangerous Profession

When I retired from the Metropolitan Police after service in the Traffic Department, I took up another job which was nearly as dangerous.

I retired from Bow Garage in 1960, and the following morning reported at the Ministry of Transport Training Branch at Stanmore for a four week course of instruction, before being accepted as a Driving Examiner. Three of the Instructors had not long before been Sergeants with me at Bow for some years, and I was somewhat surprised to be told on my arrival, 'Don't call me John.' The reasons were later obvious but had not occurred to me at the initial meeting.

At that time the driving instruction was based on the procedures at Hendon, but on a reduced scale with very poor and small vehicles. I must confess it came as quite a shock to learn that I could fail and would then be out of a job; after 25 years in the Police Service the thought of being out of work was something I had not considered.

At this time probably at least half of the examiners were ex-police and were tailor-made for dealing with the public. I served at Ilford, Dartford and Lee Green in London, and then Chichester and Worthing, on car and motor cycle tests; and later on HGV at Botley, Lancing, Reading and Poole.

All the car routes were carefully worked out to take in about five miles and 35 minutes driving time, and when I was working, the day consisted of nine tests for each examiner when employed on car tests. On Heavy Goods Vehicles we only had three tests on most days, with four on Mondays, each test lasting two hours.

Accidents and incidents were almost a daily occurrence. With the experience most examiners had, it was usually possible to avoid too many collisions but not always. In my early days there were not many dual-control cars and it often meant taking the wheel and/or applying the handbrake to prevent some collisions.

Some people took a failure in a sensible way, but others have attacked me before I could leave the car; indeed, in one case the senior examiner was slapped in the face by an Italian woman in the waiting room because she thought he had said, 'You have failed,' and they hadn't even started the test. It was not unusual to have a candidate start off, get out of control immediately and crash into a parked car in front; or as in one incident, we moved off from the car park, crossed the road outside without turning, and went through the hedge on the other side and ended up in a field.

One day I was standing on the pavement, writing out a pass certificate for a man recently returned from Kenya, when the car behind us revved up, chased the examiner across the road, and the woman driver then rammed several cars parked on the offside pushing them on to the pavement, and then her own car turned over on its side.

When I realised it was a deliberate act I went into the office to phone the police, and she followed me in, kicked open the door and chopped up her licence with nail scissors. She then ran out shouting and screaming at everyone, and being a woman, the Inspector and PC who had by then arrived, seemed unwilling to use force to get her into the police car. But after some hesitation she was taken to the police station where she tore lumps out of the cell mattress and the blankets.

The badly damaged cars belonged to Income Tax officers working nearby, and we were never too popular after that. My candidate from Kenya stood outside all the time this was taking place and could only say, 'I can't believe it.'

Some people came for a test so often we were almost like old friends; one old country man came 36 times, doing something like going up a one-way street or round a roundabout the wrong way, but on his 36th attempt I realised near the end that he was going to make it. When I said the magic words he showed no emotion at all and said, 'I like horses better than cars, they do what you want them to do.' He said he had only learned to drive so that he could take out his disabled wife, and we all offered up a little prayer for her that day.

In London one day I signed up a woman of about 60 years with a West End address. She told me she was a 'resting' actress and when I told her the pekinese would have to stay in the waiting room, she said, 'But darling, without her I shall feel awful.' We staggered from one stall to another and on being given the instructions for the Emergency Stop she looked at me and said, 'What beautiful blue eyes you have darling;' and when I gave the signal she just looked at me and said, 'Do you mean now darling?'

Before the days of white lines at junctions, cross road collisions were frequent and I was once knocked unconscious for a few seconds when the mini I was in turned over and we had to climb out of a side window. The husband of the candidate, when told of the accident, said, 'Is the car damaged much?' making no enquiry about his wife.

Supervision was fairly frequent both by the Senior Examiner and the visiting Supervisor, who sat in the back of the car and took no part in the test. It has been known for an examiner when under supervision to take a route with several cross roads and to feel the Supervisor braced in the back and holding on to anything available to prepare himself for the inevitable collision.

Eventually I became an Instructor at the Training School on all vehicles, and we sometimes had foreign examiners on courses, not to pass or fail them but to let them see how we carried out the tests in this country. On one course I was given the Chief Driving Examiner and his deputy of a Middle East country, and I had a Jordanian acting as interpreter in the back of the car.

At that time tests in their country took only a few minutes and their examiners would deal with 30 or 40 candidates a day. These two were the most dangerous drivers I have ever been with in a car, and after the first two hours I had to return and ask for a car with dual controls.

The Jordanian in the back would crouch down behind the front seat if he felt a collision was about to happen. I was very relieved when Friday came and they were given another Instructor on the Monday. These two examiners held quite high positions in their own country as all tests there were conducted by the Police.

If it was obvious some candidates were dangerous and the examiner had to physically prevent collisions, we were allowed to stop the test in the interest of public safety and fail the candidate. Then we had to walk back to the office to be greeted by a worried car owner anxious to know whether we had had a collision. As any ex-examiner will know, I have only mentioned a small sample of what used to happen, and looking back on it I think we earned our salary, some days several times over.

Geoffrey Taylor, H, DT7

Jellied Eels by Scroby Sands

The combined Social Clubs of Old Street and Commercial Street set off for an outing to Great Yarmouth in June 1935. The two manors were covered in our absence by aid from GD, GI, and GP.

We left Liverpool Street Station about 9am. The reserved rail carriages for our outing were nearly full and if one walked through the tobacco smoke in each compartment, voices could be heard calling 'Royal Flush,' 'Abundance,' 'Solo,' 'Rummy', 'Up for none' and 'Fifteen 9 and one for his knob' etc.

After a while, windows were opened and the smoke gave way to the fragrant smell from the countryside, quite a change from the smells of Hoxton and Petticoat Lane. Unfortunately, on arrival at Great Yarmouth at about 11.30am, our fresh air was soon dispersed, and we were treated to the smell of fish packed in boxes on the station for delivery to London.

The first port of call was a pub, which was easy to find as you nearly fall over them in Yarmouth, and after a refresher, about 20 of us made our way down to the seafront where we hired six horse-drawn open carriages for a ride along the seafront and back, with much good humoured banter with pedestrian holiday-makers.

The inner man was calling and a lunch of fish and chips (G division traditional menu), followed by apple tart and custard was quickly devoured, followed by a stroll along the seafront.

My serenity was shattered when Jim Spearing GS (who passed away in 1939) suggested a boat trip to Scroby Sands, a three mile trip to see the seals. My heart sank in my boots, for although I like watching the sea waves break on the shore, or swimming, or paddling in the sea, I am no sailor, and boat trips always upset me.

My protests were of no avail and fifteen of us boarded a small fishing smack. When we were half a mile offshore, Jim started collecting the fare of 2/- each. On offering my share, Jim refused saying it was good of me to keep the party together. He flatly refused my protests, then he asked everyone to correct their watches and asked each one in turn, except me, what time they preferred. These times were put down against each man's name, mine not included; then Jim explained they were having a bet on an event, and the event was me, the winner being the man whose time corresponded with the time I was expected to feed the fishes.

Directly this was announced, I was subjected to the most diabolical description of eating greasy, fatty food, in an effort to make me sick. I was determined to try to outwit them by concentrating my mind on other things, but half a mile off Scroby Sands, one of then demonstrated how he swallowed three raw eggs in one gulp. My resistance was up, and over the side went my fish and chips etc, all colour left me, and my face felt like damp blotting paper. A great cheer went up, but I was oblivious to everything, and to land was my greatest desire.

On leaving the boat they left me lying on the sand to sleep it off, while they visited the Fun Fair. About an hour later they returned, nearly all eating jellied eels, and in true East End fashion spitting out the bones on the sand. This did not affect me and we adjourned to a nearby pub till it was time to assemble at the railway station for the return to London.

Once again, out came the cards and a PC whose name escapes me, treated me to whisky and soda, costing about one shilling and three-pence.

We had a lovely dinner on the train and, being hungry, I enjoyed supplementary portions. About 10pm we arrived at Liverpool Street and dispersed to our homes and Section Houses, all agreeing it had been a smashing day's outing, but I had mixed feelings.

Ted Aram, G, K, J, Chigwell Club

Laughter in Court

Tragedy and comedy often run hand in hand, as all policemen are aware, and this is sometimes manifested in the law courts, an unlikely venue for humour.

At the opening of the Surrey Assizes at Kingston, their Lordships go to church in full panoply and on their return to the County Hall the proceedings are formally opened. All persons having reason to be there are required by the usher 'to draw near and give their attendance', a feat difficult to separate surely. A number of VIP's remain on the dais beside the judge to see 'What's on', the number who remain when the first case is called reflecting (let it be whispered) an unhealthy interest in the frailties of their fellow men.

One judge had peevishly complained of the noise made by those who, after a time, pushed their chairs back and left. A War Reserve constable of suitable mien and deferential approach was furnished with a pair of white gloves and instructed to make himself as inconspicuous as possible at the back of the dais, while at the same time remaining on the alert to lift the chair back of anyone preparing to leave.

In due course a VIP in dress uniform stood up, apparently to leave, but in fact to adjust his sword belt. His chair was deftly removed from behind him and he sat back in thin air. His impact with the floor occasioned an agonising yell suggesting the hilt of the sword had played some part in his landing. With sympathetic help from the chair attendant, he was assisted from the dais. The judge seemed to find it necessary to study his notes, whilst the KC addressing the Court had difficulty in maintaining his measured tone. The experiment was not repeated.

Less robust factors contributed to a chuckle in Court during a case tried by Judge Sir Edward Bruce Charles, an ardent angler whose photo can be seen in the Deal boating club which he founded. The case concerned a young Canadian soldier during the last war who was charged with committing a carnal offence against a girl he had met at a dance, which he contended she had not resisted.

His Lordship had evidently formed his own opinion of the case and asked the girl in a gentle way, 'You met this soldier for the first time at a dance?' Witness: 'Yes my Lord.' Judge: 'You danced with him many times?' Witness: 'Yes my Lord.' Judge: 'You went into a field and allowed him to fondle you?' Witness: 'Ye-es my Lord.' Judge, pushing his wig back: 'And all this happened the very first time you met him?' Witness: 'Yes my Lord.' Judge: 'Ah! I would that it were so in my day!'

The spectacle of his Lordship, a confirmed bachelor, as an ardent Romeo, caused a titter around the Court, whilst the verdict of 'Not Guilty' received general assent.

No wisecracks fell from the lips of Lord Chief Justice Hewart, who nevertheless caused an unintentional snigger when trying the case of a man named Hobbs at the Assizes. Hobbs, then about 65, was charged with obtaining money by false pretences from a lady of mature age on the pretext of forming a business partnership with her and, as an added inducement, had offered marriage, a prospect which, romance having so far passed her by, the lady was willing to accept.

Lord Hewart's first wife died in 1933 and, unknown to Hobbs, he had recently remarried in 1934, an adventure cynically referred to by confirmed bachelors as 'the triumph of hope over experience'. Hobbs had 'form' and ably defended himself to the extent that the issue was in doubt. He then played what he obviously thought to be his trump card with Lord

Hewart, about his own age, whom he imagined as a fellow senior citizen and widower had, perforce, renounced all desires of the flesh and would appreciate his argument.

Turning to the judge he exclaimed: 'And as regards this allegation that I promised marriage, I am a man of 65. What have I to offer at my age?' In icy calm Lord Hewart replied: 'Are you suggesting the married state has no attractions for a man of your age?' Hobbs, thinking he had made his point replied, 'Quite so my Lord, that is what I do mean.' The impact on those aware of his Lordship's remarriage caused a gasp and a very subdued snigger. In the subsequent scrupulously fair summing up, the jury were invited to decide whether Hobbs was as naive as he pretended, or a plausible rogue. Their decision resulted in a severe term of imprisonment, wherein Hobbs was able to cogitate on the pitfalls of over-playing your hand.

The Irishman's 'gift of the gab' is proverbial, often attributed to having kissed the Blarney Stone, but such gift is possibly only bestowed on the indigenous population. As a mere tourist who has attempted this feat, lying with his head dangling downwards, on his back from the top of Blarney Castle, held by the ankles by an individual whose countenance did not inspire confidence, I found the experience more conducive to prayer than oratory.

However, a prime benefactor of the gift displayed his talent in a case in the 1930s at Kingston where I was often in charge of the jury. Two Irish brothers of magnificent physique, Michael and Joseph Murphy, members of a gang of navvies, were charged with causing an affray and nearly wrecking a pub in Guildford.

Their defence counsel, anticipating the result, had prudently brought the foreman of the gang to say a word on their behalf before sentence. The foreman had been primed as to his role and on being asked to 'tell the Court what manner of man is Michael Murphy' launched into a recitation of his many virtues and peaceful personality which, to the foreman's personal observation had often caused Michael to cross the road rather than be involved in a brawl. He continued in this vein for some time ending with the assertion, and suitable gesture, that Michael would rather chop off his right arm than use it in violence.

Giving the judge time to digest this intelligence, counsel then asked, 'and what manner of man is Joseph Murphy?' It was difficult to imagine what sacrifice Joseph could offer to match his brother's saintliness, but the foreman was equal to the occasion. Without hesitation or falter he turned to the judge and declared 'Well of the two, Sorr, I would say he is the quieter.' What more could be said?

Bert Blake Wt 118324/234V

Nailed in Spain

In 1969 I was detailed to investigate the first Spanish real estate fraud to land up in the Fraud Squad office. You know the type - 'Buy your retirement Home in the Sunshine'. There were so many legal and logistical complications present it was daunting to say the least. In fact the advice from the DPP's man was 'just go through the motions as there's no chance of nailing these men'.

Having read up the papers I knew that over 200 British people had lost nearly all their money. Within that number were two who committed suicide and a number of families had broken up under the trauma. I was not in the frame of mind to heed the advice.

My first trip to Spain was disastrous. The interpreter was well below standard and the Spanish authorities had a chip on their shoulder about Gibraltar. In fact in two weeks I managed to get only one statement.

When I returned to England Roy Ives replaced the other interpreter and everything changed. After months of meticulous preparation I returned to Spain with Roy. Not only did he speak the language like a native, he could even use the local dialect. He opened doors hitherto barred, we met people who had the year before been too important to approach, and in one case a witness's address was given to us in a bar within five minutes of asking whereas the year before she was untraceable. He dug out significant clauses in documents that were later to play a major part in the subsequent trial.

After our return, following plenty more work, we nicked the team concerned and following a three month trial at the Old Bailey secured convictions. Justifiably the judge commended Roy on his ability during the investigation and during the trial where he had to interpret for witnesses and I was surprised to see all defence counsels rise to ask to be associated with the commendation.

Roy was an extrovert and a man of many talents but he was brilliant at his job. I shall never forget the emotional pleasure Roy and I got over the next few days as we rang all of the victims to tell them that the 'untouchables' were starting prison sentences. Roy was the man who got that 'impossible' result.

Bob Roach, DCI, RID

The Marquis of Granby Rules

'Wot abaht it then?,' said Fred. 'Wot abaht wot?' said Alf. 'Wot abaht us hiring a coach and taking some of the lads up to the Albert Hall to see the amateur police boxing between the 'Itie police and the City and Met teams?' 'Should be a good night out'. 'Right, ye'r on', said Alf. 'I know a geezer in Lewisham with some cheap transport'.

We negotiated a coach, or rather a charabanc for 7/6d a head and on the great night we were embussed in what appeared to be a pre-war two-tone vehicle with solid tyres and displaying a faded sign to Brighton.

We left in good time and high spirits for the night's entertainment but having travelled barely a couple of miles in the New Cross area, the engine started misfiring and came to an abrupt halt.

The driver, wiping the sweat from his brow with his cap said 'I fink it's the timing,' and immediately lugged out a tool box from under his seat and started to attack the problem with the comforting words, 'It won't take long, you blokes might just as well go for a wet'. We retired to the pub opposite, *The Marquis of Granby*, but by the time our driver re-appeared, nearly everyone in our party had had time to buy a round of drinks and we couldn't have cared less if he had taken us on to Brighton!

We finally arrived at the Albert Hall just in time to see the final eliminating rounds of the few battered and bleeding British police teams against the very fit and professional-looking Italians but not before we had staggered the full circumference of the hall in order to locate our seats. Our vantage point was next to the great organ pit and Stanley, a younger member of our party with a somewhat classical background education and a musical bent declared, 'You must feel like God to be able to play that great organ!'

We settled down in our happy fuddled state of intoxication, cheering and applauding as most of our team were carried out feet-first with George Marlow, the well known amateur referee apparently bowing to Mecca, 'Nine, ten, out' every few minutes. The final round at heavy weight was between Mad Murdock of the Transport police, an individual with a large neckless battered head, massive hairy arms, and a large beer belly and matching backside. His opponent was a tall slim athletic Italian with an unpronounceable name, but it ended in an 'i'.

The bout commenced with someone throwing a bucket of water over Murdock, I suppose to make him angry. It certainly did, for he threw a vicious right hander to the Italian's face, but his swipe was easily side-stepped. The memento of the swing, plus the wet floor, caused Murdock to pirouette full circle, the punch catching the ref a clout behind the left ear! The Italian hit Murdock in the stomach who crashed to the floor, grabbing the Itie by the ankles. He in turn crashed to the floor and rico-cheted into the ref who was trying to pick himself up and all three lay in a heap of flailing arms and sitting punches.

The bruiser-type Seconds from both camps joined in the melee and the 'free for all' developed and then extended to the first two rows of ring-side seats. Suddenly the cat calls of 'Kill him', and 'Mamma Mia's were rudely interrupted by the sounds of the mighty organ crashing out the opening bars of Bach's *Toccata and Fugue* played of course by our eru-dite friend Stanley who had somehow found his way into the organ ros-trum.

At this point, someone shouted 'Call the police!', so we pulled the slightly inebriated 'God' from his throne and did a quick bunk to our awaiting vehicle.

The Italians won 12 bouts to our 2, George Marlow 1!

Alan Marshall (The Baron) ex 560P

London Police Pensioner magazine

London Police Pensioner magazine is sent out free of charge to all members of London Branch NARPO four times a year. The magazine is mailed to the home address of subscribers.

To receive details of joining London Branch, please write to

John Beck
London Branch Secretary
16 Shawley Way
Epsom Downs
Surrey KT18 5NZ

Those wishing to subscribe to *London Police Pensioner* magazine but not eligible to join NARPO should please also contact John Beck or write to

Karen McCall
Editor, LPP magazine
Palmers House
7 Corve Street
Ludlow
Shropshire SY8 1DB

Glossary of Police Terms & Abbreviations

AD Code name for Cannon Row police station
ARDs Additional Rest Days
Aid A uniform PC helping the CID on a specific case
Aid to District Officers called in to help out another District, usually for ceremonial dutyin central London, or called in to help out at rallys, large crowd events etc
A Division Westminster
Arbour Square Stepney Divisional station
Assistant Commissioners The Met had 4
Beat Small area patrolled on foot duty
Beak Street Training Establishment, prior to Peel House
Bobby Police officer. Derived from Robert Peel, founder
Body Police slang for an arrested person
Borstal Young offenders establishment
CID Criminal Investigation Department
C Dept Overall responsibility for criminal investigation
Copper Slang for police officer
Constables' Rep PCs and Sergeants Federation Representative
Comms Room Communications Room with telephone switchboard
Commercial Street Police station near Aldgate
Commissioner Highest rank in the Metropolitan Police
Charge Room Where the arrested person is taken.
Chief Constable Highest rank outside Met Police Force
City of London Police Independent police force covering one square mile within the Metropolitan Police District
CM Great Marlborough Street Police station
CCC Central Criminal Court: The Old Bailey

CO New Scotland Yard, the Commissioner's Office
Charge Sheet Details of an arrested person
Cycle Patrol Paid a small amount extra to cover the beat by bike
Courtesy Cops Traffic Patrols in open-top cars, wore white gauntlets to distinguish them, late 1930s
DAC Deputy Assistant Commissioner
Dep. Comm. Deputy Commissioner
DI Detective Inspector
DS Detective Sergeant
DC Detective Constable
DT4 Thornton Heath District
DT7 Bow District Garage, H Division
DT8 Lewisham District Garage, P Division
DPG Diplomatic Protection Group
Duty Officer In charge at the police station
Echo 11 Call sign of a particular radio car or Q car. They have a plain clothes crew,
EG Grays Inn Road police station
EK Kings Cross police station
ET Early Turn
Early Turn First shift usually 6am-2pm
FH Notting Hill
Form 29 Form required for dealing with injured horses
Group Reserve Centre Temporary wartime police station
GD City Road
GI Islington Police station
GO General Orders, the Bible of policing
HD Arbour Square police station
HI Isle of Dogs police station
HH Limehouse police station
HL Leman Street police station
Instruction Book Police Training Manual
Incidentals Various expenses of CID officers
IR Scotland Yard's Information Room
Job The Police Force

KW West Ham police station
KF Forest Gate police station
Knock Off To arrest, to finish duty, to steal
L/T Late Turn, second shift in the day, often 2pm-10pm
LT Relief The group of officers on late turn
LPP *London Police Pensioner* magazine
Manor Slang for the area covered by a police station
MF Child Protection Branch
MT Tower Bridge Police station
MR Rotherhithe Police station
M Division An area just south of the Thames
Met Police Metropolitan Police, covers Greater London
Metropolitan Police Driving School Based at Hendon
Mike Microphone
MD Southwark police station
MP (Redcap variety) Military Police
MPD Metropolitan Police District
Nick Police station
Night Duty Third shift in 24 hours, usually about 10pm-6am
9 Beat Station area divided into several smaller, numbered beats
No 1s Ceremonial dress, the best police uniform, belt, tunic etc
ND Relief Night Duty Relief ie the shift on nights
OB Occurrence Book, where every incident is reported
Obbo Keeping a secret observation
Old Bill Slang for police service
Occurrence Book see OB
P P Division, South East London
Panda Small Morris Minor police cars for patrolling
PC Police Constable
Peel House Police Training School
Polacc An accident involving a police vehicle
Police Box Obsolete, navy blue, flashing light & First Aid box
Portsmouth Dockyard All Royal Dockyards policed by the Met until 1933
Process Summonses for offences

Process Books Details of offenders in the Summons Book
Protection Posts Standing on the door of 10 Downing St etc.
Police Constable Lowest rank of police officer
PS Sergeant
Relief The full complement at a station: early/late/night duty
R/T Radio Telephone: Before the radio, messages were sent in Morse Code.
Royal Stags Police Boots with straps, issued from Peel House
2nd Reserve Posted to man the telephones at the station
Sect. 66 Power to stop, search and detain a suspected person.
728s Report form to explain a problem/irregularity
SD Sub Division
Sgt Sergeant, next rank up from PC
Shadwell Station Stepney, East London
Shout Slang for a call over the radio for urgent assistance
Section House Where unmarried police officers live
Sectional Stations A station on a sub-division
Section Sergeant In charge of a number of beats
Special Constabulary Volunteer police officers
Station Sergeant Now obsolete. 3 stripes with a crown above
Station Officer Could be a Sergeant or Inspector
SHAPE HQ Combined Military HQ in Paris just after the war
Silver Token Carried by senior officers in lieu of a Warrant Card,as proof of identity
6/90 Wolseley Car, with gear change on the right side
SPS Station Sergeant
Sub Division See SD
Super Supt Abbreviation for Superintendent
Superintendent The rank above Chief Inspector
TA car Traffic & Accident car (Traffic Patrol) T Division
Thames Police Court Arbour Square, H Division
Thames Division River police, stationed at Wapping, Blackwall and Erith
Third Reserve General duties at the police station: driving, manning phones etc

Thornton Heath A police garage
Traffic Branch Code originally COB8
Traffic Police Stationed at the various Garages, working on motorcycle or by car
TrafPols Traffic Police
TAG car Traffic Accident Group: 1 car and 2 motorcycles
Trenchard House Section House in London's West End
Wapping Station Part of Thames Division, river police
West End Central Police station at Savile Row
Wellington Arch Smallest police station/Section house in London
WPC Woman Police Constable, now simply PC
Warrant Card Identity Card for plain clothes officers
Uniform Worn by all but the CID
Q car Plain clothes car, 4 man team consisting of Traffic Patrol driver and three police officers in plain clothes
X Division Uxbridge area
Yard's Special Squad A team of officers who worked on various Divisions to combat illegal bookmakers and persistant criminals
YE Edmonton Police Station
ZD Croydon Police Station. Z is one of the most out-lying Districts policed by the Met